W9-AUJ-056

AMERICAN MEN

1st EDITION

AMERICAN MEN

Who They Are & How They Live

BY THE NEW STRATEGIST EDITORS

New Strategist Publications, Inc.
Ithaca, New York

New Strategist Publications, Inc.
P.O. Box 242, Ithaca, New York 14851
800-848-0842
www.newstrategist.com

ISBN 1-885070-44-6

Printed in the United States of America

Table of Contents

Chapter 4. Health

Chapter 5. Income

List of Tables

Chapter 1. Attitudes

Chapter 2. Business

Chapter 3. Education

Chapter 4. Health

Chapter 5. Income

Chapter 6. Labor Force

Chapter 7. Living Arrangements

Chapter 8. Population

Chapter 9. Spending

Chapter 10. Wealth

List of Charts

Chapter 4. Health

Chapter 5. Income

Chapter 6. Labor Force

Introduction

Men's lives have changed dramatically over the past few decades. Behind the change is the rise of a new economy based on services rather than manufacturing, an economy that rewards the well-educated and encourages women to go to work. As women moved out of the home and into the labor force, men's roles expanded from breadwinner and handyman to nurturer and home manager. As women became more independent of husbands and children, men became more involved in home and family. The changes in the roles of men and women have been nothing short of revolutionary, affecting every institution in our society, from the family to the workplace, from politics to the consumer marketplace.

American Men: Who They Are and How They Live is a benchmark of men's lives in the year 2000. Included in these pages are all-important census data showing the size, age distribution, and racial composition of American males.

As men's roles have changed, their attitudes have adjusted accordingly. Men's new perspectives on work, family, religion, personal happiness, and other facets of their lives are revealed in *American Men*, based on data from the 2000 General Social Survey.

As we publish *American Men*, a rapidly growing volume of demographic data— including 2000 census data—are becoming available online. Not only does online access make government statistics more readily available, it allows people to manipulate numbers more easily. But the abundance of numbers and their many iterations creates a daunting task for those who want to keep up with the trends. The government's web sites are of great value to researchers with the time and skills to extract the needed nuggets of information. The shift from printed reports to web sites over the past decade, while convenient for number crunchers, has made demographic analysis a bigger chore.

American Men has done the work for you. It has the numbers and the stories behind them. Thumbing through these pages, you can gain more insight into men's lives than you could by spending an afternoon surfing databases on the Internet. By having *American Men* on your bookshelf, you can get the answers to your questions even faster than you can online.

How to Use This Book

American Men is designed for easy use. It is divided into ten chapters, organized alphabetically: Attitudes and Behavior, Business, Education, Health, Income, Labor Force, Living Arrangements, Population, Spending, and Wealth.

Most of the tables in the book are based on data collected and published by the federal government, in particular the Census Bureau, the Bureau of Labor Statistics, the National Center for Education Statistics, and the National Center for Health Statistics. The federal government continues to be the best source of up-to-date, reliable information on the changing characteristics of Americans.

One of the most important sources of data about American men is the 2000 census, taken on April 1, 2000. The 2000 census was the first in modern history to allow Americans to identify themselves as multiracial. As 6 million people did so, the old rigid racial classification system gave way to a new, more elastic reality. Other government data collection efforts must offer the multiracial option by 2003. The census counts of men by the new racial categories are shown in the Population chapter.

Perhaps the most important source of data in *American Men* is the Current Population Survey. The CPS is a nationally representative survey of the civilian noninstitutional population aged 15 or older. It is taken monthly by the Census Bureau, collecting information from 50,000 households on employment and unemployment. Each year, the March survey includes a demographic supplement which is the source of most national data on the characteristics of Americans, such as their educational attainment, living arrangements, and incomes. Because the March 2000 demographic supplement did not allow respondents to identify with more than one race, racial counts differ between the 2000 census and the 2000 Current Population Survey.

Most of the attitudinal data in *American Men* are from the 2000 General Social Survey. The GSS is a biennial attitudinal survey taken by the University of Chicago's National Opinion Research Center. NORC is the oldest nonprofit, university-affiliated national survey research facility in the nation. It conducts the GSS through face-to-face interviews with an independently drawn, representative sample of 1,500 to 3,000 noninstitutionalized English-speaking people aged 18 or older living in the United States. The questions shown in quotation marks are as asked by the GSS interviewers, with occasional editing for space or style.

The spending data in *American Men* are from the 2000 Consumer Expenditure Survey (CEX), an ongoing study of the day-to-day spending of American households administered by the Bureau of Labor Statistics. The survey is used to update prices for the Consumer Price Index. The CEX includes an interview and a diary survey. The average spending figures shown in the Spending chapter are the integrated data from both the diary and interview components of the survey. Two separate, nationally representative samples are used for the interview and diary surveys. For the interview survey, 7,500 consumer units are interviewed on a rotating panel basis each quarter for five consecutive quarters. For the diary survey, another 7,500 consumer units keep weekly diaries of spending for two consecutive weeks. Because spending data are collected from households rather than from individuals, the spending patterns of men must be gleaned by examining the spending of men who live alone and of married couples. The great majority of men live in one of these households types, and their spending is detailed in *American Men*.

The data in the Wealth chapter are from the Survey of Consumer Finances, a triennial survey taken by the Federal Reserve Board. It collects data on the assets, debt, and net worth of American households. The latest data available are for 1998. In taking the survey, the Federal Reserve Board interviewed a random sample of 2,813 households and a supplemental sample of 1,496 wealthy households based on tax-return data. As with spending data, wealth data are collected from households rather than individuals. Therefore, researchers must extrapolate the wealth of men from household figures.

While most of the data in *American Men* were collected by the government, the tables published here are not simple reprints of the government's spreadsheets, as is the case in many reference books. Instead, New Strategist's editors spent hundreds of hours scouring web sites, downloading publications and datasets, compiling numbers into meaningful statistics, and creating tables with calculations and descriptive text that reveal the trends. Researchers who want more information than the tables and text provide can use the source listed at the bottom of each table to locate the original data. The book contains a lengthy table list to help readers locate the information they need. For a more detailed search, use the index at the back of the book. Also in the back of the book is the glossary, which defines most of the terms commonly used in the tables and text. A contact list also appears at the back of the book as a handy reference allowing researchers to contact government specialists and web sites.

American Men will help you understand the wants and needs of nearly half the U.S. population. Those wanting to know about the demographics and lifestyles of women should examine New Strategist's companion volume, *American Women: Who They Are and How They Live*, available in hard copy or as a PDF download at www.newstrategist.com.

1

Attitudes

Most men find life exciting.

At least 50 percent of men aged 25 to 64 say life is exciting. Most also say they are "very" or "pretty" happy.

Men are ambivalent about working mothers.

Fifty-three percent say preschoolers suffer if their mother works. Most men under age 35 disagree, however.

Men socialize with relatives frequently.

More than one-third of men say they spend a social evening with relatives at least once a week.

Men say their standard of living is better than their parents' was at their age.

They believe their children's standard of living will be even better than their own is today.

Few men would stop working if rich.

Most are "pretty well" or "more or less" satisfied with their financial situation.

The majority of men believe in God without any doubts.

Forty-three percent pray at least once a day. Only 22 percent attend religious services regularly, however.

The largest share of men are independents.

Independents outnumber Republicans and Democrats in all but the oldest age group.

Most Men Are "Pretty Happy"

Most men also find life exciting.

Happiness rises fairly steadily with age among men. The percentage of men who are "very happy" is lowest among those aged 18 to 24, at just 21 percent. It peaks at a much larger 47 percent among men aged 65 or older. Most of the oldest men are retired and enjoying their leisure time, boosting happiness.

The 52 percent majority of men find life exciting. The figure is lowest among men aged 18 to 24, only 44 percent of whom find life exciting. Many in the age group are going to college and working at entry-level jobs. In contrast, the 55 percent majority of men aged 25 to 34 say life is exciting. Most are becoming fathers and embarking on careers, boosting life's excitement. At the peak of their career, most men aged 45 to 64 also find life exciting.

Men aged 18 to 24 are much more cynical than older men, with 64 percent believing other people mostly look out for themselves and only 25 percent believing others try to be helpful. Men aged 25 or older are less cynical, with a larger share believing others try to be helpful.

■ The easing of family responsibilities may contribute to men's growing happiness with age.

Most men find life exciting

(percent distribution of men by their attitude toward life's excitement, 2000)

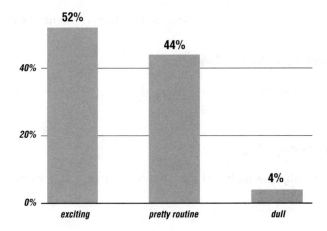

Personal Happiness, 2000

"Taken all together, how would you say things are these days—
would you say that you are very happy, pretty happy, or not too happy?"

(percent of men aged 18 or older responding, by age, 2000)

	very happy	pretty happy	not too happy
Total men	**33%**	**57%**	**10%**
Aged 18 to 24	21	63	16
Aged 25 to 34	31	63	6
Aged 35 to 44	33	57	10
Aged 45 to 54	31	60	9
Aged 55 to 64	40	52	9
Aged 65 or older	47	44	9

Note: Percentages may not add to 100 because "don't know" is not shown.
Source: 2000 General Social Survey, National Opinion Research Center, University of Chicago; calculations by New Strategist

Is Life Exciting? 2000

"In general, do you find life exciting, pretty routine, or dull?"

(percent of men aged 18 or older responding, by age, 2000)

	exciting	pretty routine	dull
Total men	**52%**	**44%**	**4%**
Aged 18 to 24	44	51	5
Aged 25 to 34	55	43	2
Aged 35 to 44	50	46	3
Aged 45 to 54	56	40	3
Aged 55 to 64	55	41	4
Aged 65 or older	48	46	5

Note: Percentages may not add to 100 because "don't know" is not shown.
Source: 2000 General Social Survey, National Opinion Research Center, University of Chicago; calculations by New Strategist

Helpfulness of People, 2000

"Would you say that most of the time people try to be helpful,
or that they are mostly just looking out for themselves?"

(percent of men aged 18 or older responding, by age, 2000)

	try to be helpful	just look out for themselves	depends*
Total men	**43%**	**47%**	**9%**
Aged 18 to 24	25	64	11
Aged 25 to 34	47	44	9
Aged 35 to 44	44	49	7
Aged 45 to 54	47	36	16
Aged 55 to 64	43	50	6
Aged 65 or older	48	43	7

* Volunteered response.
Note: Percentages may not add to 100 because "don't know" is not shown.
Source: 2000 General Social Survey, National Opinion Research Center, University of Chicago; calculations by New Strategist

Most Men Had Working Mothers

Most think working mothers are a problem for preschoolers.

Most men were raised by a working mother. The 62 percent majority of men say their mother worked for as long as a year while they were growing up. The percentage is highest among the youngest men, with 82 percent of men under age 25 saying their mother worked. The figure falls with age to just 34 percent among men aged 65 or older.

The majority of men believe preschoolers suffer if their mother works. Overall, 53 percent think working mothers are a problem for preschoolers. The proportion is smallest among the youngest men, at 35 percent. The figure rises to the 55 percent majority among men aged 35 to 44. Among men aged 55 or older, more than two-thirds think preschoolers suffer if their mother works.

■ Men are more likely than women to believe preschoolers suffer if their mother works, a potential source of marital strife.

Most men aged 35 or older think preschoolers suffer if their mother works

(percent of men who believe preschoolers suffer if their mother works, by age, 2000)

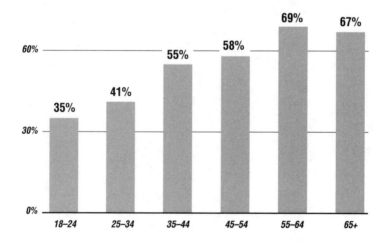

Did Your Mother Work? 2000

"Did your mother ever work for pay for as long as a year,
while you were growing up?"

(percent of men aged 18 or older responding, by age, 2000)

	yes	no
Total men	**62%**	**38%**
Aged 18 to 24	82	18
Aged 25 to 34	70	29
Aged 35 to 44	72	27
Aged 45 to 54	57	43
Aged 55 to 64	44	56
Aged 65 or older	34	64

Note: Percentages may not add to 100 because "don't know" is not shown.
Source: 2000 General Social Survey, National Opinion Research Center, University of Chicago; calculations by New Strategist

Do Young Children Suffer if Mother Works? 2000

"A preschool child is likely to suffer if his or her mother works—
do you agree or disagree?"

(percent of men aged 18 or older responding, by age, 2000)

	strongly agree	agree	disagree	strongly disagree
Total men	11%	42%	37%	7%
Aged 18 to 24	6	29	51	9
Aged 25 to 34	7	34	51	7
Aged 35 to 44	9	46	35	7
Aged 45 to 54	14	44	33	6
Aged 55 to 64	16	53	24	4
Aged 65 or older	23	44	22	7

Note: Percentages may not add to 100 because "don't know" is not shown.
Source: 2000 General Social Survey, National Opinion Research Center, University of Chicago; calculations by New Strategist

Most Men Say Their Marriage Is "Very Happy"

Most do not believe a traditional marriage is best.

Among men who are currently married, 64 percent say their marriage is "very happy." Another one-third say it is "pretty happy." Only 3 percent of husbands describe their marriage as "not too happy." Marital happiness is greatest among the oldest men, with 70 percent of those aged 65 or older saying their marriage is very happy.

Men's attitude toward marriage has changed dramatically over the past few decades. This shift is evident in the variation by age in men's attitude toward the roles of husband and wife. The 75 percent majority of men aged 65 or older believe a traditional marriage—where the man is the achiever outside the home and the women takes care of home and family— is best. Among men under age 45, more than 60 percent disagree that traditional roles are best.

■ Although many men are ambivalent about the effect of working mothers on preschoolers, most men think working wives are OK.

The oldest men think traditional marriages are best

(percent of men who believe it is better if the man is the achiever outside the home and the woman takes care of home and family, by age, 2000)

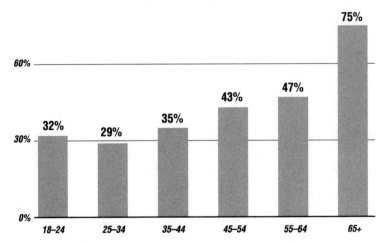

Marital Happiness, 2000

"Taking things all together, how would you describe your marriage? Would you say that your marriage is very happy, pretty happy, or not too happy?"

(percent of men aged 18 or older responding, by age, 2000)

	very happy	pretty happy	not too happy
Total men	**64%**	**33%**	**3%**
Aged 18 to 24	–	–	–
Aged 25 to 34	60	38	2
Aged 35 to 44	63	35	2
Aged 45 to 54	66	31	3
Aged 55 to 64	64	34	2
Aged 65 or older	70	26	3

Note: Asked only of respondents who were currently married; percentages may not add to 100 because "don't know" is not shown; (–) means sample was too small to make a reliable estimate.
Source: 2000 General Social Survey, National Opinion Research Center, University of Chicago; calculations by New Strategist

Female Homemakers and Male Breadwinners, 2000

"It is much better for everyone involved if the man is the achiever
outside the home and the woman takes care of the home
and family—do you agree or disagree?"

(percent of men aged 18 or older responding, by age, 2000)

	strongly agree	agree	disagree	strongly disagree
Total men	**10%**	**30%**	**42%**	**16%**
Aged 18 to 24	7	25	41	27
Aged 25 to 34	6	23	53	15
Aged 35 to 44	8	27	45	18
Aged 45 to 54	11	32	40	14
Aged 55 to 64	13	34	36	13
Aged 65 or older	24	51	20	3

Note: Percentages may not add to 100 because "don't know" is not shown.
Source: 2000 General Social Survey, National Opinion Research Center, University of Chicago; calculations by New Strategist

Most Men Are Fathers

The majority of fathers had their first child between the ages of 21 and 29.

Among men aged 18 or older, 34 percent are childless. Fourteen percent have had one child, 25 percent have had two children, and 27 percent have had three or more children. The majority of men under age 35 have not yet had children, but only 24 percent of 35-to-44-year-olds are childless. Men aged 65 or older have had the most children, 56 percent having had three or more. Many are the fathers of the baby-boom generation.

Sixty-three percent of men had their first child between the ages of 21 and 29. Most women had their first child before age 25 because they tend to marry at a younger age than men. Only 18 percent of men and 10 percent of women had their first child at age 30 or older.

Only 5 percent of men do not have siblings (including step-siblings). Fully 26 percent have five or more siblings. The youngest men are most likely to have only one or two siblings. Among baby boomers, aged 35 to 54, only 17 to 18 percent have fewer than two siblings.

■ Baby-boom men will be able to share the burden of caring for aging parents among their many siblings.

Most men have had three or more children

(percent distribution of men by number of children ever born, 2000)

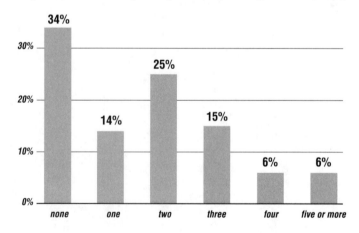

Number of Children Ever Born, 2000

"How many children have you ever had? Please count all that were born alive at any time including any you had from a previous marriage."

(percent of men aged 18 or older responding, by age, 2000)

	none	one	two	three	four	five or more
Total men	**34%**	**14%**	**25%**	**15%**	**6%**	**6%**
Aged 18 to 24	84	12	3	0	1	0
Aged 25 to 34	51	20	18	10	0	0
Aged 35 to 44	24	16	36	13	7	4
Aged 45 to 54	20	12	32	20	7	9
Aged 55 to 64	12	7	37	22	7	16
Aged 65 or older	14	12	18	24	18	14

Source: 2000 General Social Survey, National Opinion Research Center, University of Chicago; calculations by New Strategist

Age When First Child Was Born, 2000

"How old were you when your first child was born?"

(percent of people aged 18 or older responding, by age and sex, 2000)

	men	women
Under age 18	4%	12%
Aged 18 to 20	15	29
Aged 21 to 24	31	28
Aged 25 to 29	32	21
Aged 30 to 34	13	7
Aged 35 or older	5	3

Note: Asked only of parents.
Source: 2000 General Social Survey, National Opinion Research Center, University of Chicago; calculations by New Strategist

How Many Brothers and Sisters? 2000

"How many brothers and sisters did you have? Please count those born alive but no longer living, as well as those alive now. Also include stepbrothers and stepsisters and children adopted by your parents."

(percent of men aged 18 or older responding, by age, 2000)

	none	one	two	three	four	five or more
Total men	**5%**	**18%**	**22%**	**19%**	**10%**	**26%**
Aged 18 to 24	3	30	30	10	7	19
Aged 25 to 34	6	20	25	21	12	16
Aged 35 to 44	2	15	20	22	11	30
Aged 45 to 54	4	14	23	22	8	29
Aged 55 to 64	7	12	20	20	9	31
Aged 65 or older	5	17	14	14	13	37

Source: 2000 General Social Survey, National Opinion Research Center, University of Chicago; calculations by New Strategist

Men Socialize Most Frequently with Relatives

Going to bars is less popular than visiting with relatives.

More than one-third of men say they spend a social evening with relatives at least once a week. Twenty-four percent spend a social evening with friends that often, and 23 percent do so with neighbors. Only 12 percent of men say they go to a bar or tavern at least once a week. The youngest men socialize most frequently. Forty-one percent of men aged 18 to 24 spend a social evening with relatives at least weekly. About half spend an evening with friends or neighbors that often, and 22 percent go to a bar at least once a week. The majority of men aged 55 or older say they never go to a bar.

Most men say they have had a lot of energy "all" or "most of" the time during the past four weeks. The majority also say they have felt calm and peaceful "all" or "most of" the time. Few have felt downhearted or blue, and the great majority say physical or emotional problems have not interfered with their social activities.

■ Relatives are an important part of men's social life at all ages.

Men visit their relatives frequently

(percent of men who spend a social evening with relatives at least once a week, by age, 2000)

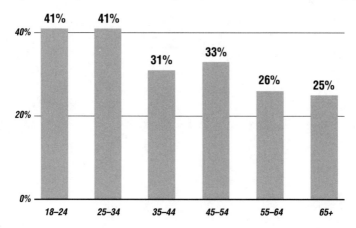

Frequency of Socializing, 2000

"Which comes closest to how often you do the following?"

(percent of men aged 18 or older responding, by age, 2000)

	almost every day	once or twice a week	several times a month	about once a month	several times a year	about once a year	never
Spend a social evening with relatives							
Total men	10%	24%	20%	18%	18%	6%	4%
Aged 18 to 24	15	26	15	22	13	6	3
Aged 25 to 34	14	27	21	18	13	5	3
Aged 35 to 44	5	26	22	16	18	9	4
Aged 45 to 54	11	22	19	15	25	6	3
Aged 55 to 64	9	17	20	21	19	5	8
Aged 65 or older	6	19	21	20	23	5	5
Spend a social evening with someone who lives in your neighborhood							
Total men	6	17	10	14	13	13	26
Aged 18 to 24	19	29	5	16	4	3	23
Aged 25 to 34	5	25	11	10	11	13	25
Aged 35 to 44	4	13	10	16	15	13	29
Aged 45 to 54	4	10	11	20	12	14	29
Aged 55 to 64	8	9	7	10	20	25	21
Aged 65 or older	1	18	10	12	20	12	27
Spend a social evening with friends who live outside the neighborhood							
Total men	5	19	18	21	21	8	7
Aged 18 to 24	19	31	27	8	7	5	4
Aged 25 to 34	6	27	23	21	14	8	2
Aged 35 to 44	3	16	14	27	22	10	7
Aged 45 to 54	1	18	19	22	29	4	6
Aged 55 to 64	5	10	15	24	32	6	9
Aged 65 or older	1	15	10	17	23	20	15
Go to a bar or tavern							
Total men	1	11	9	12	13	13	40
Aged 18 to 24	0	22	17	15	2	10	35
Aged 25 to 34	1	17	12	11	20	14	24
Aged 35 to 44	1	10	10	17	17	13	32
Aged 45 to 54	3	9	7	10	11	17	43
Aged 55 to 64	1	4	7	5	13	15	53
Aged 65 or older	0	3	3	5	5	7	77

Note: Percentages may not add to 100 because "don't know" is not shown.
Source: 2000 General Social Survey, National Opinion Research Center, University of Chicago; calculations by New Strategist

Men's Feelings, 2000

"These questions are about how you feel and how things have been with you during the past four weeks. For each question, please give the one answer that comes closest to the way you have been feeling. How much of the time during the past four weeks have you felt: "

(percent of men aged 18 or older responding, by age, 2000)

	all of the time	most of the time	a good bit of the time	some of the time	a little bit of the time	none of the time
A lot of energy?						
Total men	**13%**	**39%**	**20%**	**16%**	**8%**	**2%**
Aged 18 to 24	11	33	27	18	11	0
Aged 25 to 34	16	40	18	17	8	1
Aged 35 to 44	16	41	22	13	6	1
Aged 45 to 54	10	45	16	18	8	3
Aged 55 to 64	14	33	24	12	13	4
Aged 65 or older	9	38	17	21	8	8
Calm and peaceful?						
Total men	**11**	**44**	**17**	**20**	**6**	**2**
Aged 18 to 24	2	52	18	21	5	2
Aged 25 to 34	12	38	16	29	4	1
Aged 35 to 44	13	36	23	21	7	1
Aged 45 to 54	7	48	16	20	6	3
Aged 55 to 64	12	50	21	12	5	1
Aged 65 or older	24	55	7	5	6	3
Downhearted and blue?						
Total men	**1**	**2**	**3**	**16**	**37**	**41**
Aged 18 to 24	0	3	8	16	34	38
Aged 25 to 34	0	1	4	15	43	36
Aged 35 to 44	1	3	2	12	39	44
Aged 45 to 54	1	5	1	20	40	33
Aged 55 to 64	1	1	4	19	29	46
Aged 65 or older	0	0	4	17	29	50
Physical or emotional problems interfered with social activities?						
Total men	**2**	**2**	**3**	**8**	**13**	**72**
Aged 18 to 24	0	5	2	4	19	71
Aged 25 to 34	0	1	2	8	16	73
Aged 35 to 44	2	1	2	10	12	73
Aged 45 to 54	3	5	5	6	15	67
Aged 55 to 64	3	2	2	12	5	76
Aged 65 or older	5	2	5	8	10	71

Note: Percentages may not add to 100 because "don't know" is not shown.
Source: 2000 General Social Survey, National Opinion Research Center, University of Chicago; calculations by New Strategist

Most Men Say Their Standard of Living Is Better than Their Parents'

Most think their children's standard of living will be even better.

Sixty-eight percent of men believe their standard of living is higher than their parents' standard of living was at the age they are now. The proportion of men who feel this way is greatest in the older age groups. Eighty percent of men aged 65 or older say their standard of living is higher than their parents' was.

A different pattern emerges when men are asked whether their children's standard of living will be better than theirs. Men aged 25 to 34 are most likely to believe their children's standard of living will be better than theirs is now (73 percent). Men in this age group have been struggling to progress in the shadow of the large baby-boom generation. Many may feel their children are certain to be better off. Men aged 65 or older are least likely to feel their children's standard of living will be better than their own is now. Most probably know that the boomers (their children) are unlikely to live as well in retirement as the current generation of older Americans.

■ The American belief in economic progress is deeply rooted, few men believe they are worse off than their parents were or that their children will be worse off than they are today.

Most men believe their children will be better off

(percent of men who believe their children's standard of living will be better, by age, 2000)

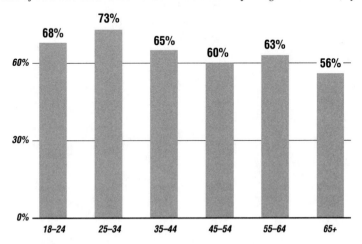

Standard of Living Relative to Parents', 2000

"Compared to your parents when they were the age you are now, do you think your own standard of living now is much better, somewhat better, about the same, somewhat worse, or much worse than theirs was?"

(percent of men aged 18 or older responding, by age, 2000)

	better	about the same	worse
Total men	**68%**	**18%**	**11%**
Aged 18 to 24	68	25	4
Aged 25 to 34	65	21	13
Aged 35 to 44	66	15	18
Aged 45 to 54	66	19	12
Aged 55 to 64	73	18	9
Aged 65 or older	80	11	5

Note: Percentages may not add to 100 because "don't know" is not shown.
Source: 2000 General Social Survey, National Opinion Research Center, University of Chicago; calculations by New Strategist

Children's Future Standard of Living, 2000

"When your children are at the age you are now, do you think their standard of living will be much better, somewhat better, about the same, somewhat worse, or much worse than yours is now?"

(percent of men aged 18 or older responding, by age, 2000)

	better	about the same	worse
Total men	**65%**	**19%**	**13%**
Aged 18 to 24	68	18	9
Aged 25 to 34	73	15	7
Aged 35 to 44	65	18	12
Aged 45 to 54	60	19	17
Aged 55 to 64	63	22	14
Aged 65 or older	56	21	17

Note: Percentages may not add to 100 because "don't know" is not shown.
Source: 2000 General Social Survey, National Opinion Research Center, University of Chicago; calculations by New Strategist

Most Men Are Satisfied with Their Financial Situation

Even if they were rich, the majority would still work.

Thirty-two percent of men say they are "pretty well" satisfied with their financial situation, and another 45 percent are "more or less" satisfied. Only 22 percent of men are "not at all" satisfied with their finances. Those least satisfied are men aged 25 to 34. Most in the age group are starting a career, having children, and buying a home, often finding it a struggle to make ends meet. Those most satisfied with their finances are men aged 65 or older, the majority of whom are retired and living on Social Security, pensions, and savings.

More than two-thirds of working men (69 percent) say they would continue to work even if they had enough money to live comfortably for the rest of their lives. Just 29 percent of men would stop working. Older men are most likely to say they would stop working. Many are near retirement and looking forward to more leisure time.

■ Although older men depend on Social Security and other fixed sources of income, they are much more satisfied with their finances than men working their way up the career ladder.

Most men would work even if they didn't need the money

(percent of working men who would continue to work even if they had enough money to live comfortably for the rest of their life, by age, 2000)

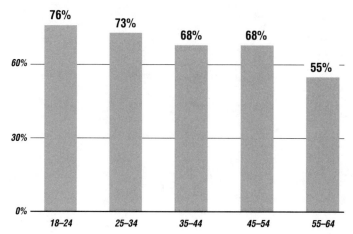

Satisfaction with Financial Situation, 2000

"So far as you and your family are concerned, would you say that you are pretty well satisfied with your present financial situation, more or less satisfied, or not satisfied at all?"

(percent of men aged 18 or older responding, by age, 2000)

	pretty well satisfied	more or less satisfied	not at all satisfied
Total men	**32%**	**45%**	**22%**
Aged 18 to 24	33	43	24
Aged 25 to 34	19	51	30
Aged 35 to 44	27	49	23
Aged 45 to 54	34	47	19
Aged 55 to 64	46	36	18
Aged 65 or older	48	38	14

Note: Percentages may not add to 100 because "don't know" is not shown.
Source: 2000 General Social Survey, National Opinion Research Center, University of Chicago; calculations by New Strategist

Would You Work if You Were Rich? 2000

"If you were to get enough money to live as comfortably as you would like for the rest of your life, would you continue to work or would you stop working?"

(percent of men aged 18 to 64 responding, by age, 2000)

	continue to work	stop working
Total men	**69%**	**29%**
Aged 18 to 24	76	21
Aged 25 to 34	73	26
Aged 35 to 44	68	29
Aged 45 to 54	68	29
Aged 55 to 64	55	45

Note: Asked only of people who are currently working; percentages may not add to 100 because "don't know" is not shown.
Source: 2000 General Social Survey, National Opinion Research Center, University of Chicago; calculations by New Strategist

Most Men Support Affirmative Action for Women

Many men (and women) think men could be hurt by affirmative action, however.

The 60 percent majority of men think that, because of past discrimination, employers should make special efforts to hire and promote qualified women. A slightly larger 67 percent of women agree. Only 27 percent of men and 22 percent of women do not support affirmative action for women.

Sixty-three percent of men think it is "somewhat" or "very likely" that a woman won't get a job or promotion while an equally or less qualified man gets one instead. Seventy-six percent of women think this scenario is somewhat or very likely. But both men and women see the potential harm of affirmative action. Fifty-three percent of men and 43 percent of women say it is somewhat or very likely that a man won't get a job or promotion while an equally or less qualified woman gets one instead. Forty-two percent of men say this situation is somewhat or very unlikely.

■ Men support affirmative action because most have working wives.

Most think employers should make special efforts to hire and promote women

(percent of people who agree that employers should make special efforts to hire and promote qualified women, by sex, 2000)

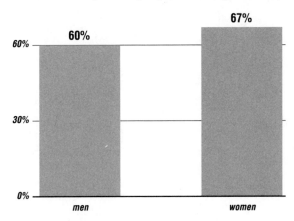

Affirmative Action for Women, 2000

"Because of past discrimination, employers should make special efforts
to hire and promote qualified women—do you agree or disagree?"

(percent of people aged 18 or older responding, by sex, 2000)

	men	women
Strongly agree	15%	23%
Agree	45	44
Neither agree nor disagree	11	10
Disagree	21	18
Strongly disagree	6	4

Note: Percentages may not add to 100 because "don't know" is not shown.
Source: 2000 General Social Survey, National Opinion Research Center, University of Chicago; calculations by New Strategist

Job Discrimination against Women, 2000

"What do you think the chances are these days that a woman won't get a job or promotion while an equally or less qualified man gets one instead?"

(percent of people aged 18 or older responding, by sex, 2000)

	men	women
Very likely	17%	30%
Somewhat likely	46	46
Somewhat unlikely	24	15
Very unlikely	10	6

Note: Percentages may not add to 100 because "don't know" is not shown.
Source: 2000 General Social Survey, National Opinion Research Center, University of Chicago; calculations by New Strategist

Job Discrimination against Men, 2000

"What do you think the chances are these days that a man won't get a job or promotion while an equally or less qualified woman gets one instead?"

(percent of people aged 18 or older responding, by sex, 2000)

	men	women
Very likely	12%	13%
Somewhat likely	41	30
Somewhat unlikely	31	30
Very unlikely	11	21

Note: Percentages may not add to 100 because "don't know" is not shown.
Source: 2000 General Social Survey, National Opinion Research Center, University of Chicago; calculations by New Strategist

Many Men Pray at Least Once a Day

Only 22 percent attend religious services at least weekly, however.

The 53 percent majority of men believe in God without a doubt, the proportion rising from a low of 39 percent among men aged 18 to 24 to a high of 72 percent among those aged 65 or older. Forty-three percent of men pray at least once a day. Again the proportion rises with age, from 34 percent of men aged 18 to 34 to 64 percent of men aged 65 or older.

Only 22 percent of men attend religious services at least once a week. Those most likely to attend regularly are men aged 65 or older, 36 percent of whom attend at least weekly. Most men have a high opinion of their local church. The majority say their church's worship service, preaching, respect for women's rights, work with young people, and sympathetic counseling are "very good" or "excellent."

■ Although many men have doubts about God and do not attend religious services regularly, the majority believe in God without a doubt and pray regularly.

Many men pray every day

(percent of men who pray at least once a day, by age, 2000)

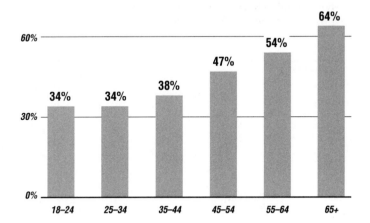

Belief about God, 2000

"Please tell me which of these statements comes closest to expressing what you believe about God: I don't believe in God; I don't know whether there is a God and I don't believe there is any way to find out; I don't believe in a personal God, but I do believe in a Higher Power of some kind; I find myself believing in God some of the time, but not at others; while I have doubts, I feel that I do believe in God; I know God really exists and I have no doubts about it."

(percent of men aged 18 or older responding, by age, 2000)

	don't know, don't believe	no way to find out	believe in Higher Power	believe only some of the time	believe, but have doubts	believe, have no doubts
Total men	**4%**	**6%**	**7%**	**5%**	**21%**	**53%**
Aged 18 to 24	3	10	11	3	28	39
Aged 25 to 34	5	5	9	6	22	49
Aged 35 to 44	5	6	5	4	24	53
Aged 45 to 54	7	8	4	3	14	59
Aged 55 to 64	1	3	12	7	27	47
Aged 65 or older	0	7	6	6	5	72

Note: Percentages may not add to 100 because "don't know" is not shown.
Source: 2000 General Social Survey, National Opinion Research Center, University of Chicago; calculations by New Strategist

Frequency of Prayer, 2000

"About how often do you pray?"

(percent of men aged 18 or older responding, by age, 2000)

	at least once a day	one or more times a week	less than once a week	never
Total men	**43%**	**23%**	**33%**	**1%**
Aged 18 to 24	34	25	42	0
Aged 25 to 34	34	28	36	2
Aged 35 to 44	38	26	37	0
Aged 45 to 54	47	20	29	4
Aged 55 to 64	54	17	29	0
Aged 65 or older	64	17	19	1

Note: Percentages may not add to 100 because "don't know" is not shown.
Source: 2000 General Social Survey, National Opinion Research Center, University of Chicago; calculations by New Strategist

Frequency of Attending Religious Services, 2000

"How often do you attend religious services?"

(percent of men aged 18 or older responding, by age, 2000)

	at least weekly	at least monthly, but less than once a week	once to several times a year	less than once a year or never
Total men	**22%**	**19%**	**27%**	**31%**
Aged 18 to 24	17	22	31	30
Aged 25 to 34	15	20	33	32
Aged 35 to 44	21	21	27	30
Aged 45 to 54	24	19	25	31
Aged 55 to 64	24	13	28	35
Aged 65 or older	36	18	19	28

Note: Percentages may not add to 100 because "don't know" is not shown.
Source: 2000 General Social Survey, National Opinion Research Center, University of Chicago; calculations by New Strategist

Opinion of Local Church, 2000

"How do you rate how your local church does each of the following? Would you say your local church does an excellent, very good, good, fair, or poor job of:"

(percent of men aged 18 or older responding, by age, 2000)

	excellent	very good	good	fair	poor
Worship services	30%	35%	25%	5%	1%
Preaching	26	30	31	6	2
Respecting rights of women	35	32	22	4	1
Working with young people	32	33	20	7	1
Sympathetic counseling	28	30	23	6	2

Note: Percentages may not add to 100 because "don't know" is not shown.
Source: 2000 General Social Survey, National Opinion Research Center, University of Chicago; calculations by New Strategist

Men Support Abortion, Gun Permits, Death Penalty

Most also support physician-assisted suicide.

While the debate over abortion, gun control, and physician-assisted suicide may rage among politicians, men are solidly in favor of all three. The majority of men support abortion if a woman's health is endangered by pregnancy, if pregnancy is the result of rape, and if there is a chance the baby will be born with a serious defect. Only 37 percent support abortion for any reason, however.

Sixty-eight percent of men support physician-assisted suicide for people with an incurable disease. Support is highest among young adults (87 percent) and falls with age to the slim 51 percent majority of those aged 65 or older.

Seventy percent of men favor requiring gun buyers to obtain police permits. Seventy-one percent favor the death penalty. Support for these measures does not vary much by age.

■ Although so many men (and women) favor gun control, the issue is surprisingly difficult to legislate.

Support for physician-assisted suicide falls with age

(percent of men who think doctors should be allowed by law to end a patient's life by some painless means if the patient and his family request it, by age, 2000)

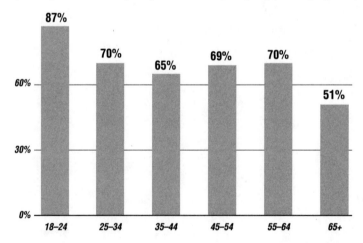

Opinions about Abortion, 2000

"Please tell me whether or not you think it should be possible for a pregnant woman to obtain a legal abortion for the following reasons:"

(percent of men aged 18 or older responding, 2000)

	yes	no
If the woman's own health is seriously endangered by the pregnancy	87%	10%
If she became pregnant as a result of rape	79	16
If there is a strong chance of serious defect in the baby	77	18
If she is married and does not want any more children	41	54
If the family has a very low income and cannot afford more children	41	55
If she is not married and does not want to marry the man	38	57
If the woman wants it for any reason	37	58

Note: Percentages may not add to 100 because "don't know" is not shown.
Source: 2000 General Social Survey, National Opinion Research Center, University of Chicago; calculations by New Strategist

Physician-Assisted Suicide, 2000

"When a person has a disease that cannot be cured, do you think doctors should be allowed by law to end the patient's life by some painless means if the patient and his family request it?"

(percent of men aged 18 or older responding, by age, 2000)

	yes	no
Total men	**68%**	**27%**
Aged 18 to 24	87	13
Aged 25 to 34	70	25
Aged 35 to 44	65	30
Aged 45 to 54	69	26
Aged 55 to 64	70	28
Aged 65 or older	51	43

Note: Percentages may not add to 100 because "don't know" is not shown.
Source: 2000 General Social Survey, National Opinion Research Center, University of Chicago; calculations by New Strategist

Opinion of Requiring Gun Permits, 2000

"Would you favor or oppose a law that would require a person
to obtain a police permit before he or she could buy a gun?"

(percent of men aged 18 or older responding, by age, 2000)

	favor	oppose
Total men	**70%**	**27%**
Aged 18 to 24	74	25
Aged 25 to 34	71	27
Aged 35 to 44	72	26
Aged 45 to 54	65	29
Aged 55 to 64	66	30
Aged 65 or older	74	26

Note: Percentages may not add to 100 because "don't know" is not shown.
Source: 2000 General Social Survey, National Opinion Research Center, University of Chicago; calculations by New Strategist

Opinion of the Death Penalty, 2000

"Do you favor or oppose the death penalty for persons convicted of murder?"

(percent of men aged 18 or older responding, by age, 2000)

	favor	oppose	don't know
Total men	**71%**	**23%**	**6%**
Aged 18 to 24	71	23	5
Aged 25 to 34	69	24	6
Aged 35 to 44	71	22	7
Aged 45 to 54	72	24	4
Aged 55 to 64	69	27	4
Aged 65 or older	77	18	5

Source: 2000 General Social Survey, National Opinion Research Center, University of Chicago; calculations by New Strategist

Many Men Put Environment First, but Some Are Doubters

The majority of older men think claims about environmental threats are exaggerated.

Environmental protection has become an important political issue over the past few decades, with many Americans regarding themselves as environmentalists. But a substantial share still have their doubts. Thirty-one percent of men believe that many of the claims about environmental threats are exaggerated. Twenty-seven percent neither agree nor disagree, while the largest share (40 percent) disagree that claims are exaggerated. The 53 percent majority of men aged 65 or older think claims are exaggerated. Those most likely to disagree that threats are exaggerated are baby boomers, aged 35 to 54.

Men are also split on the importance of protecting the environment. Twenty-two percent agree that there are more important things to do in life than to protect the environment. The figure is largest among men aged 65 or older (29 percent). The majority of men aged 35 to 54 (baby boomers) disagree that there are more important things to do than to protect the environment.

■ The environment has always been an important issue for baby boomers, making it an important issue for politicians.

Older men are most likely to think environmental threats are exaggerated

(percent of men who agree that many of the claims of environmental threats are exaggerated, by age, 2000)

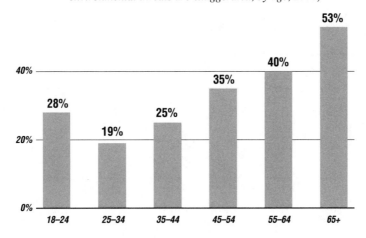

Environmental Threats Are Exaggerated, 2000

"Many of the claims about environmental threats are exaggerated—
how much do you agree or disagree?"

(percent of men aged 18 or older responding, by age, 2000)

	agree	neither	disagree
Total men	**31%**	**27%**	**40%**
Aged 18 to 24	28	32	38
Aged 25 to 34	19	39	40
Aged 35 to 44	25	24	45
Aged 45 to 54	35	20	43
Aged 55 to 64	40	22	34
Aged 65 or older	53	18	29

Note: Percentages may not add to 100 because "can't choose" is not shown.
Source: 2000 General Social Survey, National Opinion Research Center, University of Chicago; calculations by New Strategist

Importance of Protecting the Environment, 2000

"There are more important things to do in life than protect the environment—
how much do you agree or disagree?"

(percent of men aged 18 or older responding, by age, 2000)

	agree	neither	disagree
Total men	**22%**	**28%**	**48%**
Aged 18 to 24	18	34	45
Aged 25 to 34	19	29	50
Aged 35 to 44	22	24	51
Aged 45 to 54	23	25	51
Aged 55 to 64	22	34	42
Aged 65 or older	29	28	44

Note: Percentages may not add to 100 because "don't know" is not shown.
Source: 2000 General Social Survey, National Opinion Research Center, University of Chicago; calculations by New Strategist

The Largest Share of Men Say They Are Independents

Men accounted for 47 percent of voters in the 2000 presidential election.

The Democratic and Republican parties constantly struggle to attract the independent voter, and with good reason. The largest share of men (42 percent) identify themselves as independent rather than Democrat or Republican. Among men, independents outnumber Democrats and Republicans in all but the oldest age group. Men aged 65 or older are most likely to identify themselves as Democrats. In the 45-to-54 age group, Democrats and Republicans are neck-and-neck (29 and 28 percent, respectively).

Fifty-three percent of men say they voted in the November 2000 presidential election. The voting rate ranged from just 30 percent among men aged 18 to 24 to a high of 72 percent among men aged 75 or older. Among men who did not vote in the election, the largest share (22 percent) said they were too busy. Thirteen percent said they were out of town, and another 13 percent said they were not interested or their vote would not make a difference.

■ Among people under age 65, women are more likely to vote than men. Among people aged 65 or older, the opposite is true.

Few young men went to the polls in November 2000

(percent of men who voted in the November 2000 presidential election, by age)

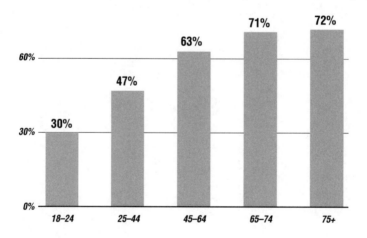

Political Party Identification, 2000

"Generally speaking, do you usually think of yourself as a
Republican, Democrat, independent, or what?"

(percent of men aged 18 or older responding, by age, 2000)

	Democrat	independent	Republican
Total men	**27%**	**42%**	**29%**
Aged 18 to 24	19	57	24
Aged 25 to 34	21	50	27
Aged 35 to 44	29	36	33
Aged 45 to 54	29	41	28
Aged 55 to 64	23	40	32
Aged 65 or older	40	27	33

Note: Percentages may not add to 100 because "don't know" and "other party" are not shown.
Source: 2000 General Social Survey, National Opinion Research Center, University of Chicago; calculations by New Strategist

Voting by Sex and Age, November 2000

(total number of people aged 18 or older, number and percent distribution of those voting in the election of November 2000, and voter share of total, by sex and age; numbers in thousands)

| | total | voters | | |
		number	percent distribution	share of total
Total people	202,609	110,826	100.0%	54.7%
Aged 18 to 24	26,712	8,635	7.8	32.3
Aged 25 to 44	81,780	40,738	36.8	49.8
Aged 45 to 64	61,352	39,301	35.5	64.1
Aged 65 to 74	17,819	12,450	11.2	69.9
Aged 75 or older	14,945	9,702	8.8	64.9
Total men	**97,087**	**51,542**	**46.5**	**53.1**
Aged 18 to 24	13,338	4,005	3.6	30.0
Aged 25 to 44	40,109	18,952	17.1	47.3
Aged 45 to 64	29,693	18,624	16.8	62.7
Aged 65 to 74	8,079	5,756	5.2	71.2
Aged 75 or older	5,868	4,205	3.8	71.7
Total women	**105,523**	**59,284**	**53.5**	**56.2**
Aged 18 to 24	13,375	4,630	4.2	34.6
Aged 25 to 44	41,671	21,785	19.7	52.3
Aged 45 to 64	31,659	20,677	18.7	65.3
Aged 65 to 74	9,740	6,695	6.0	68.7
Aged 75 or older	9,077	5,497	5.0	60.6

Source: Bureau of the Census, Voting and Registration in the Election of November 2000, *detailed tables from Current Population Report P20-542, 2002; Internet site <www.census.gov/population/www/socdemo/voting/p20-542.html>; calculations by New Strategist*

Reasons for Not Voting, by Sex, November 2000

(percent distribution of people registered to vote who did not vote by reason and sex, November 2000)

	total	men	women
Total reasons	**100.0%**	**100.0%**	**100.0%**
Too busy, conflicting schedule	20.9	22.5	19.5
Illness or disability (own or family's)	14.8	9.9	19.1
Not interested, felt vote would not make difference	12.2	12.9	11.6
Out of town or away from home	10.2	13.3	7.5
Other reasons	10.2	10.1	10.2
Did not like candidates or campaign issues	7.7	7.7	7.7
Don't know	7.5	9.2	6.0
Registration problems	6.9	6.1	7.5
Forgot to vote or to send in absentee ballot	4.0	3.8	4.1
Inconvenient polling place, hours, or lines too long	2.6	2.6	2.6
Transportation problems	2.4	1.6	3.1
Bad weather conditions	0.6	0.2	1.0

Source: Bureau of the Census, Voting and Registration in the Election of November 2000, *detailed tables from Current Population Report P20-542, 2002; Internet site <www.census.gov/population/www/socdemo/voting/p20-542.html>; calculations by New Strategist*

Older Men Are More Likely to Read Newspapers

Younger men are more likely to be online.

Older men are big consumers of newspapers. The majority of men aged 55 or older read a newspaper every day. Among men under age 35, fewer than one in four reads a newspaper daily. With television, the oldest and youngest men are the most avid viewers. More than half of men aged 18 to 24 and aged 65 or older watch TV for at least three hours a day. This compares with only 40 to 42 percent of men aged 25 to 54.

Men under age 50 are much more likely than those aged 50 or older to use computers and go online. Among men aged 25 to 49, fully 62 percent use the Internet compared with 40 percent of men aged 50 or older. Married couples with children under age 18 are most likely to be computer and Internet users.

■ Increasingly, young and middle-aged adults are getting their information from the Internet rather than from traditional media such as newspapers and television.

Few young adults read a newspaper every day

(percent of men who read a newspaper every day, by age, 2000)

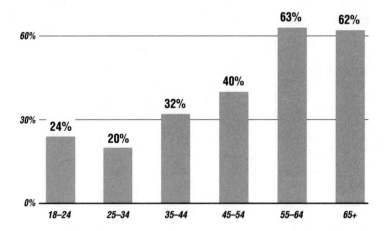

Newspaper Readership, 2000

"How often do you read the newspaper—every day, a few times
a week, once a week, less than once a week, or never?"

(percent of men aged 18 or older responding, by age, 2000)

	every day	a few times a week	once a week	less than once a week	never
Total men	37%	27%	14%	14%	9%
Aged 18 to 24	24	38	11	19	8
Aged 25 to 34	20	38	16	18	9
Aged 35 to 44	32	30	16	16	6
Aged 45 to 54	40	21	14	13	12
Aged 55 to 64	63	16	7	7	6
Aged 65 or older	62	10	12	5	12

Note: Percentages may not add to 100 because "don't know" is not shown.
Source: 2000 General Social Survey, National Opinion Research Center, University of Chicago; calculations by New Strategist

Television Viewing, 2000

"On the average day, about how many hours
do you personally watch television?"

(percent of men aged 18 or older responding, by age, 2000)

	none	1 to 2 hours	3 to 4 hours	5 or more hours
Total men	**4%**	**51%**	**29%**	**16%**
Aged 18 to 24	5	42	32	22
Aged 25 to 34	4	56	25	15
Aged 35 to 44	5	52	27	15
Aged 45 to 54	1	57	29	13
Aged 55 to 64	4	50	35	11
Aged 65 or older	2	44	33	21

Note: Percentages may not add to 100 because "don't know" is not shown.
Source: 2000 General Social Survey, National Opinion Research Center, University of Chicago; calculations by New Strategist

Computer and Internet Use by Age and Sex, 2001

(percent of people aged 3 or older who use computers or go online, by age and sex, 2001)

	total	male	female
Computer users			
Total people	**65.6%**	**65.5%**	**65.8%**
Under age 18	70.7	70.3	71.1
Aged 18 to 24, attending school or college	80.7	81.9	89.1
Aged 18 to 24, not attending school or college	52.4	–	–
Aged 25 to 49	70.2	67.3	73.0
Aged 50 or older	42.5	45.1	40.2
Internet users			
Total people	**53.9**	**53.9**	**53.8**
Under age 18	41.2	41.1	41.2
Aged 18 to 24, attending school or college	68.0	69.4	66.8
Aged 18 to 24, not attending school or college	24.0	–	–
Aged 25 to 49	63.9	61.8	66.0
Aged 50 or older	37.1	39.9	34.6

Note: Percentages for people under age 18 are for computer and Internet use at home; (–) means data are not available.
Source: National Telecommunications and Information Administration, A Nation Online: How Americans Are Expanding Their Use of the Internet, *2002, Internet site <www.ntia.doc.gov/ntiahome/dn/index.html>*

Computer and Internet Use by Household Type, 2001

(percent of people aged 3 or older who use computers or go online, by household type, 2001)

	computer users	Internet users
Married couple with children under age 18	78.5%	62.0%
Male householder with children under age 18	62.6	45.8
Female householder with children under age 18	66.0	45.3
Family household, no children under age 18	56.6	50.5
Nonfamily household	51.8	47.6

Source: National Telecommunications and Information Administration, A Nation Online: How Americans Are Expanding Their Use of the Internet, *2002, Internet site <www.ntia.doc.gov/ntiahome/dn/index.html>*

2

Business

Most businesses are owned by men.

Men own the 55 percent majority of the nation's 21 million businesses. Women own another 26 percent, while the remainder are owned jointly by equal numbers of men and women. Men own the largest share of businesses in the construction industry.

Most firms owned by men are individual proprietorships.

Of the 11 million firms owned by men, 70 percent are individual proprietorships. Sixty-one percent of firms owned by men had sales and receipts of less than $50,000 in 1997. Only 30 percent had employees.

Nearly 40 percent of businesses owned by men are in just five states.

California is home to 12 percent of all businesses owned by men. New York has another 8 percent. Men own 63 percent of all businesses in New York and New Jersey, but only 47 percent of businesses in Idaho.

Men Own 55 Percent of the Nation's Businesses

In the construction industry, men own 78 percent of firms.

Men own 55 percent of the nation's 21 million businesses. Women own another 26 percent, while the remainder are owned jointly by equal numbers of men and women, according to the Survey of Women-Owned Business Enterprises, a part of the 1997 Economic Censuses. The survey counts a firm as male-owned if the majority of owners are men. It determines ownership for a firm in its entirety rather than at individual locations.

Men own a 43 percent minority of firms in the retail trade industry. They own only 35 percent of apparel stores, for example. While men own slightly more than half the firms in the service industries, they own just 21 percent of social service firms. Men own more than 91 percent of pipeline firms, 88 percent of coal mining businesses, and 80 percent of insurance carriers.

■ As women have entered the workforce by the millions over the past few decades, the percentage of businesses owned by men has been shrinking.

In most industries, men own the majority of firms

(percent of firms owned by men, by industry, 1997)

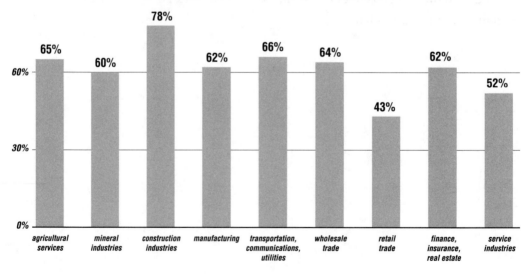

Number and Percent Distribution of Businesses Owned by Men, 1997

(total number of firms, number and percent distribution of firms owned by men, and male share of total, by industry, 1997)

SIC code		total firms	firms owned by men		
			number	percent distribution	share of total
	All industries	**20,821,935**	**11,382,000**	**100.0%**	**54.7%**
	Agricultural services, forestry, fishing	**496,164**	**322,754**	**2.8**	**65.0**
07	Agricultural services	412,852	263,329	2.3	63.8
08	Forestry	14,051	9,641	0.1	68.6
09	Fishing, hunting, and trapping	69,271	49,794	0.4	71.9
	Mineral industries	**126,809**	**76,349**	**0.7**	**60.2**
10	Metal mining	1,819	1,295	0.0	71.2
12	Coal mining	2,242	1,982	0.0	88.4
13	Oil and gas extraction	115,953	68,131	0.6	58.8
14	Nonmetallic minerals, except fuels	6,862	5,004	0.0	72.9
	Construction industries, subdividers, and developers	**2,333,424**	**1,831,090**	**16.1**	**78.5**
15	Building construction, general contractors, and operative builders	472,111	361,411	3.2	76.6
16	Heavy construction contractors other than buildings	64,314	47,133	0.4	73.3
17	Special trade contractors	1,739,060	1,379,404	12.1	79.3
6552	Subdividers and developers not elsewhere classified (excl. cemeteries)	58,362	43,527	0.4	74.6
	Manufacturing	**688,782**	**429,205**	**3.8**	**62.3**
20	Food and kindred products	30,256	17,247	0.2	57.0
21	Tobacco products	133	108	0.0	81.2
22	Textile mill products	8,213	4,744	0.0	57.8
23	Apparel and other textile products	54,889	20,604	0.2	37.5
24	Lumber and wood products	106,569	75,683	0.7	71.0
25	Furniture and fixtures	28,712	19,387	0.2	67.5
26	Paper and allied products	7,186	4,985	0.0	69.4
27	Printing and publishing	119,936	65,366	0.6	54.5
28	Chemicals and allied products	10,941	8,466	0.1	77.4
29	Petroleum and coal products	1,434	1,179	0.0	82.2
30	Rubber and miscellaneous plastics	16,296	12,466	0.1	76.5

(continued)

(continued from previous page)

SIC code		total firms	firms owned by men		
			number	percent distribution	share of total
31	Leather and leather products	5,251	2,993	0.0%	57.0%
32	Stone, clay, and glass products	29,262	14,325	0.1	49.0
33	Primary metal industries	7,703	5,800	0.1	75.3
34	Fabricated metal products	63,141	44,585	0.4	70.6
35	Industrial machinery, equipment	85,401	20,029	0.2	70.7
36	Electronic and other electric equip.	28,324	20,029	0.2	70.7
37	Transportation equipment	13,673	10,253	0.1	75.0
38	Instruments and related products	12,423	9,411	0.1	75.8
39	Misc. manufacturing industries	65,185	34,659	0.3	53.2
	Transportation, communications, and utilities	**919,570**	**604,368**	**5.3**	**65.7**
41	Local and interurban passenger transportation	116,993	87,882	0.8	75.1
42	Motor freight transportation and warehousing	544,523	368,301	3.2	67.6
44	Water transportation	15,788	10,781	0.1	68.3
45pt.	Transportation by air	20,706	15,430	0.1	74.5
46	Pipelines, except natural gas	136	125	0.0	91.9
47	Transportation services	129,652	61,931	0.5	47.8
48	Communications	61,180	38,140	0.3	62.3
49	Electric, gas, and sanitary services	31,345	22,434	0.2	71.6
	Wholesale trade	**797,856**	**511,094**	**4.5**	**64.1**
50	Durable goods	489,308	326,926	2.9	66.8
51	Nondurable goods	309,731	185,227	1.6	59.8
	Retail trade	**2,889,041**	**1,232,599**	**10.8**	**42.7**
52	Building materials, hardware, garden supply, and mobile home dealers	85,060	48,845	0.4	57.4
53	General merchandise stores	35,027	13,689	0.1	39.1
54	Food stores	216,067	104,500	0.9	48.4
55	Automotive dealers and gasoline service stations	255,259	179,615	1.6	70.4
56	Apparel and accessory stores	127,848	45,206	0.4	35.4
57	Home furniture, furnishings, and equipment stores	153,248	85,543	0.8	55.8
58	Eating and drinking places	493,313	244,273	2.1	49.5
59	Miscellaneous retail	1,528,857	515,160	4.5	33.7

(continued)

(continued from previous page)

SIC code		total firms	firms owned by men		
			number	percent distribution	share of total
	Finance, insurance, and real estate (excl. subdividers, developers)	**2,237,675**	**1,378,604**	**12.1%**	**61.6%**
60	Depository institutions	24,616	20,974	0.2	85.2
61	Nondepository credit institutions	45,905	31,049	0.3	67.6
62	Security and commodity brokers, dealers, exchanges, and services	91,446	68,694	0.6	75.1
63pt.	Insurance carriers	9,108	7,315	0.1	80.3
64	Insurance agents, brokers, services	411,902	291,493	2.6	70.8
65pt.	Real estate (excl. subdividers and developers)	1,503,438	856,787	7.5	57.0
67pt.	Holding and other investment offices, except trusts	157,652	108,082	0.9	68.6
	Service industries (excl. membership organizations, private household)	**8,891,023**	**4,590,818**	**40.3**	**51.6**
70	Hotels, rooming houses, camps, and other lodging places	93,380	37,094	0.3	39.7
72	Personal services	1,348,554	503,967	4.4	37.4
73	Business services	2,221,046	1,086,759	9.5	48.9
75	Automotive repair, services, parking	448,584	329,112	2.9	73.4
76	Miscellaneous repair services	231,371	162,351	1.4	70.2
78	Motion pictures	87,700	53,306	0.5	60.8
79	Amusement and recreation services	603,896	370,825	3.3	61.4
80	Health services	1,004,672	583,561	5.1	58.1
81	Legal services	353,147	259,637	2.3	73.5
82	Educational services	270,648	110,488	1.0	40.8
83	Social services	665,067	141,581	1.2	21.3
84	Museums, art galleries, botanical and zoological gardens	5,205	4,893	0.0	94.0
87	Engineering, accounting, research, management, and related services	1,446,195	898,907	7.9	62.2
89	Services not elsewhere classified	119,931	55,582	0.5	46.3
	Industries not classified	**1,480,003**	**819,357**	**7.2**	**55.4**

Note: Among businesses owned by men, industry subcategories include 382,000 publicly held, foreign-owned, and nonprofit companies.
Source: Bureau of the Census, Women-Owned Businesses, *1997 Economic Census, Survey of Women-Owned Business Enterprises, Company Statistics Series, EC97CS-2, 2001; calculations by New Strategist*

Most Firms Owned by Men Are Small

Only 3 million male-owned firms have employees.

Most businesses in the U.S. are small, with only one person running the operation. Of the 11 million businesses owned by men, 70 percent are individual proprietorships. Only 25 percent are corporations. Just 30 percent of male-owned firms have paid employees. Most of those have fewer than four employees.

Most businesses are small and do not generate much revenue. Fully 61 percent of firms owned by men had sales and receipts of less than $50,000 in 1997. Only 7 percent had sales and receipts of $1,000,000 or more. Male-owned businesses account for 76 percent of all firms with sales and receipts of $1,000,000 or more—greater than the 55 percent male share of all firms.

■ Because most businesses are small, government efforts to aid small businesses are of interest to millions.

Most businesses owned by men have sales and receipts below $50,000

(percent distribution of sales and receipts for firms owned by men, 1997)

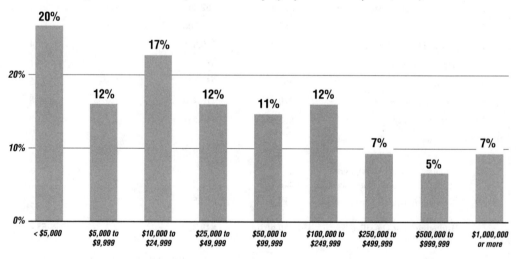

Characteristics of Male-Owned Businesses by Legal Form of Organization, Receipt Size, and Employees, 1997

(total number of firms, number and percent distribution of firms owned by men and male share of total, by legal form of organization, size of receipts, and number of employees, 1997)

		firms owned by men		
	total	number	percent distribution	share of total
Total firms	**20,821,934**	**11,382,000**	**100.0%**	**54.7%**
Legal form of organization				
C corporations	2,390,478	1,667,932	14.7	69.8
Subchapter S corporations	1,979,425	1,196,669	10.5	60.5
Individual proprietorships	15,122,882	8,006,370	70.3	52.9
Partnerships	1,226,455	803,695	7.1	65.5
Other	102,694	88,970	0.8	86.6
Size of receipts				
Under $5,000	4,625,337	2,249,662	19.8	48.6
$5,000 to $9,999	2,760,243	1,352,133	11.9	49.0
$10,000 to $24,999	3,619,150	1,927,188	16.9	53.2
$25,000 to $49,999	2,396,802	1,412,281	12.4	58.9
$50,000 to $99,999	2,106,310	1,296,943	11.4	61.6
$100,000 to $249,999	2,213,767	1,385,458	12.2	62.6
$250,000 to $499,999	1,221,990	787,807	6.9	64.5
$500,000 to $999,999	827,956	556,784	4.9	67.2
$1,000,000 or more	1,050,379	795,383	7.0	75.7
Number of employees				
Firms with employees	5,295,151	3,418,902	100.0	64.6
No employees*	819,990	581,769	17.0	70.9
1 to 3 employees	2,569,184	1,622,393	47.5	63.1
5 to 9 employees	966,871	609,076	17.8	63.0
10 to 19 employees	570,401	373,416	10.9	65.5
20 to 49 employees	359,358	260,268	7.6	72.4
50 to 99 employees	113,693	90,247	2.6	79.4
100 to 499 employees	79,688	65,094	1.9	81.7
500 employees or more	15,966	14,638	0.4	91.7

* Firms that reported annual payroll but no employees on the payroll during the specified period in 1997.
Note: Among businesses owned by men, subcategories include 382,000 publicly held, foreign-owned, and nonprofit companies.
Source: Bureau of the Census, Women-Owned Businesses, *1997 Economic Census, Survey of Women-Owned Business Enterprises, Company Statistics Series, EC97CS-2, 2001; calculations by New Strategist*

Largest Share of Male-Owned Firms Are in California

Another 8 percent of male-owned firms are in New York.

California, home to the largest number of Americans, is also where the largest share of male-owned businesses are based. Twelve percent of the 11 million firms owned by men are in California. Eight percent of male-owned businesses are in New York and another 7 percent are in Texas.

The percentage of businesses owned by men varies by state, ranging from a high of 63 percent in New York and New Jersey to a low of 47 percent in Idaho. Just because men own fewer than half of businesses in a state does not mean women own the larger share because many firms are owned by equal numbers of men and women.

■ Business growth is closely tied to population trends. The number of businesses in states with rapidly growing populations will increase faster than the number in slow-growing states.

Nearly 40 percent of businesses owned by men are in just five states.

(number of businesses owned by men in the five states with the most male-owned businesses, 1997)

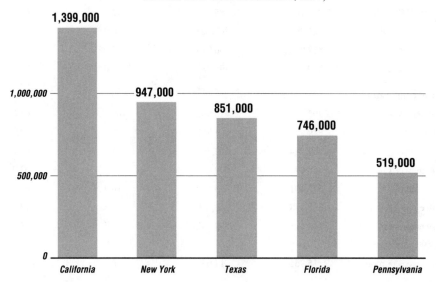

Male-Owned Businesses by State, 1997

(total number of firms, number and percent distribution of firms owned by men, and male share of total, 1997)

| | total | firms owned by men | | |
		number	percent distribution	share of total
Total firms	**20,821,934**	**11,382,000**	**100.0%**	**54.7%**
Alabama	285,206	171,871	1.5	60.3
Alaska	64,134	32,797	0.3	51.1
Arizona	329,031	160,550	1.4	48.8
Arkansas	193,424	105,612	0.9	54.6
California	2,565,734	1,399,084	12.3	54.5
Colorado	410,249	216,945	1.9	52.9
Connecticut	284,022	176,667	1.6	62.2
Delaware	56,586	34,035	0.3	60.1
District of Columbia	45,297	27,405	0.2	60.5
Florida	1,301,920	745,589	6.6	57.3
Georgia	568,552	340,204	3.0	59.8
Hawaii	93,981	52,465	0.5	55.8
Idaho	109,758	51,460	0.5	46.9
Illinois	882,053	493,185	4.3	55.9
Indiana	413,400	223,441	2.0	54.0
Iowa	227,562	117,409	1.0	51.6
Kansas	213,392	106,543	0.9	49.9
Kentucky	281,551	164,554	1.4	58.4
Louisiana	295,679	169,339	1.5	57.3
Maine	127,467	73,376	0.6	57.6
Maryland	400,203	227,446	2.0	56.8
Massachusetts	537,150	333,916	2.9	62.2
Michigan	677,473	380,611	3.3	56.2
Minnesota	410,634	225,542	2.0	54.9
Mississippi	167,907	100,345	0.9	59.8
Missouri	411,403	214,418	1.9	52.1
Montana	93,677	47,443	0.4	50.6
Nebraska	138,762	68,782	0.6	49.6
Nevada	129,757	69,354	0.6	53.4
New Hampshire	115,747	70,445	0.6	60.9
New Jersey	654,227	410,194	3.6	62.7

(continued)

(continued from previous page)

| | total | firms owned by men | | |
		number	percent distribution	share of total
New Mexico	131,685	63,295	0.6%	48.1%
New York	1,509,829	946,810	8.3	62.7
North Carolina	570,484	335,648	2.9	58.8
North Dakota	55,266	30,394	0.3	55.0
Ohio	781,284	462,826	4.1	59.2
Oklahoma	280,722	149,890	1.3	53.4
Oregon	291,596	143,017	1.3	49.0
Pennsylvania	837,756	518,660	4.6	61.9
Rhode Island	80,934	49,370	0.4	61.0
South Carolina	260,342	159,967	1.4	61.4
South Dakota	65,791	33,546	0.3	51.0
Tennessee	415,934	244,797	2.2	58.9
Texas	1,525,972	850,779	7.5	55.8
Utah	169,164	93,295	0.8	55.2
Vermont	67,488	36,504	0.3	54.1
Virginia	480,122	279,833	2.5	58.3
Washington	447,433	214,654	1.9	48.0
West Virginia	111,737	64,106	0.6	57.4
Wisconsin	366,436	200,864	1.8	54.8
Wyoming	49,376	23,919	0.2	48.4

Note: Among businesses owned by men, state subcategories include 382,000 publicly held, foreign-owned, and nonprofit companies. Numbers will not add to total because firms located in more than one state are counted only once in the total.
Source: Bureau of the Census, Women-Owned Businesses, *1997 Economic Census, Survey of Women-Owned Business Enterprises, Company Statistics Series, EC97CS-2, 2001; calculations by New Strategist*

3

Education

Men have made strides in education.

Between 1950 and 2000, the proportion of men with a high school diploma climbed from 33 to 84 percent. The proportion of men with a college degree rose from 7 to 28 percent.

Middle-aged men are better educated than those younger or older.

Thirty-four percent of men aged 50 to 54 have a college degree compared with 27 to 29 percent of men under age 45.

Asian men are most likely to be college graduates.

Forty-eight percent of Asian men have a college degree compared with 31 percent of non-Hispanic whites.

Men are a minority of college students.

Among the nation's 15 million college students in 2000, only 44 percent were men. This share is down slightly from 45 percent in 1990.

Many men in college are Asian, black, or Hispanic.

Non-Hispanic whites accounted for 71 percent of college students in 2000, down from 73 percent in the early 1990s.

Male and female college students have similar objectives.

Among college freshmen, 76 percent of men and 71 percent of women say it is very important or essential to be "very well off financially."

Men earn most doctoral and first-professional degrees.

Men earned a minority of associate's, bachelor's, and master's degrees in 2000, but more than half of doctoral and first-professional degrees.

Men's Educational Attainment Has Grown

In 2000, more than one in four men had a college degree.

The educational attainment of the U.S. population has grown dramatically as the baby-boom and younger generations of Americans entered adulthood, replacing older, less-educated generations. In 1950, few men had even graduated from high school—only 33 percent had a high school diploma. In 1967, the proportion passed the 50 percent threshold for the first time. By 2000, fully 84 percent of men aged 25 or older were high school graduates.

The proportion of men with a college degree also climbed sharply between 1950 and 2000. In 1950, just 7 percent of men were college graduates. By 2000, the figure had climbed to 28 percent.

■ As men's educational attainment has grown, so have white-collar jobs and the service economy.

Men are much better educated today than in 1950

(percent of men who are high school or college graduates, 1950 and 2000)

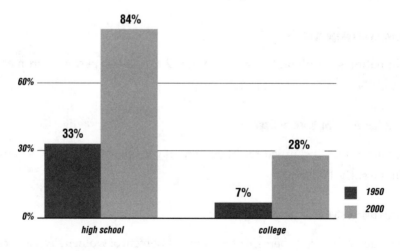

Educational Attainment of Men, 1950 to 2000

(percent of men aged 25 or older who are high school or college graduates, 1950 to 2000)

	high school	college
2000	84.2%	27.8%
1995	81.7	26.0
1990	77.7	24.4
1985	74.4	23.1
1980	69.2	20.9
1975	63.1	17.6
1970	55.0	14.1
1965	48.0	12.0
1959	42.2	10.3
1950	32.6	7.3

Source: Bureau of the Census, Current Population Surveys, Internet site <www.census.gov/population/socdemo/education/tableA-2.txt>

Middle-Aged Men Are the Best Educated

More than one-third of men aged 50 to 54 have a college degree.

Graduating from high school has been a nearly universal experience for baby boomers and younger generations of men. Today, nearly 90 percent of men under age 55 (the oldest boomers turned 54 in 2000) are high school graduates. Older men are not as likely to be high school graduates. Only 70 percent of those aged 65 or older have a high school diploma.

The percentage of men with a bachelor's degree peaks in middle age, at 34 percent among those aged 50 to 54. Men in this age group are better educated than others because many went to college to avoid the Vietnam War. Without such an incentive, younger men have been less likely to graduate from college. Only 27 to 29 percent of men under age 45 have a college degree.

■ Young men are less likely to be college graduates than their female counterparts, a fact that may affect the lifestyles of younger generations of Americans.

Men in their fifties are most likely to be college graduates

(percent of men with a bachelor's degree, by age, 2000)

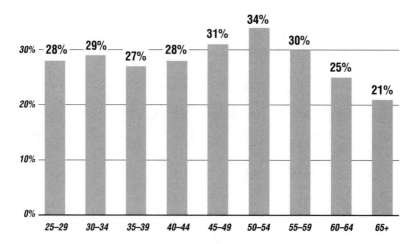

Male High School and College Graduates by Age, 2000

(percent of men aged 25 or older who are high school or college graduates by age, 2000)

	high school	*college*
Total men	**84.2%**	**27.8%**
Aged 25 to 29	86.7	27.9
Aged 30 to 34	87.5	29.3
Aged 35 to 39	88.2	27.3
Aged 40 to 44	88.2	27.5
Aged 45 to 49	89.3	30.7
Aged 50 to 54	88.4	34.2
Aged 55 to 59	85.0	29.9
Aged 60 to 64	78.5	25.5
Aged 65 or older	69.6	21.4
Aged 65 to 69	75.4	23.4
Aged 70 to 74	70.1	22.3
Aged 75 or older	64.9	19.3

Source: Bureau of the Census, Educational Attainment in the United States: March 2000 (Update), *detailed tables for Current Population Report P20-536, 2000; Internet site <www.census.gov/population/socdemo/ education/p20-536/tab01a.txt>*

Asian Men Are Most Likely to Be College Graduates

Hispanic men are least likely to have a high school diploma or college degree.

Only 57 percent of Hispanic men have a high school diploma, a much lower share than the 84 percent of all men who graduated from high school. Asian and non-Hispanic white men are most likely to be high school graduates, at 88 percent. Only 11 percent of Hispanic men are college graduates compared with 16 percent of black men, 31 percent of non-Hispanic white men, and 48 percent of Asian men.

Young men are more likely than older men to be high school graduates, regardless of race or Hispanic origin. The pattern is different at the college level. The percentage of men with a college degree varies by age, with men aged 50 to 54 most likely to have a degree among Hispanics (17 percent), blacks (21 percent), and non-Hispanic whites (37 percent). For Asians, the percentage of men with a college degree ranges between 46 and 55 percent for men under age 60.

■ The educational attainment of Hispanic men is much lower than that of other racial and ethnic groups because many are recent immigrants from countries with poorly educated populations.

Hispanic men are least likely to have a college degree

(percent of men aged 25 or older with a college degree, by race and Hispanic origin, 2000)

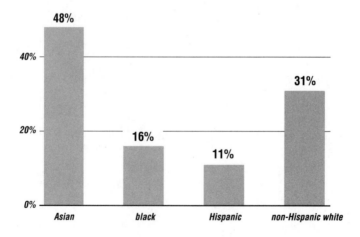

Male High School and College Graduates by Race and Hispanic Origin, 2000

(percent of men aged 25 or older who are high school or college graduates, by race and Hispanic origin, 2000)

	high school	college
Total men	**84.2%**	**27.8%**
Asian	88.2	47.6
Black	78.7	16.3
Hispanic	56.6	10.7
White	84.8	28.5
Non-Hispanic white	88.5	30.8

Source: Bureau of the Census, Educational Attainment in the United States: March 2000 (Update), *detailed tables for Current Population Report P20-536, 2000; Internet site <www.census.gov/population/socdemo/education/p20-536/tab01a.txt>*

Male High School and College Graduates by Age, Race, and Hispanic Origin, 2000

(percent of men aged 25 or older who are high school or college graduates, by age, race, and Hispanic origin, 2000)

	Asian	black	Hispanic	white total	white non-Hispanic
High school graduates					
Total men	**88.2%**	**78.7%**	**56.6%**	**84.8%**	**88.5%**
Aged 25 to 29	91.9	86.6	59.2	86.6	92.9
Aged 30 to 34	93.4	89.1	58.6	87.1	93.2
Aged 35 to 39	89.7	89.6	59.8	88.0	92.8
Aged 40 to 44	89.4	87.6	60.1	88.3	91.8
Aged 45 to 49	89.7	83.5	59.2	90.1	93.4
Aged 50 to 54	90.8	77.8	57.5	89.5	92.7
Aged 55 to 59	92.1	69.8	53.6	86.7	89.7
Aged 60 to 64	84.4	55.6	42.2	80.8	84.1
Aged 65 or older	70.5	44.7	41.0	71.9	73.8
Aged 65 to 69	72.6	54.5	48.1	77.7	79.9
Aged 70 to 74	79.1	46.5	41.8	72.2	74.1
Aged 75 or older	62.6	35.1	32.6	67.6	69.3
College graduates					
Total men	**47.6**	**16.3**	**10.7**	**28.5**	**30.8**
Aged 25 to 29	55.3	18.1	8.3	27.8	32.3
Aged 30 to 34	45.7	17.9	8.9	30.3	34.8
Aged 35 to 39	50.2	19.0	10.3	27.5	30.4
Aged 40 to 44	54.4	15.1	12.6	28.3	30.3
Aged 45 to 49	45.6	18.5	12.0	31.9	33.9
Aged 50 to 54	50.2	21.0	16.8	35.1	37.0
Aged 55 to 59	48.5	15.3	12.3	31.0	32.6
Aged 60 to 64	39.1	11.4	9.4	26.5	28.0
Aged 65 or older	32.2	7.4	9.3	22.4	23.2
Aged 65 to 69	31.5	9.9	10.6	24.6	25.5
Aged 70 to 74	32.9	7.4	9.0	23.5	24.4
Aged 75 or older	32.4	5.3	8.2	20.2	20.7

Source: Bureau of the Census, Educational Attainment in the United States: March 2000 (Update), detailed tables for Current Population Report P20-536, 2000; Internet site <www.census.gov/population/socdemo/education/p20-536/tab01a.txt>

Source: Bureau of the Census, Educational Attainment in the United States: March 2000 (Update), *detailed tables for Current Population Report P20-536, 2000; Internet site <www.census.gov/population/socdemo/education/p20-536/tab01a.txt>*

The Majority of Men Have College Experience

Many men have attended college but do not have a bachelor's degree.

Twenty-eight percent of men have a bachelor's degree, 7 percent have an associate's degree, and 17 percent have attended college but failed to earn a degree. Altogether, 52 percent of men aged 25 or older have at least some college experience. Among men aged 50 to 54 (the best educated age group), fully 62 percent have college experience.

The proportion of men with a bachelor's degree peaks among those aged 50 to 54 at 34 percent. The proportion of men with a master's degree also peaks in the same age group at 9 percent. There is little variation by age in the percentage of men with a doctoral or first-professional degree.

■ The Vietnam War not only boosted the educational attainment of men, it also shaped the attitudes of the baby-boom generation, which came of age during those years.

Six percent of men have a master's degree

(percent distribution of men by educational attainment, 2000)

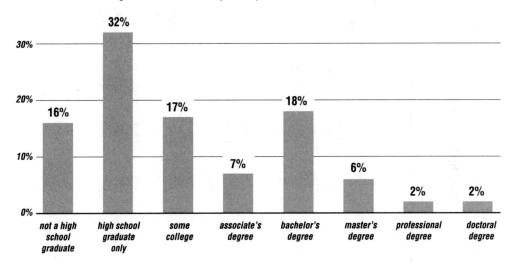

Educational Attainment of Men by Age, 2000

(number and percent distribution of men aged 25 or older by age and educational attainment, 2000; numbers in thousands)

	total	not a high school graduate	total	high school graduate only	some college	associate's degree	total	bachelor's degree only	master's degree	professional degree	doctoral degree
							high school graduate or more			bachelor's degree or more	
Total men	83,611	13,216	70,396	26,651	14,540	5,953	23,252	14,909	5,166	1,752	1,425
Aged 25 to 29	8,942	1,186	7,756	2,831	1,770	657	2,498	2,079	287	96	36
Aged 30 to 34	9,621	1,199	8,421	3,158	1,713	730	2,820	2,055	514	145	106
Aged 35 to 39	11,032	1,306	9,726	3,861	1,978	872	3,015	2,018	654	185	158
Aged 40 to 44	11,103	1,316	9,789	3,785	1,956	992	3,056	1,959	707	204	186
Aged 45 to 49	9,654	1,030	8,624	3,002	1,832	828	2,962	1,802	754	237	169
Aged 50 to 54	8,235	960	7,276	2,197	1,584	674	2,821	1,657	741	230	193
Aged 55 to 59	6,105	913	5,191	1,982	1,015	369	1,825	965	495	195	170
Aged 60 to 64	5,032	1,083	3,948	1,609	745	311	1,283	694	359	136	94
Aged 65 or older	13,886	4,223	9,662	4,225	1,947	519	2,971	1,679	655	324	313
Aged 65 to 69	4,376	1,075	3,300	1,413	665	198	1,024	559	239	94	132
Aged 70 to 74	3,673	1,099	2,576	1,098	507	150	821	454	197	82	88
Aged 75 or older	5,837	2,049	3,787	1,714	775	171	1,127	667	219	147	94

(continued)

(continued from previous page)

| | total | not a high school graduate | high school graduate or more | | | | | | | | |
| | | | total | high school graduate only | some college | associate's degree | bachelor's degree or more | | | | |
							total	bachelor's degree only	master's degree	professional degree	doctoral degree
Total men	**100.0%**	**15.8%**	**84.2%**	**31.9%**	**17.4%**	**7.1%**	**27.8%**	**17.8%**	**6.2%**	**2.1%**	**1.7%**
Aged 25 to 29	100.0	13.3	86.7	31.7	19.8	7.3	27.9	23.2	3.2	1.1	0.4
Aged 30 to 34	100.0	12.5	87.5	32.8	17.8	7.6	29.3	21.4	5.3	1.5	1.1
Aged 35 to 39	100.0	11.8	88.2	35.0	17.9	7.9	27.3	18.3	5.9	1.7	1.4
Aged 40 to 44	100.0	11.9	88.2	34.1	17.6	8.9	27.5	17.6	6.4	1.8	1.7
Aged 45 to 49	100.0	10.7	89.3	31.1	19.0	8.6	30.7	18.7	7.8	2.5	1.8
Aged 50 to 54	100.0	11.7	88.4	26.7	19.2	8.2	34.3	20.1	9.0	2.8	2.3
Aged 55 to 59	100.0	15.0	85.0	32.5	16.6	6.0	29.9	15.8	8.1	3.2	2.8
Aged 60 to 64	100.0	21.5	78.5	32.0	14.8	6.2	25.5	13.8	7.1	2.7	1.9
Aged 65 or older	100.0	30.4	69.6	30.4	14.0	3.7	21.4	12.1	4.7	2.3	2.3
Aged 65 to 69	100.0	24.6	75.4	32.3	15.2	4.5	23.4	12.8	5.5	2.1	3.0
Aged 70 to 74	100.0	29.9	70.1	29.9	13.8	4.1	22.4	12.4	5.4	2.2	2.4
Aged 75 or older	100.0	35.1	64.9	29.4	13.3	2.9	19.3	11.4	3.8	2.5	1.6

Source: Bureau of the Census, Educational Attainment in the United States: March 2000 (Update), detailed tables for Current Population Report P20-536, 2000; Internet site <www.census.gov/population/socdemo/education/p20-536/tab01.txt> ; calculations by New Strategist

Many Older Men Are in School

The majority of boys are also in school.

The value Americans place on education is apparent in school enrollment statistics. Virtually all children aged 5 to 17 are enrolled in school. And although it was once rare for children to be in preschool, today slightly more than half of 3- and 4-year-old boys are in school. School enrollment among boys exceeds 90 percent from ages 7 to 17. It falls to 58 percent among 18- and 19-year-olds as a substantial portion of young adults choose not to go to college.

Many men are students well into their twenties and thirties. Nearly one-fourth of 22-to-24-year-olds are in school, as are 10 percent of those aged 25 to 29 and 6 percent of 30-to-34-year-olds. Among men aged 35 or older, nearly 1 million are students.

■ Increasingly, Americans view education as a lifelong pursuit rather than something reserved for the young.

Among men aged 18 or older, many are in school

(percent of men aged 18 or older enrolled in school, by age, 2000)

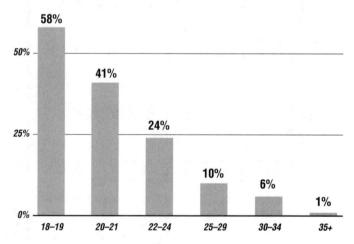

School Enrollment of Males by Age, 2000

(total number of males aged 3 or older, and number and percent enrolled in school, by age, 2000; numbers in thousands)

	total	enrolled in school	
		number	percent
Total males	**128,044**	**35,838**	**28.0%**
Aged 3 and 4	4,007	2,035	50.8
Aged 5 and 6	4,105	3,903	95.1
Aged 7 to 9	6,304	6,177	98.0
Aged 10 to 13	8,449	8,308	98.3
Aged 14 and 15	4,103	4,050	98.7
Aged 16 and 17	4,064	3,767	92.7
Aged 18 and 19	4,037	2,353	58.3
Aged 20 and 21	3,777	1,548	41.0
Aged 22 to 24	5,525	1,320	23.9
Aged 25 to 29	8,566	860	10.0
Aged 30 to 34	9,547	536	5.6
Aged 35 to 44	22,021	651	3.0
Aged 45 to 54	18,238	250	1.4
Aged 55 or older	25,300	80	0.3

Source: Bureau of the Census, School Enrollment: Social and Economic Characteristics of Students: October 2000, *Current Population Report PPL-148, 2001; Internet site <www.census.gov/population/socdemo/school/ppl-148/tab01.txt>*

Men's College Enrollment Rate Grew during the 1990s

But the male share of college students fell slightly.

In 2000, 60 percent of men graduating from high school continued their education by enrolling in college, up from 58 percent in 1990. Among women, the proportion rose from 62 percent in 1990 to 66 percent in 2000. The enrollment rate of men was below that of women in most years during the 1990s.

Men accounted for the 44 percent minority of college students in 2000, down from 45 percent in 1990. While overall college enrollment climbed 12 percent between 1990 and 2000, the number of men enrolled rose only 8 percent, from 6.2 million to 6.7 million.

■ Although more than 60 percent of men enroll in college, many never earn a bachelor's degree.

Men's college enrollment grew by less than 500,000 during the 1990s

(total number of people enrolled in college and number of men enrolled, 1990 and 2000; numbers in millions)

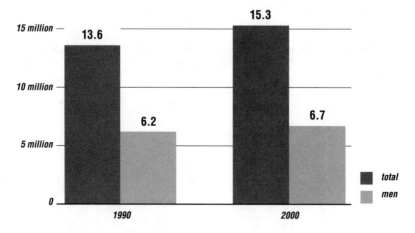

College Enrollment Rates by Sex, 1990 to 2000

(percent of people aged 16 to 24 who graduated from high school in the previous 12 months and were enrolled in college as of October of each year, by sex; percentage point difference in enrollment rates between men and women, 1990 to 2000)

	men	women	percentage point difference
2000	59.9%	66.2%	–6.3
1999	61.4	64.4	–3.0
1998	62.4	69.1	–6.7
1997	63.5	70.3	–6.8
1996	60.1	69.7	–9.6
1995	62.6	61.4	1.2
1994	60.6	63.2	–2.6
1993	59.7	65.4	–5.7
1992	59.6	63.8	–4.2
1991	57.6	67.1	–9.5
1990	57.8	62.0	–4.2

Source: National Center for Education Statistics, Digest of Education Statistics 2001; *Internet site <http://nces.ed.gov/pubsearch/pubsinfo.asp?pubid=2002130>; calculations by New Strategist*

College Enrollment of Men, 1990 to 2000

(total number of people aged 14 or older enrolled in college, number of men enrolled, and male share of total, 1990 to 2000; percent change, 1990–2000; numbers in thousands)

	total	*men*	
		number	*share of total*
2000	15,314	6,682	43.6%
1999	15,203	6,956	45.8
1998	15,546	6,905	44.4
1997	15,436	6,843	44.3
1996	15,226	6,820	44.8
1995	14,715	6,703	45.6
1994	15,022	6,764	45.0
1993	14,394	6,599	45.8
1992	14,035	6,192	44.1
1991	14,057	6,439	45.8
1990	13,621	6,192	45.5
Percent change			
1990–2000	12.4%	7.9%	—

Source: Bureau of the Census, Internet site <www.census.gov/population/socdemo/school/tabA-6.txt>; calculations by New Strategist

Most Men in College Are in the Traditional Age Group

Older men are also a growing share of students.

As the large millennial generation entered its twenties during the 1990s, the number of male college students in the traditional college-going age group, 18 to 24, expanded by more than 400,000. Overall, 65 percent of male college students were aged 18 to 24 in 2000, up from 63 percent in 1990.

The number of male college students aged 25 to 29 fell 7 percent between 1990 and 2000 as the small generation X entered the 25-to-34 age group. The number of male college students aged 30 to 34 rose only 3 percent during those years. The biggest percentage increase among male college students was in the 35-or -older age group, which posted a 19 percent gain during the 1990s and grew to nearly 1 million. This age group accounted for 14 percent of male college students in 2000, up from 12 percent in 1990.

■ Older college students will rise as a share of all students as the millennial generation ages into its late twenties and thirties.

Most male college students are under age 24

(percent distribution of male college students by age, 2000)

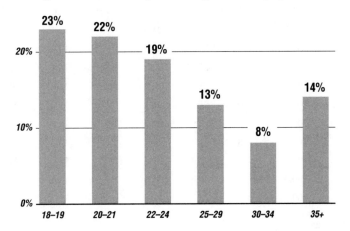

Men in College by Age, 1990 to 2000

(number and percent distribution of men aged 14 or older enrolled in college by age, 1990 to 2000; percent change in number and percentage point change in distribution, 1990–2000; numbers in thousands)

	total	14–17	18–19	20–21	22–24	25–29	30–34	35+
Number								
2000	6,682	61	1,570	1,472	1,300	844	517	918
1999	6,956	78	1,648	1,525	1,224	911	547	1,023
1998	6,905	48	1,667	1,517	1,219	979	521	953
1997	6,843	59	1,561	1,521	1,292	1,052	457	899
1996	6,820	97	1,489	1,379	1,319	1,038	485	1,013
1995	6,703	68	1,431	1,423	1,235	1,008	553	985
1994	6,764	65	1,416	1,414	1,322	972	617	958
1993	6,599	55	1,407	1,405	1,425	892	534	880
1992	6,192	97	1,325	1,344	1,243	845	547	789
1991	6,439	49	1,326	1,390	1,238	1,018	587	832
1990	6,192	86	1,443	1,364	1,115	910	502	772
Percent change								
1990–2000	7.9%	–29.1%	8.8%	7.9%	16.6%	–7.3%	3.0%	18.9%
Percent distribution								
2000	100.0%	0.9%	23.5%	22.0%	19.5%	12.6%	7.7%	13.7%
1999	100.0	1.1	23.7	21.9	17.6	13.1	7.9	14.7
1998	100.0	0.7	24.1	22.0	17.7	14.2	7.5	13.8
1997	100.0	0.9	22.8	22.2	18.9	15.4	6.7	13.1
1996	100.0	1.4	21.8	20.2	19.3	15.2	7.1	14.9
1995	100.0	1.0	21.3	21.2	18.4	15.0	8.3	14.7
1994	100.0	1.0	20.9	20.9	19.5	14.4	9.1	14.2
1993	100.0	0.8	21.3	21.3	21.6	13.5	8.1	13.3
1992	100.0	1.6	21.4	21.7	20.1	13.6	8.8	12.7
1991	100.0	0.8	20.6	21.6	19.2	15.8	9.1	12.9
1990	100.0	1.4	23.3	22.0	18.0	14.7	8.1	12.5
Percentage point change								
1990–2000	–	–0.5	0.2	0.0	1.4	–2.1	–0.4	1.3

Note: (–) means not applicable.
Source: Bureau of the Census, Current Population Surveys, Internet site <www.census.gov/population/socdemo/school/tabA-6.txt>; calculations by New Strategist

Thirty Percent of Male College Students Are Minorities

Non-Hispanic whites are a shrinking share of college students.

Non-Hispanic whites accounted for 71 percent of men enrolled in college in 2000, down from 73 percent in the early 1990s. Twelve percent of male college students are black, up from 9 percent in 1990. The Hispanic share of male college students grew from 6 to 9 percent between 1990 and 2000. Asians accounted for 8 percent of male college students in 2000.

The number of men enrolled in college grew 8 percent between 1990 and 2000. The number of black men in college grew much faster, rising 39 percent during those years to 815,000. The number of Hispanic men in college rose an even larger 70 percent during the 1990s.

■ Financial aid to low-income families is boosting the minority share of college students.

Blacks are the largest minority on campus

(percent distribution of male college students by race and Hispanic origin, 2000)

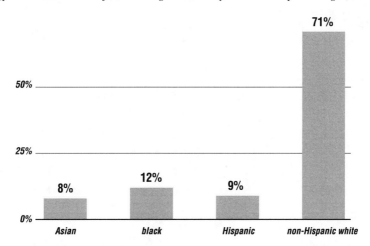

College Enrollment of Men by Race and Hispanic Origin, 1990 to 2000

(number and percent distribution of men aged 14 or older enrolled in college by race and Hispanic origin, 1990 to 2000; percent change in number and percentage point change in distribution, 1990–2000; numbers in thousands)

	total	Asian	black	Hispanic	white total	white non-Hispanic
Number						
2000	6,682	517	815	619	5,311	4,716
1999	6,956	506	833	568	5,562	5,033
1998	6,905	–	770	550	5,602	5,035
1997	6,843	–	723	555	5,552	5,007
1996	6,820	–	764	529	5,453	4,926
1995	6,703	–	710	568	5,535	5,046
1994	6,764	–	745	529	5,524	5,008
1993	6,599	–	652	539	5,403	4,838
1992	6,192	–	527	388	5,210	–
1991	6,439	–	629	347	5,304	–
1990	6,192	–	587	364	5,235	–
Percent change						
1990–2000	7.9%	–	38.8%	70.1%	1.5%	–
Percent distribution						
2000	100.0%	7.7%	12.2%	9.3%	79.5%	70.6%
1999	100.0	7.3	12.0	8.2	80.0	72.4
1998	100.0	–	11.2	8.0	81.1	72.9
1997	100.0	–	10.6	8.1	81.1	73.2
1996	100.0	–	11.2	7.8	80.0	72.2
1995	100.0	–	10.6	8.5	82.6	75.3
1994	100.0	–	11.0	7.8	81.7	74.0
1993	100.0	–	9.9	8.2	81.9	73.3
1992	100.0	–	8.5	6.3	84.1	–
1991	100.0	–	9.8	5.4	82.4	–
1990	100.0	–	9.5	5.9	84.5	–
Percentage point change						
1990–2000	–	–	2.7	3.4	–5.1	–

Note: (–) means data not available or not applicable.
Source: Bureau of the Census, Current Population Surveys, Internet site <www.census.gov/population/socdemo/school/tabA-6.txt>; calculations by New Strategist

Most Older Students Are Part-Timers

Younger students are likely to attend school full-time.

Among male undergraduates attending four-year colleges, the 80 percent majority are full-time students. The proportion of students at four-year schools who attend full-time ranges from a high of more than 90 percent among those under age 20 to a low of 43 percent among those aged 35 or older.

In graduate school, part-timers outnumber full-timers. Overall, 53 percent of men in graduate school attend only part-time as they try to juggle family, career, and schooling. Among men aged 35 or older in graduate school, fully 79 percent are part-time students.

■ Graduate schools are adapting to the busy schedules of older students, allowing many to take courses online.

Most younger men attending four-year colleges are full-time students

(percent of men attending four-year undergraduate schools who are full-time students, by age, 2000)

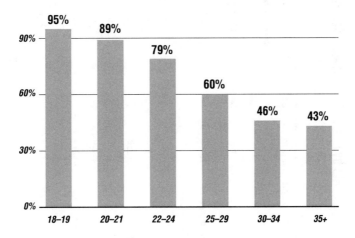

Male College Students by Age and Attendance Status, 2000

(number and percent distribution of men aged 14 or older enrolled in college by age and attendance status, 2000; numbers in thousands)

| | undergraduate | | | | | | graduate | | |
| | two-year college | | four-year college | | | | | | |
	total	full-time	part-time	total	full-time	part-time	total	full-time	part-time
Number									
Total men in college	**1,654**	**969**	**685**	**3,866**	**3,090**	**776**	**1,163**	**546**	**617**
Aged 14 to 17	36	31	5	22	22	–	3	3	–
Aged 18 to 19	575	449	126	973	920	53	23	18	5
Aged 20 to 21	274	198	76	1,154	1030	124	46	41	5
Aged 22 to 24	252	131	121	843	667	176	204	151	53
Aged 25 to 29	164	63	101	408	243	165	271	151	120
Aged 30 to 34	89	20	69	200	92	108	227	100	127
Aged 35 or older	219	77	186	272	116	150	389	82	307

(continued)

(continued from previous page)

Percent distribution by attendance status

	two-year college			four-year college			graduate		
	total	full-time	part-time	total	full-time	part-time	total	full-time	part-time
Total men in college	100.0%	58.6%	41.4%	100.0%	79.9%	20.1%	100.0%	46.9%	53.1%
Aged 15 to 17	100.0	86.1	13.9	100.0	100.0	–	100.0	100.0	–
Aged 18 to 19	100.0	78.1	21.9	100.0	94.6	5.4	100.0	78.3	21.7
Aged 20 to 21	100.0	72.3	27.7	100.0	89.3	10.7	100.0	89.1	10.9
Aged 22 to 24	100.0	52.0	48.0	100.0	79.1	20.9	100.0	74.0	26.0
Aged 25 to 29	100.0	38.4	61.6	100.0	59.6	40.4	100.0	55.7	44.3
Aged 30 to 34	100.0	22.5	77.5	100.0	46.0	54.0	100.0	44.1	55.9
Aged 35 or older	100.0	15.1	84.9	100.0	42.6	55.1	100.0	21.1	78.9

Percent distribution by age

	two-year college			four-year college			graduate		
	total	full-time	part-time	total	full-time	part-time	total	full-time	part-time
Total men in college	100.0%	100.0%	100.0%	100.0%	100.0%	100.0%	100.0%	100.0%	100.0%
Aged 15 to 17	2.2	3.2	0.7	0.6	0.7	–	0.3	0.5	–
Aged 18 to 19	34.8	46.3	18.4	25.2	29.8	6.8	2.0	3.3	0.8
Aged 20 to 21	16.6	20.4	11.1	29.8	33.3	16.0	4.0	7.5	0.8
Aged 22 to 24	15.2	13.5	17.7	21.8	21.6	22.7	17.5	27.7	8.6
Aged 25 to 29	9.9	6.5	14.7	10.6	7.9	21.3	23.3	27.7	19.4
Aged 30 to 34	5.4	2.1	10.1	5.2	3.0	13.9	19.5	18.3	20.6
Aged 35 or older	13.2	7.9	27.2	7.0	3.8	19.3	33.4	15.0	49.8

Note: (–) means sample is too small to make a reliable estimate.
Source: Bureau of the Census, School Enrollment: Social and Economic Characteristics of Students: October 2000, detailed tables for Current Population Report PPL-148, 2001; Internet site <www.census.gov/population/socdemo/school/ppl-148/tab09.txt>; calculations by New Strategist

Full-Time Attendance Varies by Race and Hispanic Origin

In graduate school, Asian men are most likely to attend full-time.

At four-year colleges, 80 percent of male students pursuing an undergraduate degree attend school full-time. Among Hispanics, however, only 68 percent of male undergraduates are full-timers. The figure is a slightly higher 69 percent for blacks. At the other extreme, fully 87 percent of Asians attend full-time.

In graduate school, part-timers outnumber full-timers. But among Asian men in graduate school, the 64 percent majority are full-time students. The proportion is lowest among black men attending graduate school, only 31 percent of whom are full-time students. This compares with 46 percent of non-Hispanic whites and 49 percent of Hispanics.

■ Students attend school part-time rather than full-time for a variety of reasons, including demands of work and family as well as ability to pay.

Regardless of race, most men attending four-year colleges are full-time students

(percent of male undergraduates attending four-year schools who are full-time students, by race and Hispanic origin, 2000)

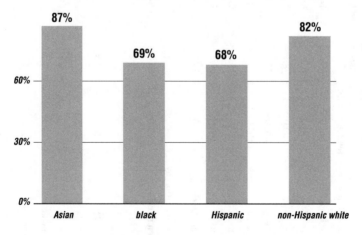

Male College Students by Race, Hispanic Origin, and Attendance Status, 2000

(number and percent distribution of men aged 14 or older enrolled in college by race, Hispanic origin, and attendance status, 2000; numbers in thousands)

| | undergraduate | | | | | | graduate | | |
| | two year college | | | four-year college | | | | | |
	total	full-time	part-time	total	full-time	part-time	total	full-time	part-time
Total men enrolled									
in college	**1,654**	**969**	**685**	**3,866**	**3,090**	**776**	**1,163**	**546**	**617**
Asians	107	61	46	304	265	39	106	68	38
Blacks	217	131	86	504	349	155	94	29	65
Hispanics	246	157	89	288	195	93	84	41	43
Whites	1,322	772	550	3,033	2458	575	958	444	514
Non-Hispanic whites	1,085	621	464	2,759	2273	486	871	401	470

Percent distribution by attendance status

Total men enrolled									
in college	**100.0%**	**58.6%**	**41.4%**	**100.0%**	**79.9%**	**20.1%**	**100.0%**	**46.9%**	**53.1%**
Asians	100.0	57.0	43.0	100.0	87.2	12.8	100.0	64.2	35.8
Blacks	100.0	60.4	39.6	100.0	69.2	30.8	100.0	30.9	69.1
Hispanics	100.0	63.8	36.2	100.0	67.7	32.3	100.0	48.8	51.2
Whites	100.0	58.4	41.6	100.0	81.0	19.0	100.0	46.3	53.7
Non-Hispanic whites	100.0	57.2	42.8	100.0	82.4	17.6	100.0	46.0	54.0

Percent distribution by race and Hispanic origin

Total men enrolled									
in college	**100.0%**	**100.0%**	**100.0%**	**100.0%**	**100.0%**	**100.0%**	**100.0%**	**100.0%**	**100.0%**
Asians	6.5	6.3	6.7	7.9	8.6	5.0	9.1	12.5	6.2
Blacks	13.1	13.5	12.6	13.0	11.3	20.0	8.1	5.3	10.5
Hispanics	14.9	16.2	13.0	7.4	6.3	12.0	7.2	7.5	7.0
Whites	79.9	79.7	80.3	78.5	79.5	74.1	82.4	81.3	83.3
Non-Hispanic whites	65.6	64.1	67.7	71.4	73.6	62.6	74.9	73.4	76.2

Source: Bureau of the Census, School Enrollment: Social and Economic Characteristics of Students: October 2000, *detailed tables for Current Population Report PPL-148, 2001; Internet site <www.census.gov/ population/socdemo/school/ppl-148/tab09.txt>; calculations by New Strategist*

Objectives of Male and Female College Students Are Similar

Making money and raising a family are the most important objectives.

The goals of male and female college freshmen are similar, and few objectives show significant gaps between the sexes. Seventy-three percent of both male and female college freshmen say raising a family is a top priority for them. Even more important to men is "being very well off financially," with 76 percent saying this is essential or very important. Women rate this objective slightly lower than raising a family, with 71 percent saying it is essential or very important.

Men are more likely than women to want to "be successful in my own business." Forty-five percent of men cite this as an essential or very important objective compared with only 35 percent of women. Men are much less likely than women to say helping others in difficulty is a top objective. Fifty-three percent of men hold this as an essential or very important goal, 16 percentage points lower than the 69 percent of female college freshmen for whom helping other is a top priority.

■ Today's young men will be pairing up with ambitious young women who want it all—family, meaningful career, and financial security.

Family and financial security are the two top objectives of college freshmen

(percent of college freshmen who cite "raising a family" and "being very well off financially" as essential or very important objectives, by sex, 2000)

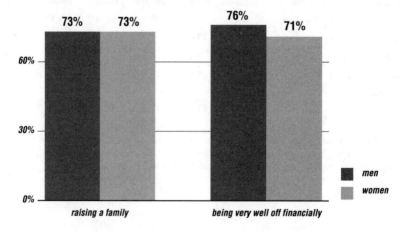

Objectives of College Freshmen by Sex, 2000

(percent of college freshmen who say the objective is essential or very important, by sex, and percentage point difference between men and women, 2000; ranked by importance to men)

	men	women	percentage point difference between men and women
Being very well off financially	76.1%	71.1%	5.0
Raising a family	72.7	73.4	–0.7
Becoming an authority in my field	61.6	58.1	3.5
Helping others who are in difficulty	52.8	68.8	–16.0
Being successful in a business of my own	45.1	34.6	10.5
Developing a meaningful philosophy of life	43.1	41.8	1.3
Integrating spirituality into my life	41.3	48.1	–6.8
Influencing social values	33.5	40.9	–7.4
Keeping up to date with political affairs	31.8	25.1	6.7
Becoming a community leader	31.4	30.4	1.0
Helping to promote racial understanding	28.1	32.9	–4.8
Influencing the political structure	20.4	15.3	5.1
Making a theoretical contribution to science	18.9	13.7	5.2
Participating in a community action program	18.5	26.1	–7.6
Becoming involved in programs to clean up the environment	17.4	17.5	–0.1
Writing original works	15.2	14.4	0.8
Creating artistic work	13.7	15.7	–2.0

Source: The American Freshman: National Norms for Fall 2000, *Linda J. Sax, Alexander W. Astin, William S. Korn, and Kathryn M. Mahoney, Higher Education Research Institute, UCLA, 2001; calculations by New Strategist*

Among College Freshmen, Men Are More Confident than Women

College men may overestimate their abilities, while women underestimate theirs.

Among college freshmen, men are far more likely than women to believe they are above average on a wide range of characteristics including academic ability, leadership ability, self-understanding, intellectual self-confidence, emotional health, physical health, and popularity, according to a survey by UCLA's Higher Education Research Institute. Men are less confident than women in only four areas—drive to achieve, understanding of others, writing ability, and spirituality.

More than half of both men and women say they are above average in their drive to achieve, understanding of others, academic ability, leadership ability, self-understanding, and intellectual self-confidence. A minority of both sexes feel confident in such qualities as their writing ability, spirituality, popularity, and—surprisingly—computer skills.

■ Building self-esteem is an important part of today's elementary and secondary curricula. It appears to be working, especially for boys.

Among college freshmen, men are far more confident than women

(percent of college freshmen who rate themselves above average for selected abilities, by sex, 2000)

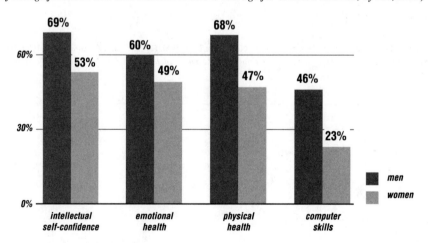

Self-Confidence of College Freshmen by Sex, 2000

(percentage of college freshmen rating themselves above average for selected abilities compared with the average person his/her age, by sex, 2000; percentage point difference between men and women)

	men	women	percentage point difference between men and women
Academic ability	70.5%	64.8%	5.7
Drive to achieve	69.4	71.7	–2.3
Self-confidence (intellectual)	69.1	53.1	16.0
Physical health	67.7	47.2	20.5
Leadership ability	63.9	58.2	5.7
Understanding of others	62.7	68.0	–5.3
Self understanding	61.7	53.3	8.4
Emotional health	60.2	48.6	11.6
Self-confidence (social)	57.3	47.8	9.5
Popularity	48.5	34.3	14.2
Computer skills	46.4	23.2	23.2
Writing ability	44.3	47.2	–2.9
Spirituality	43.3	46.1	–2.8
Public speaking ability	40.3	35.0	5.3
Artistic ability	29.9	28.9	1.0

Source: The American Freshman: National Norms for Fall 2000, *Linda J. Sax, Alexander W. Astin, William S. Korn, and Kathryn M. Mahoney, Higher Education Research Institute, UCLA, 2001; calculations by New Strategist*

Men Earn a Minority of College Degrees

They earn the majority of doctoral and first-professional degrees, however.

Of the 2.4 million degrees awarded by institutions of higher education in 1999–2000, men earned only 43 percent. Among blacks, men earned just 34 percent of degrees awarded that year, while among American Indians the figure was 38 percent. Among foreign students (called nonresident aliens) who earned degrees in 1999–2000, however, men accounted for the 57 percent majority.

Men earned only 40 percent of associate's degrees awarded in 1999–2000. They earned 43 percent of bachelor's degrees and 42 percent of master's degrees. But men accounted for the 56 percent majority of doctoral degrees and 55 percent of first-professional degrees awarded in 1999–2000. Among blacks, however, men earned a minority of doctoral and first-professional degrees.

■ Many of today's young men will marry women who are better-educated than they are, changing the dynamics of families.

Men's share of bachelor's degrees varies by race and Hispanic origin

(men's share of bachelor's degrees, by race and Hispanic origin, 1999–2000)

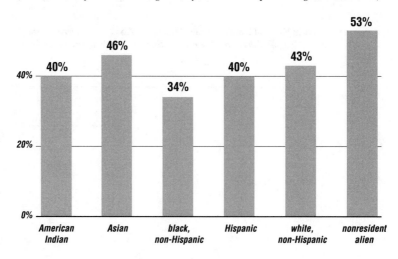

Degrees Earned by Men by Level of Degree, Race, and Hispanic Origin, 1999–2000

(total number of degrees conferred by institutions of higher education, number and percent distribution of degrees earned by men, and male share of total, by level of degree, race, and Hispanic origin, 1999–2000)

		degrees earned by men		
	total	number	percent distribution	share of total
Total degrees	**2,384,729**	**1,016,147**	**100.0%**	**42.6%**
American Indian	18,160	6,853	0.7	37.7
Asian	139,412	64,340	6.3	46.2
Black, non-Hispanic	211,469	72,191	7.1	34.1
Hispanic	150,753	61,429	6.0	40.7
White, non-Hispanic	1,741,641	741,310	73.0	42.6
Nonresident alien	123,294	70,024	6.9	56.8
Associate's degrees	**564,933**	**224,721**	**100.0**	**39.8**
American Indian	6,494	2,224	1.0	34.2
Asian	27,764	12,001	5.3	43.2
Black, non-Hispanic	60,181	20,951	9.3	34.8
Hispanic	51,541	20,933	9.3	40.6
White, non-Hispanic	408,508	164,197	73.1	40.2
Nonresident alien	10,445	4,415	2.0	42.3
Bachelor's degrees	**1,237,875**	**530,367**	**100.0**	**42.8**
American Indian	8,711	3,459	0.7	39.7
Asian	77,793	35,789	6.7	46.0
Black, non-Hispanic	107,891	36,972	7.0	34.3
Hispanic	74,963	30,255	5.7	40.4
White, non-Hispanic	928,013	402,368	75.9	43.4
Nonresident alien	40,504	21,524	4.1	53.1
Master's degrees	**457,056**	**191,792**	**100.0**	**42.0**
American Indian	2,232	829	0.4	37.1
Asian	22,899	10,853	5.7	47.4
Black, non-Hispanic	35,625	11,093	5.8	31.1
Hispanic	19,093	7,543	3.9	39.5
White, non-Hispanic	317,999	126,522	66.0	39.8
Nonresident alien	59,208	34,952	18.2	59.0

(continued)

(continued from previous page)

	total	degrees earned by men		
		number	percent distribution	share of total
Doctoral degrees	**44,808**	**25,028**	**100.0%**	**55.9%**
American Indian	159	56	0.2	35.2
Asian	2,380	1,329	5.3	55.8
Black, non-Hispanic	2,220	863	3.4	38.9
Hispanic	1,291	603	2.4	46.7
White, non-Hispanic	27,520	14,241	56.9	51.7
Nonresident alien	11,238	7,936	31.7	70.6
First-professional degrees	**80,057**	**44,239**	**100.0**	**55.3**
American Indian	564	285	0.6	50.5
Asian	8,576	4,368	9.9	50.9
Black, non-Hispanic	5,552	2,312	5.2	41.6
Hispanic	3,865	2,095	4.7	54.2
White, non-Hispanic	59,601	33,982	76.8	57.0
Nonresident alien	1,899	1,197	2.7	63.0

Note: American Indians include Alaska Natives; Asians include Pacific Islanders.
Source: National Center for Education Statistics, Digest of Education Statistics 2001; *Internet site <http://nces.ed.gov/pubsearch/pubsinfo.asp?pubid=2002130>; calculations by New Strategist*

Men Earn Most Engineering Degrees

The percentage of degrees awarded to men varies greatly by field.

Although women earn most of the associate's, bachelor's, and master's degrees awarded each year, men earn the majority of degrees in many fields.

The share of associate's degrees awarded to men ranged from a low of 8 percent in library science to a high of 95 percent in construction trades. Among bachelor's degrees awarded in 1999-00, men earned more than 80 percent of those in engineering and 70 percent of degrees in theological studies. In contrast, men earned only 24 percent of bachelor's degrees in education in 1999-00. At the master's level, men earned 67 percent of degrees awarded in computer and information sciences, 65 percent of those in physical sciences, and 62 percent of degrees in philosophy and religion.

Men earned the majority of doctoral degrees awarded in 1999-00. But they earned a minority of doctoral degrees in such fields as communications, education, English, health professions, library science, and psychology.

■ Because men and women choose different fields of study in college, their career paths diverge upon graduation.

Men earn most computer science degrees

(men's share of computer science degrees, by degree level, 1999–2000)

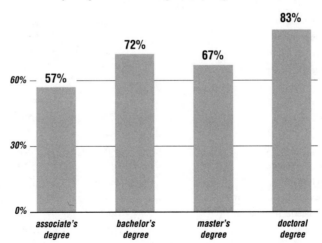

Associate's Degrees Earned by Men by Field of Study, 1999–2000

(total number of associate's degrees conferred and number and percent earned by men, by field of study, 1999–2000)

	total	earned by men number	earned by men percent
Total associate's degrees	**564,933**	**224,721**	**39.8%**
Agriculture and natural resources	6,667	4,353	65.3
Architecture and related programs	392	101	25.8
Area, ethnic, and cultural studies	259	56	21.6
Biological, life sciences	1,434	481	33.5
Business management and administrative services	92,274	27,584	29.9
Communications	2,754	1,435	52.1
Communications technologies	1,709	1,059	62.0
Computer and information sciences	20,450	11,700	57.2
Construction trades	2,337	2,220	95.0
Consumer and personal services	9,570	5,560	58.1
Education	8,226	1,702	20.7
Engineering	1,752	1,509	86.1
Engineering-related technologies	35,395	30,736	86.8
English language and literature, letters	947	333	35.2
Foreign languages and literatures	501	235	46.9
Health professions and related sciences	84,081	11,728	13.9
Home economics	8,381	704	8.4
Law and legal studies	7,265	881	12.1
Liberal arts and sciences, general studies, and humanities	187,454	69,746	37.2
Library science	98	8	8.2
Marketing operations, marketing, and distribution	5,557	1,381	24.9
Mathematics	675	408	60.4
Mechanics and repairers	11,614	10,791	92.9
Multi/interdisciplinary studies	11,784	5,521	46.9
Parks, recreation, leisure and fitness	855	511	59.8
Philosophy and religion	63	32	50.8
Physical sciences	2,460	1,299	52.8
Precision production trades	11,814	9,200	77.9
Protective services	16,298	10,507	64.5
Psychology	1,455	326	22.4
Public administration and services	3,656	555	15.2
R.O.T.C. and military technoloiges	65	54	83.1
Social sciences and history	5,136	1,791	34.9
Theological studies, religious vocations	636	355	55.8
Transportation and material moving	1,021	870	85.2
Visual and performing arts	17,100	7,999	46.8
Not classified	2,798	990	35.4

Source: National Center for Education Statistics, Digest of Education Statistics 2001*; Internet site <http://nces.ed.gov/pubsearch/pubsinfo.asp?pubid=2002130>; calculations by New Strategist*

Bachelor's Degrees Earned by Men by Field of Study, 1999–2000

(total number of bachelor's degrees conferred and number and percent earned by men, by field of study, 1999–2000)

	total	earned by men number	earned by men percent
Total bachelor's degrees	**1,237,875**	**530,367**	**42.8%**
Agriculture and natural resources	24,247	13,850	57.1
Architecture and related programs	8,462	5,193	61.4
Area, ethnic, and cultural studies	6,381	2,064	32.3
Biological sciences, life sciences	63,532	26,504	41.7
Business management, administrative services, marketing	257,709	129,664	50.3
Communications and communications technologies	56,910	22,063	38.8
Computer and information sciences	36,195	26,042	71.9
Education	108,168	26,124	24.2
Engineering and engineering related technologies	72,555	59,145	81.5
English language and literature, letters	50,920	16,341	32.1
Foreign languages and literatures	14,968	4,375	29.2
Health professions and related sciences	78,458	12,727	16.2
Home economics	17,779	2,160	12.1
Law and legal studies	1,925	520	27.0
Liberal arts and sciences, general studies, and humanities	36,104	12,250	33.9
Library science	154	77	50.0
Mathematics	12,070	6,382	52.9
Multi/interdisciplinary studies	27,460	9,136	33.3
Parks, recreation, leisure and fitness	19,111	9,170	48.0
Philosophy and religion	8,366	5,228	62.5
Physical sciences and science technologies	18,385	10,972	59.7
Precision production trades	393	281	71.5
Protective services	24,877	14,069	56.6
Psychology	74,060	17,430	23.5
Public administration and services	20,185	3,816	18.9
R.O.T.C. and military technologies	7	6	85.7
Social sciences and history	127,101	62,062	48.8
Theological studies, religious vocations	6,809	4,791	70.4
Transportation and material moving	3,395	2,985	87.9
Visual and performing arts	58,791	24,003	40.8
Not classified	2,398	937	39.1

Source: National Center for Education Statistics, Digest of Education Statistics 2001; *Internet site <http:// nces.ed.gov/pubsearch/pubsinfo.asp?pubid=2002130>; calculations by New Strategist*

Master's Degrees Earned by Men by Field of Study, 1999–2000

(total number of master's degrees conferred and number and percent earned by men, by field of study, 1999–2000)

	total	earned by men	
		number	percent
Total master's degrees	**457,056**	**191,792**	**42.0%**
Agriculture and natural resources	4,375	2,362	54.0
Architecture and related programs	4,268	2,508	58.8
Area, ethnic, and cultural studies	1,591	644	40.5
Biological sciences, life sciences	6,198	2,773	44.7
Business management, administrative services, marketing	112,258	67,544	60.2
Communications and communications technologies	5,605	2,059	36.7
Computer and information sciences	14,264	9,512	66.7
Education	124,240	29,321	23.6
Engineering and engineering related technologies	26,522	20,968	79.1
English language and literature, letters	7,230	2,393	33.1
Foreign languages and literatures	2,780	845	30.4
Health professions and related sciences	42,456	9,624	22.7
Home economics	2,830	457	16.1
Law and legal studies	3,750	2,192	58.5
Liberal arts and sciences, general studies, and humanities	3,256	1,143	35.1
Library science	4,577	947	20.7
Mathematics	3,412	1,881	55.1
Multi/interdisciplinary studies	3,064	1,173	38.3
Parks, recreation, leisure and fitness	2,478	1,238	50.0
Philosophy and religion	1,329	827	62.2
Physical sciences and science technologies	4,841	3,126	64.6
Precision production trades	5	3	60.0
Protective services	2,609	1,534	58.8
Psychology	14,465	3,552	24.6
Public administration and services	25,594	6,808	26.6
R.O.T.C. and military technologies	–	–	–
Social sciences and history	14,066	7,024	49.9
Theological studies, religious vocations	5,576	3,352	60.1
Transportation and material moving	697	629	90.2
Visual and performing arts	10,918	4,672	42.8
Not classified	1,802	681	37.8

Note: (–) means no degrees were awarded in field.
Source: National Center for Education Statistics, Digest of Education Statistics 2001; *Internet site <http://nces.ed.gov/pubsearch/pubsinfo.asp?pubid=2002130>; calculations by New Strategist*

Doctoral Degrees Earned by Men by Field of Study, 1999–2000

(total number of doctoral degrees conferred and number and percent earned by men, by field of study, 1999–2000)

	total	earned by men	
		number	percent
Total doctoral degrees	**44,808**	**25,028**	**55.9%**
Agriculture and natural resources	1,181	811	68.7
Architecture and related programs	129	85	65.9
Area, ethnic, and cultural studies	217	106	48.8
Biological sciences, life sciences	4,867	2,722	55.9
Business management, administrative services, marketing	1,196	814	68.1
Communications and communications technologies	357	168	47.1
Computer and information sciences	777	646	83.1
Education	6,830	2,419	35.4
Engineering and engineering related technologies	5,390	4,555	84.5
English language and literature, letters	1,628	671	41.2
Foreign languages and literatures	915	375	41.0
Health professions and related sciences	2,676	1,038	38.8
Home economics	357	83	23.2
Law and legal studies	74	49	66.2
Liberal arts and sciences, general studies, and humanities	83	41	49.4
Library science	68	19	27.9
Mathematics	1,106	830	75.0
Multi/interdisciplinary studies	384	203	52.9
Parks, recreation, leisure and fitness	134	75	56.0
Philosophy and religion	586	381	65.0
Physical sciences and science technologies	4,018	2,994	74.5
Precision production trades	–	–	–
Protective services	52	28	53.8
Psychology	4,310	1,405	32.6
Public administration and services	537	227	42.3
R.O.T.C. and military technologies	–	–	–
Social sciences and history	4,095	2,407	58.8
Theological studies, religious vocations	1,643	1,307	79.5
Transportation and material moving	–	–	–
Visual and performing arts	1,127	537	47.6
Not classified	71	32	45.1

Note: (–) means no degrees were awarded in field.

Source: National Center for Education Statistics, Digest of Education Statistics 2001*; Internet site <http://nces.ed.gov/pubsearch/pubsinfo.asp?pubid=2002130>; calculations by New Strategist*

Men Still Dominate Many Professional Degree Programs

They earn the majority of degrees in medicine and law.

Among the 80,057 first-professional degrees awarded in 1999–2000, men earned the 55 percent majority. In most professional degree programs, men outnumber women, although the gap is shrinking.

In 1999–2000, men earned 71 percent of first-professional degrees in chiropractic medicine, 71 percent of degrees in theology, and 70 percent of degrees in osteopathic medicine. They accounted for a minority of degrees in veterinary medicine (32 percent), pharmacy (34 percent), and optometry (47 percent) however. Men earned the 60 percent majority of degrees in dentistry, 57 percent of those in medicine, and 54 percent of law degrees.

■ Although men's dominance of first-professional degree programs is waning, they remain the majority of graduates and practicing professionals in most fields.

Men earn the majority of first-professional degrees in most fields

(men's share of first-professional degrees in selected fields, 1999–2000)

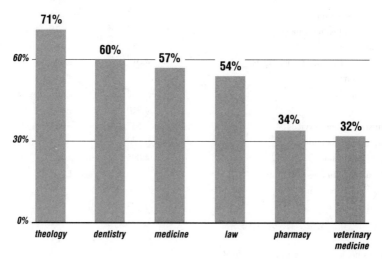

First-Professional Degrees Earned by Men by Field of Study, 1999–2000

(total number of first-professional degrees conferred and number and percent earned by men, by field of study, 1999–2000)

		earned by men	
	total	number	percent
Total first-professional degrees	**80,057**	**44,239**	**55.3%**
Dentistry (D.D.S. or D.M.D.)	4,250	2,547	59.9
Medicine (M.D.)	15,286	8,761	57.3
Optometry (O.D.)	1,293	604	46.7
Osteopathic medicine (D.O.)	2,236	1,399	62.6
Pharmacy (Pharm.D.)	5,669	1,943	34.3
Podiatry (Pod.D., D.P., or D.P.M.)	569	396	69.6
Veterinary medicine (D.V.M.)	2,251	710	31.5
Chiropractic (D.C. or D.C.M.)	3,809	2,718	71.4
Law (LL.B. or J.D.)	38,152	20,638	54.1
Theology (M.Div., M.H.L., B.D., or Ord. and M.H.L./Rav.)	6,129	4,337	70.8
Other	413	186	45.0

Source: National Center for Education Statistics, Digest of Education Statistics 2001; *Internet site <http://nces.ed.gov/pubsearch/pubsinfo.asp?pubid=2002130>; calculations by New Strategist*

Men's Share of College Students Will Decline

Only at the doctoral and first-professional degree levels will men account for the majority of degrees awarded in 2011.

Men's share of the nation's college students is projected to fall from 44 to 42 percent between 2000 and 2011, according to projections by the National Center for Education Statistics. Regardless of age, men will account for fewer than half of students. Only 30 percent of students aged 35 or older will be male in 2011, down from 37 percent today.

Men now earn 43 percent of all degrees awarded by institutions of higher education. By 2011, they will earn an even smaller 41 percent. Regardless of the degree, men's share will shrink. But men will continue to earn most doctoral and first-professional degrees. The government projects the proportion of first-professional degrees awarded to men to be 52 percent in 2011. Men will earn 56 percent of doctoral degrees in that year.

■ As women become better educated than men, more changes are on the way for families and workplaces.

Men will continue to earn most doctoral and first-professional degrees in 2011

(percent of degrees awarded to men, by level of degree, 2011)

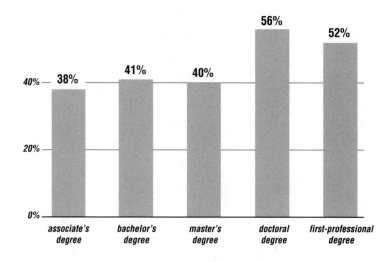

Projections of Men's College Enrollment by Age, 2000 and 2011

(total number of people enrolled in institutions of higher education, number and percent distribution of men enrolled, and male share of total, by age, 2000 and 2011; numbers in thousands)

	total	men number	men percent distribution	men share of total
2000				
Total people enrolled	**15,314**	**6,682**	**100.0%**	**43.6%**
Aged 14 to 17	149	61	0.9	40.9
Aged 18 to 19	3,599	1,570	23.5	43.6
Aged 20 to 21	3,169	1,472	22.0	46.4
Aged 22 to 24	2,683	1,300	19.5	48.5
Aged 25 to 29	1,962	844	12.6	43.0
Aged 30 to 34	1,244	517	7.7	41.5
Aged 35 or older	2,507	918	13.7	36.6
2011				
Total people enrolled	**17,688**	**7,401**	**100.0**	**41.8**
Aged 14 to 17	224	108	1.5	48.2
Aged 18 to 19	4,111	1,783	24.1	43.4
Aged 20 to 21	3,716	1,665	22.5	44.8
Aged 22 to 24	2,928	1,346	18.2	46.0
Aged 25 to 29	2,355	1,051	14.2	44.6
Aged 30 to 34	1,405	559	7.6	39.8
Aged 35 or older	2,948	889	12.0	30.2

Source: Bureau of the Census, Internet site <www.census.gov/population/socdemo/school/tabA-6.txt>; and National Center for Education Statistics, Projections of Education Statistics NCES 2001-083, 2001; calculations by New Strategist

Projections of Degrees Earned by Men, 2000 and 2011

(total number of degrees earned, number earned by men, and male share of total, by level of degree, 2000 and 2011)

	total	earned by men	
		number	share of total
2000			
Total degrees	**2,334,100**	**992,500**	**42.5%**
Associate's degree	569,000	217,000	38.1
Bachelor's degree	1,193,000	519,000	43.5
Master's degree	444,000	185,000	41.7
Doctoral degree	47,100	26,700	56.7
First-professional degree	81,000	44,800	55.3
2011			
Total degrees	**2,631,400**	**1,067,700**	**40.6**
Associate's degree	625,000	236,000	37.8
Bachelor's degree	1,392,000	568,000	40.8
Master's degree	477,000	190,000	39.8
Doctoral degree	49,100	27,600	56.2
First-professional degree	88,300	46,100	52.2

Source: National Center for Education Statistics, Projections of Education Statistics NCES 2001-083, 2001; calculations by New Strategist

4

Health

Most men rate their health as good or excellent.

The percentage of men who say their health is only fair or poor rises with age but remains below the majority even in the oldest age group.

The eating habits of men vary by age.

Young adults prefer soft drinks, while older men prefer coffee.

Most men eat away from home on an average day.

Fast-food restaurants are more popular than sit-down establishments among men under age 50, while men aged 50 or older prefer sit-down restaurants.

Many young men lack health insurance coverage.

Among men aged 18 to 24, 30 percent lack health insurance. A substantial 24 percent of 25-to-34-year-olds also are without coverage.

Males are a minority of doctor and hospital patients.

Men account for 41 percent of physician visits, and they constitute only 40 percent of hospital patients.

Most AIDS victims are men.

Men account for fully 83 percent of Americans diagnosed with AIDS. Among teenagers with the disease, males are a smaller 59 percent.

Heart disease is the biggest killer of males.

Thirty percent of males who died in 1999 succumbed to heart disease, and another 24 percent died of cancer.

Most Men Rate Their Health as Good or Excellent

Even in old age, most give high marks to their health.

The majority of men say their health is good or excellent. The largest percentage (49 percent) say it is good, while another 33 percent say they are in excellent health. Fifteen percent say their health is fair, while 3 percent describe their health as poor.

Men aged 25 to 34 are most likely to rate their health as excellent, with 41 percent saying so. The figure falls with age. Among men aged 65 or older, 21 percent say they are in excellent health and another 40 percent say their health is good. The proportion of men who describe their health as only fair or poor rises from 7 percent among men aged 25 to 34 to 38 percent among those aged 65 or older.

■ Older Americans rate their health more highly today than they did in the past thanks to better management of chronic conditions.

Few men say their health is poor

(percent distribution of men by health status, 2000)

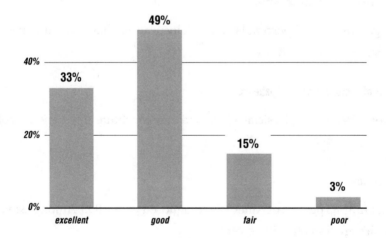

Health Status of Men by Age, 2000

"Would you say your own health, in general, is excellent, good, fair, or poor?"

(percent of men aged 18 or older responding by age, 2000)

	excellent	*good*	*fair*	*poor*
Total men	**33.1%**	**49.1%**	**14.6%**	**3.2%**
Aged 18 to 24	38.7	45.5	15.0	0.8
Aged 25 to 34	40.7	51.9	7.2	0.3
Aged 35 to 44	34.1	51.5	13.9	0.4
Aged 45 to 54	29.9	54.7	10.5	4.9
Aged 55 to 64	29.6	43.5	23.5	3.5
Aged 65 or older	21.4	40.3	25.5	12.8

Source: 2000 General Social Survey, National Opinion Research Center, University of Chicago; calculations by New Strategist

Men Are Concerned about Healthy Eating

But they do not take dietary guidelines as seriously as women.

Men are less likely than women to regard a variety of dietary guidelines as "very important." From "eat a variety of foods" to "maintain a healthy weight," fewer men than women say the guidelines are "very important."

The gap between the percentages of men and women who regard specific guidelines as very important is greatest for "choose a diet with plenty of fruits and vegetables." Just 60 percent of men compared with 75 percent of women regard the guideline as very important. The gap is smallest—just 6 percentage points—for "choose a diet with plenty of breads, cereals, rice, and pasta."

Overall, the largest percentage of men and women rate "maintain a healthy weight" as most important. Sixty-eight percent of men and 77 percent of women believe the advice is very important.

■ Fewer men are concerned with dietary guidelines because they depend on their wives to provide them with a healthy diet.

A minority of men say it is "very important" to choose a low-fat diet

(percent of people who say it is "very important" to choose a diet low in saturated fat, by sex, 1994–96)

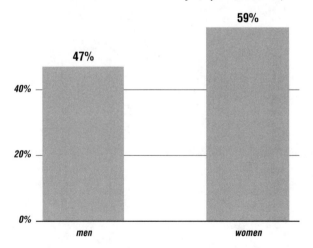

Importance of Dietary Guidelines by Sex, 1994–96

(percent of people aged 20 or older saying dietary guidelines are very important by sex, and percentage point difference between men and women, 1994–96; ranked by percentage point difference)

	men	women	percentage point difference
Choose a diet with plenty of fruits and vegetables	59.7%	75.3%	−15.6
Eat at least two servings of dairy products daily	28.2	42.6	−14.4
Choose a diet low in fat	50.6	64.5	−13.9
Choose a diet low in saturated fat	47.1	59.4	−12.3
Eat a variety of foods	54.8	66.1	−11.3
Choose a diet with adequate fiber	44.3	55.5	−11.2
Use sugars only in moderation	45.0	56.0	−11.0
Use salt or sodium only in moderation	45.6	56.1	−10.5
Choose a diet low in cholesterol	50.9	60.4	−9.5
Maintain a healthy weight	68.1	77.0	−8.9
Choose a diet with plenty of breads, cereals, rice, and pasta	28.6	34.3	−5.7

Source: U.S. Department of Agriculture, Agricultural Research Service, Data Tables: Results from USDA's Continuing Survey of Food Intakes by Individuals *and* 1994–96 Diet and Health Knowledge Survey, *Internet site <www.barc.usda.gov/bhnrc/foodsurvey/home.htm>; calculations by New Strategist*

Younger Men Are More Likely to Eat French Fries

The foods consumed by men differ by age.

During an average two-day period, 42 percent of teenage boys eat French fries. Among men aged 60 or older, the figure is a much smaller 11 percent. Conversely, 25 percent of men aged 60 or older eat fried eggs during a two-day period compared with only 15 percent of teens and young adults.

The foods men eat vary by age for a variety of reasons. Health is one, as older men watch their diet more carefully than teens and young adults. Life experience is another. Younger men are more accustomed to fast food such as French fries and pizza. A third reason for differences by age is demographic, since younger men are more racially and ethnically diverse than older men. This diversity partly explains why younger men, many of whom are Hispanic, are more likely to eat tortillas than older men. During an average two days, more than 20 percent of teen and young-adult men eat tortillas compared with only 4 percent of men aged 60 or older.

Another big difference can be seen in coffee consumption. More than 80 percent of men aged 60 or older drink coffee during an average two days compared with just 46 percent of men aged 20 to 39. On the other hand, more than 80 percent of men under age 40 have a soft drink during a two-day period versus a much smaller 43 percent of men aged 60 or older.

■ Coffee is the one item older men are most likely to consume during a two-day period. Among teenagers, soft drinks are number one.

French fries are most popular among teens and young adults

(percent of males aged 12 or older who eat French fries during an average two days, by age, 1994–96)

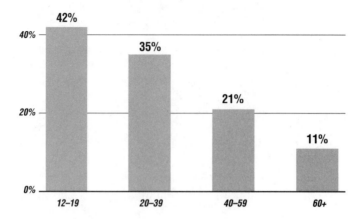

Men's Food Consumption by Age, 1994–96

(percent of total people aged 2 or older and men aged 12 or older consuming selected foods at least once in two days, by age, 1994–96)

	both sexes aged 2 or older	men aged			
		12 to 19	*20 to 39*	*40 to 59*	*60 or older*
White bread	59.6%	61.3%	63.0%	59.7%	59.3%
Whole grain and wheat bread	28.1	14.5	25.3	32.8	39.8
Rolls	48.0	61.9	62.0	47.9	37.8
Biscuits	10.9	12.2	11.5	13.4	13.0
Tortillas	15.5	22.9	20.6	13.4	4.2
Quickbreads and muffins	12.5	11.0	8.0	15.7	17.4
Doughnuts and sweet rolls	12.4	17.3	13.3	13.4	11.4
Crackers	17.4	10.6	11.9	16.6	25.6
Cookies	30.7	29.0	20.8	27.6	29.7
Cake	16.2	15.1	13.5	16.5	19.2
Pie	8.5	6.6	5.8	11.8	16.4
Pancakes or waffles	10.3	13.5	8.0	7.5	10.8
Cooked cereal	10.3	5.2	5.2	9.7	20.9
Oatmeal	6.1	2.4	2.7	6.0	13.6
Ready-to-eat cereal	40.6	45.6	26.9	29.8	44.6
Rice	28.0	24.2	30.8	29.4	23.1
Pasta	36.0	33.4	37.1	34.3	27.9
Macaroni and cheese	8.5	7.5	7.8	6.1	7.1
Spaghetti with tomato sauce	8.0	10.1	8.6	5.5	5.0
Pizza	19.9	39.6	23.7	13.0	5.3
Lettuce	53.3	56.0	63.4	55.5	48.1
Cooked broccoli	7.3	3.9	7.6	7.8	8.5
Cooked carrots	5.8	2.8	5.0	6.7	9.6
Raw carrots	14.1	9.2	12.3	14.4	13.6
Raw tomatoes	32.0	25.7	33.1	38.1	40.0
Cooked string beans	13.2	8.3	10.6	13.7	18.3
Coleslaw	5.0	2.6	3.8	7.2	9.8
Cooked peas	6.1	3.6	4.4	7.4	8.4
Cooked corn	15.1	12.8	12.7	17.1	14.2
Raw onions	14.4	11.1	17.9	19.6	19.0
French fries	25.5	41.7	35.3	20.6	11.2
Home fries or hash-browned potatoes	8.9	10.1	9.5	11.2	10.4
Baked potatoes	12.4	8.6	11.4	13.0	17.9
Boiled potatoes	5.3	2.0	3.9	6.3	11.0
Mashed potatoes	15.0	14.6	14.7	16.0	19.7
Cooked dried beans or peas	8.0	5.8	8.0	10.0	9.1
Baked beans	4.7	3.6	4.5	5.5	6.9
Raw oranges	7.9	4.3	6.6	7.4	8.9
Orange juice	27.2	30.8	24.3	24.1	30.2

(continued)

	both sexes aged 2 or older	men aged			
		12 to 19	20 to 39	40 to 59	60 or older
Raw apples	15.6%	11.7%	12.1%	14.1%	17.6%
Applesauce or cooked apples	4.6	2.3	1.3	3.1	8.1
Apple juice	7.0	7.8	4.2	4.7	4.8
Raw bananas	20.8	10.3	14.4	21.9	36.5
Fluid milk	67.8	72.3	58.0	60.5	73.9
Whole milk	25.4	30.0	22.9	20.3	22.3
Low-fat milk	35.0	39.6	29.4	31.2	40.2
Skim milk	14.3	9.7	9.3	15.1	17.7
Cheese, except cream and cottage	51.1	61.1	63.8	48.3	40.9
Ice cream or ice milk	16.6	14.2	14.7	18.0	22.7
Beef steaks	12.8	9.5	17.1	18.3	13.4
Beef roasts	7.4	5.1	6.9	9.9	11.7
Ground beef	54.0	73.4	65.3	50.0	40.7
Ham	11.3	11.6	10.8	13.5	15.2
Pork chops, steaks, roasts	12.6	11.6	12.8	14.3	16.4
Bacon	14.3	14.9	14.1	17.5	20.6
Pork breakfast sausage	6.1	6.3	6.6	6.6	10.7
Frankfurters or luncheon meats	41.8	46.7	46.2	44.9	41.6
Canned tuna	7.8	5.1	6.7	8.5	8.4
Other finfish	10.1	7.1	9.6	12.3	15.0
Chicken	35.9	34.3	37.1	34.5	32.1
Turkey	7.0	8.2	6.8	8.5	7.7
Boiled, poached, baked eggs	11.0	5.0	9.4	12.0	15.7
Fried eggs	16.9	14.9	15.2	20.9	24.6
Scrambled eggs	9.2	8.9	10.7	11.1	12.0
Peanut butter	11.4	11.4	8.3	7.9	10.3
Coffee	45.4	7.5	45.8	72.5	80.8
With caffeine	40.8	7.3	44.4	67.7	66.9
Decaffeinated	8.8	0.2	3.0	12.6	24.0
Tea	31.8	21.6	31.9	35.8	32.2
Soft drinks	66.3	83.8	81.0	68.6	43.2
Not diet, with caffeine	41.2	70.0	61.9	38.7	19.0
Not diet, caffeine-free	21.3	32.1	23.6	18.5	10.7
Diet, with caffeine	12.6	4.3	12.4	16.1	11.4
Diet, caffeine-free	8.1	4.4	5.0	11.5	9.2
Fruit drinks	28.3	42.0	25.1	21.0	14.7
Beer	10.9	3.4	28.7	22.5	11.3
Wine	5.3	0.3	4.9	8.6	9.5
Soup	22.1	17.2	18.5	22.7	30.2
Potato chips	17.1	20.2	20.1	16.9	8.8
Corn chips	16.0	26.9	16.2	12.8	4.8
Popcorn	9.5	7.8	8.1	9.6	6.1
Prepared mustard	22.2	27.8	29.7	25.5	19.9

(continued)

(continued from previous page)

	both sexes aged 2 or older	men aged			
		12 to 19	20 to 39	40 to 59	60 or older
Tomato catsup	26.5%	42.4%	35.8%	21.0%	13.3%
Soy-based sauces	15.8	17.5	19.0	15.3	10.5
Pickles (cucumber)	20.7	25.8	30.8	22.0	13.4
Margarine	32.7	26.7	23.6	32.4	44.7
Butter	14.6	11.2	15.0	17.1	19.6
Salad dressing, pourable	21.3	12.4	21.4	26.0	28.0
Mayonnaise	22.7	31.2	33.4	26.4	15.5
Mayonnaise-type dressing	8.0	8.1	9.7	8.6	5.9
Gravy	9.4	8.8	9.5	11.5	13.9
Syrup	8.8	12.3	7.5	7.1	8.4
Sugar	38.1	31.0	43.0	45.2	40.3
Candy, with chocolate	15.8	19.5	15.3	14.1	11.0
Candy, without chocolate	11.0	14.1	5.4	6.4	6.2
Jelly, jams, preserves	17.3	13.4	11.5	15.3	25.2

Source: U.S. Department of Agriculture, Foods Commonly Eaten in the United States: Quantities Consumed per Eating Occasion and in a Day, 1994–1996, *NFS Report No. 96-5, by Smiciklas-Wright, H., D. C. Mitchell, S. J. Mickle, A. J. Cook, and J. D. Goldman, 2002; Internet site <www.barc.usda.gov/bhnrc/foodsurvey/Products9496.html>*

Men Are Less Likely to Take Vitamins

The gap between the sexes is largest among people under age 60.

Overall, 42 percent of men and 56 percent of women aged 20 or older take vitamin or mineral supplements. Among men, the share taking supplements rises with age to more than 47 percent of those aged 60 or older. Among women, the share taking supplements peaks at 63 percent in the 50-to-59 age group.

Women are more likely than men to take supplements at all ages. The biggest difference occurs in the 50-to-59 age group, where women are 19 percentage points more likely to take supplements than men. Among Americans aged 60 or older, the gap between men and women shrinks to less than 10 percentage points.

■ Americans aged 50 or older are most likely to take vitamins. As the large baby-boom generation enters its fifties and sixties, sales of vitamin and mineral supplements will grow.

A minority of men take vitamins

(percent of people aged 20 or older using vitamin/mineral supplements, by sex, 1994–96)

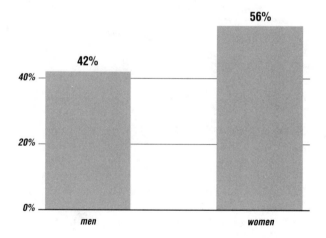

Vitamin Use by Age and Sex, 1994–96

(percent of people aged 20 or older using vitamin/mineral supplements by age and sex, and percentage point difference between men and women, 1994–96)

	men	women	percentage point difference
Aged 20 or older	**41.9%**	**55.8%**	**–13.9**
Aged 20 to 29	36.4	52.0	–15.6
Aged 30 to 39	39.7	54.4	–14.7
Aged 40 to 49	43.8	56.7	–12.9
Aged 50 to 59	43.8	62.6	–18.8
Aged 60 to 69	47.6	57.3	–9.7
Aged 70 or older	47.1	53.6	–6.5

Source: U.S. Department of Agriculture, Agricultural Research Service, Food and Nutrient Intakes by Individuals in the United States, by Sex and Age, 1994–96, *Nationwide Food Surveys Report No. 96-2, 1998; Internet site <www.barc.usda.gov/bhnrc/foodsurvey/Products9496.html>; calculations by New Strategist*

On an Average Day, Most Men Eat Out

Fast-food restaurants are most popular among young men, while older men prefer sit-down restaurants.

Overall, 61 percent of men eat away from home on an average day. The proportion eating away from home peaks at 71 percent among men in their twenties, then falls with age. Among men aged 60 or older, fewer than half eat out on an average day.

Among all men, fast-food restaurants are more popular than sit-down establishments. Among men aged 20 or older eating out on an average day, 36 percent go to a fast-food restaurant and 32 percent eat at a sit-down restaurant. Fast-food restaurants capture a larger share of men under age 50 than sit-down restaurants, while sit-down establishments are more popular than fast-food joints among men aged 50 or older.

Other eating-out venues are also popular among men. Of those who eat out on an average day, 28 percent eat at a store, perhaps the deli counter in a supermarket. Seventeen percent eat at someone else's house.

■ As Americans age, sit-down restaurants may see a resurgence of popularity.

A minority of men aged 60 or older eat out on an average day

(percent of men eating away from home on an average day, by age, 1994–96)

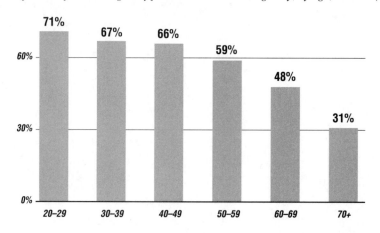

Men Eating away from Home by Age and Source of Food, 1994–96

(percent of men aged 20 or older eating food away from home on an average day by age, and percent distribution by source of food, 1994–96)

| | total eating away from home | | source of food | | | | | | |
		total	sit-down restaurant	fast-food restaurant	someone else or gift	store	school cafeteria	other cafeteria	other
Total men	61.2%	100.0%	32.2%	35.6%	17.3%	27.7%	1.7%	8.5%	29.1%
Aged 20 to 29	71.2	100.0	29.7	43.7	19.0	31.9	2.3	6.8	30.6
Aged 30 to 39	66.9	100.0	26.5	35.5	19.1	31.7	–	9.5	32.9
Aged 40 to 49	66.2	100.0	30.7	35.9	15.4	28.3	2.3	10.2	28.3
Aged 50 to 59	59.1	100.0	39.1	30.9	12.3	25.4	–	8.2	28.4
Aged 60 to 69	47.9	100.0	42.4	27.3	18.1	13.5	–	7.2	22.1
Aged 70 or older	31.3	100.0	46.7	21.0	20.1	11.4	–	7.4	17.1

Note: Percentages will not add to 100 because food may be eaten at more than one location during the day; (–) means sample is too small to make a reliable estimate.

Source: U.S. Department of Agriculture, Agricultural Research Service, Food and Nutrient Intakes by Individuals in the United States, by Sex and Age, 1994–96, Nationwide Food Surveys Report No. 96-2, 1998; Internet site <www.barc.usda.gov/bhnrc/foodsurvey/Products9496.html>; calculations by New Strategist

Men and Women Are Equally Likely to Be Overweight

The middle-aged have the biggest weight problem.

Overall, 32 percent of men and women are overweight, according to a 1994–96 survey by the United States Department of Agriculture.

Young adults are least likely to be overweight, and people aged 40 to 69 are most likely to tip the scales. Among men aged 20 to 29, only 22 percent are overweight. But fully 41 percent of men aged 60 to 69 weigh more than they should. Among women in their twenties, only 22 percent are overweight. The figure peaks at 38 percent among women aged 50 to 69.

Men in their thirties are significantly more likely than their female counterparts to be overweight. The opposite is true among people in their seventies, in which age group 33 percent of women but only 22 percent of men are considered overweight.

■ The large baby-boom generation is now entering the lifestage when maintaining a healthy weight becomes increasingly difficult.

Weight problems are greatest among the middle aged

(percent of men who are overweight, by age, 1994–96

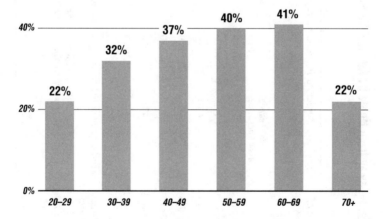

Overweight People by Age and Sex, 1994–96

(percent of people aged 20 or older who are overweight by age and sex, and percentage point difference between men and women, 1994–96)

	men	women	percentage point difference
Total people	**31.8%**	**31.5%**	**0.3**
Aged 20 to 29	21.5	22.1	–0.6
Aged 30 to 39	32.3	27.4	4.9
Aged 40 to 49	37.0	36.1	0.9
Aged 50 to 59	39.9	37.8	2.1
Aged 60 to 69	40.7	37.8	2.9
Aged 70 or older	22.1	33.4	–11.3

Note: For men, overweight is defined as having a body mass index of 27.8 or more. For women, overweight is defined as a body mass index of 27.3 or more. BMI is calculated by dividing weight in kilograms by the square of height in meters.
Source: U.S. Department of Agriculture, Agricultural Research Service, Data Tables: Results from USDA's Continuing Survey of Food Intakes by Individuals *and 1994–96 Diet and Health Knowledge Survey, Internet site <www.barc.usda.gov/bhnrc/foodsurvey/home.htm>; calculations by New Strategist*

One in Four Men Smokes Cigarettes

Young men are increasingly likely to smoke.

Public health campaigns against cigarette smoking have had an impact on some men, but not others. In 1990, 28 percent of men smoked cigarettes. By 1999, the proportion had fallen to 26 percent. But among young adults, smoking increased.

Men aged 18 to 24 and 35 to 44 are most likely to smoke, at 30 percent. Those least likely to smoke are the oldest adults. Only 11 percent of men aged 65 or older smoke cigarettes. One reason the oldest adults are least likely to smoke is that many have kicked the habit, some following doctor's orders.

While men in most age groups were less likely to smoke in 1999 than in 1990, young men are more likely to smoke. Thirty percent of men aged 18 to 24 smoked cigarettes in 1999, up from 27 percent in 1990. In contrast, men aged 35 to 44 saw the biggest decline in smoking, a drop from 35 to 30 percent.

■ Cigarette smoking should continue to decline as cigarette prices rise and smoking is increasingly restricted.

Few older men smoke cigarettes

(percent of men who smoke cigarettes, by age, 1999)

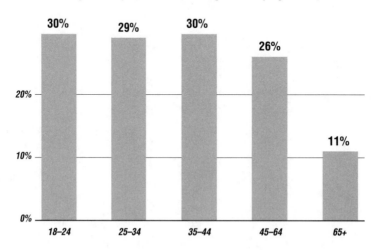

Cigarette Smoking among Men by Age, 1990 and 1999

(percent of men aged 18 or older who smoke cigarettes by age, 1990 and 1999; percentage point change, 1990–99)

	1999	1990	percentage point change
Total men	**25.7%**	**28.4%**	**–2.7**
Aged 18 to 24	29.5	26.6	2.9
Aged 25 to 34	29.1	31.6	–2.5
Aged 35 to 44	30.0	34.5	–4.5
Aged 45 to 64	25.8	29.3	–3.5
Aged 65 or older	10.5	14.6	–4.1

Source: National Center for Health Statistics, Health, United States, 2001; *calculations by New Strategist*

Most Men Drink Alcohol

Nearly one-third of men are "moderate" drinkers.

Overall, 70 percent of men currently drink alcoholic beverages, which is defined as having had at least 12 drinks in one's lifetime and at least one drink in the past year. Fifteen percent of men are former drinkers (no drinks in the past year) and another 15 percent are abstainers (fewer than 12 drinks in their lifetime and none in the past year). The men most likely to drink are aged 25 to 44. More than three out of four men in the age group are current drinkers. A smaller 69 percent of men aged 45 to 64 are drinkers, and the proportion falls to 53 percent among men aged 65 or older.

Among current drinkers, 59 percent describe their drinking as light, meaning three or fewer drinks per week. A substantial 32 percent of men are moderate drinkers (4 to 14 drinks per week). Only 9 percent are heavy drinkers (more than 14 drinks per week).

■ Older men are less likely to drink than younger adults because health problems and medications often limit alcohol consumption.

More than three-fourths of men aged 25 to 44 drink alcohol

(percent of men who are current drinkers, by age, 1999)

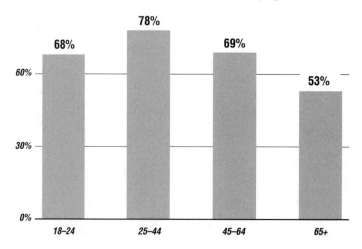

Alcohol Consumption among Men by Age, 1999

(percent distribution of men aged 18 or older by drinking status, and percent who drink alcohol by age, 1999)

	percent distribution
Total men	**100.0%**
Lifetime abstainer	14.7
Former drinker	15.3
Current drinker	70.0
All current drinkers	**100.0**
Light	58.9
Moderate	32.3
Heavy	8.7
	percent
Current drinkers by age	
Total men	**70.0%**
Aged 18 to 24	67.6
Aged 25 to 44	77.6
Aged 45 to 64	68.5
Aged 65 or older	52.6

Note: Lifetime abstainers have had fewer than 12 drinks in their lifetime. Former drinkers have had at least 12 drinks in their lifetime but none in the past year. Current drinkers have had at least 12 drinks in their lifetime and at least one drink in the past year. Among current drinkers, light drinkers have up to three drinks per week, moderate drinkers have 4 to 14 drinks per week, and heavy drinkers have more than 14 drinks per week.
Source: National Center for Health Statistics, Health United States 2001

Men Are Less Likely to Have High Cholesterol

Among men under age 45, however, the opposite is true.

Eighteen percent of men aged 20 or older have high cholesterol, according to the National Center for Health Statistics. Among women, the proportion is a larger 20 percent.

Men under age 45 are more likely to have high cholesterol than their female counterparts. The difference is a tiny 0.9 percentage points among 20-to-34-year-olds, rising to 7 percentage points among 35-to-44-year-olds.

The percentage of women with high cholesterol leaps upward in the 45-to-54 age group, closing the gap between the sexes. Among people aged 55 or older, women are 13 to 19 percentage points more likely than men to have high cholesterol.

Among men, the proportion with high cholesterol peaks at 28 percent in the 55-to-64 age group. Among women, the peak is a much higher 41 percent among those aged 55 to 74.

■ Men have lower cholesterol than women despite their lesser concern about healthy eating.

Cholesterol level peaks among men aged 55 to 64

(percent of men with high cholesterol, by age, 1988–94)

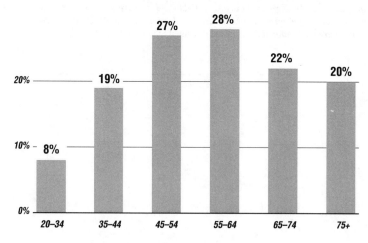

High Cholesterol by Age and Sex, 1988–94

(percent of people aged 20 or older who have high serum cholesterol by age and sex, and percentage point difference between men and women, 1988–94)

	men	women	percentage point difference
Total people	**17.6%**	**19.9%**	**–2.3**
Aged 20 to 34	8.2	7.3	0.9
Aged 35 to 44	19.4	12.3	7.1
Aged 45 to 54	26.6	26.7	–0.1
Aged 55 to 64	28.0	40.9	–12.9
Aged 65 to 74	21.9	41.3	–19.4
Aged 75 or older	20.4	38.2	–17.8

Source: National Center for Health Statistics, Health, United States, 2001, *calculations by New Strategist*

High Blood Pressure Is Common among Older Men

Most men aged 65 or older have high blood pressure.

Overall, 25 percent of men and 22 percent of women have high blood pressure. Among people under age 55, men are more likely than women to have high blood pressure. But among people aged 55 or older, women are more likely than men to have the problem.

The proportion of men and women with high blood pressure peaks in the oldest age group. Among people aged 75 or older, 64 percent of men and 77 percent of women have high blood pressure. Overall, the majority of adults aged 65 or older have high blood pressure.

Among adults aged 45 to 54, a significant one-third of men and one-fourth of women have high blood pressure. Even among men aged 35 to 44, a substantial 21 percent have a problem with blood pressure.

■ As the baby-boom generation ages, the medications and lifestyle changes necessary to alleviate high blood pressure will become commonplace in millions of American households.

High blood pressure is most common among men aged 75 or older

(percent of men with high blood pressure, by age, 1988–94)

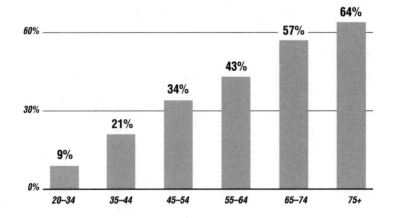

High Blood Pressure by Age and Sex, 1988–94

(percent of people aged 20 or older with hypertension by age and sex, and percentage point difference between men and women, 1988–94)

	men	women	percentage point difference
Total people	**24.7%**	**21.5%**	**3.2**
Aged 20 to 34	8.6	3.4	5.2
Aged 35 to 44	20.9	12.7	8.2
Aged 45 to 54	34.1	25.1	9.0
Aged 55 to 64	42.9	44.2	−1.3
Aged 65 to 74	57.3	60.8	−3.5
Aged 75 or older	64.2	77.3	−13.1

Source: National Center for Health Statistics, Health, United States, 2001*; calculations by New Strategist*

Most Men Exercise Vigorously at Least Twice a Week

Young men are most likely to exercise daily.

The majority of men under age 70 say they exercise vigorously at least twice a week. Twenty-five percent say they exercise vigorously on a daily basis, while another 33 percent say they get vigorous exercise from two to six times a week.

The percentage of men who engage in vigorous exercise at least twice weekly falls with age from a high of 69 percent among men aged 20 to 29 to a low of 39 percent among those aged 70 or older. Conversely, the proportion of men who say they rarely exercise vigorously rises with age from 17 percent of those in their twenties to the 55 percent majority of men aged 70 or older.

■ Most men have gotten the message that exercise is important to healthy living, but older men still lag in participation.

Most men exercise regularly

(percent of men who exercise vigorously at least twice a week, by age, 1994–96)

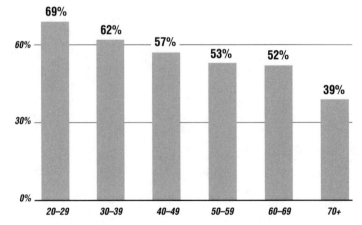

Exercise among Men by Age, 1994–96

(percent distribution of men aged 20 or older by frequency of vigorous exercise, by age, 1994–96)

	daily	5 to 6 times per week	2 to 4 times per week	1 time per week	1 to 3 times per month	rarely
Total men	**24.5%**	**7.9%**	**25.4%**	**8.1%**	**5.3%**	**28.4%**
Aged 20 to 29	30.3	9.3	29.0	8.9	5.6	16.6
Aged 30 to 39	23.5	9.0	29.7	9.2	6.8	21.8
Aged 40 to 49	21.4	8.8	26.6	9.4	5.8	27.4
Aged 50 to 59	22.4	7.2	23.4	8.8	4.2	33.4
Aged 60 to 69	27.6	5.8	18.1	4.7	3.8	39.4
Aged 70 or older	20.5	3.7	14.3	3.6	2.5	54.6

Source: U.S. Department of Agriculture, Agricultural Research Service, Data Tables: Results from USDA's Continuing Survey of Food Intakes by Individuals *and* 1994–96 Diet and Health Knowledge Survey, *Internet site <www.barc.usda.gov/bhnrc/foodsurvey/home.htm>; calculations by New Strategist*

Young Adults Are Most Likely to Be Uninsured

Three out of ten men aged 18 to 24 lack health insurance.

Most Americans have health insurance coverage, but a large share of young adults do not. Among men aged 18 to 24, 30 percent lack health insurance. A substantial 24 percent of 25-to-34-year-olds are also without coverage. Twelve percent of boys under age 18 do not have health insurance, but thanks to Medicare nearly all men aged 65 or older are covered.

Sixty-five percent of males have employment-based health insurance, and many wives and children depend on this coverage. Nine percent of males are covered through Medicaid, the health insurance program for the poor, including 20 percent of boys under age 18. Twelve percent of males have Medicare coverage, including 95 percent of men aged 65 or older. Three percent of males have health insurance through the military.

■ An employment-based health insurance system, as prevails in the United States, can be a problem for those without a job or whose companies do not offer health insurance benefits.

Older men are most likely to have health insurance coverage

(percent of males without health insurance, by age, 2000)

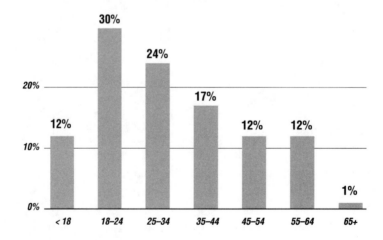

Health Insurance Coverage of Males by Age, 2000

(number and percent distribution of males by age and health insurance coverage status, 2000; numbers in thousands)

| | | covered by private or government health insurance | | | | | | | |
| | | private health insurance | | | government health insurance | | | | |
	total	total	total	employ-ment based	total	Medicaid	Medicare	Military	not covered
Total males	**135,245**	**115,096**	**98,428**	**88,308**	**30,122**	**12,672**	**16,222**	**4,431**	**20,149**
Under 18	37,133	32,739	26,094	24,501	8,756	7,608	270	1,124	4,394
Aged 18–24	13,476	9,476	8,753	7,270	1,197	801	86	358	3,999
Aged 25–34	18,451	14,107	13,216	12,467	1,276	734	244	427	4,344
Aged 35–44	22,177	18,467	17,364	16,399	1,650	927	451	564	3,709
Aged 45–54	18,578	16,353	15,143	14,191	1,900	879	716	625	2,224
Aged 55–64	11,253	9,907	8,801	7,902	1,755	577	934	463	1,346
Aged 65+	14,179	14,047	9,056	5,579	13,587	1,148	13,520	869	132

Percent distribution by type of coverage

Total males	**100.0%**	**85.1%**	**72.8%**	**65.3%**	**22.3%**	**9.4%**	**12.0%**	**3.3%**	**14.9%**
Under 18	100.0	88.2	70.3	66.0	23.6	20.5	0.7	3.0	11.8
Aged 18–24	100.0	70.3	65.0	53.9	8.9	5.9	0.6	2.7	29.7
Aged 25–34	100.0	76.5	71.6	67.6	6.9	4.0	1.3	2.3	23.5
Aged 35–44	100.0	83.3	78.3	73.9	7.4	4.2	2.0	2.5	16.7
Aged 45–54	100.0	88.0	81.5	76.4	10.2	4.7	3.9	3.4	12.0
Aged 55–64	100.0	88.0	78.2	70.2	15.6	5.1	8.3	4.1	12.0
Aged 65+	100.0	99.1	63.9	39.3	95.8	8.1	95.4	6.1	0.9

Percent distribution by age

Total males	**100.0%**	**100.0%**	**100.0%**	**100.0%**	**100.0%**	**100.0%**	**100.0%**	**100.0%**	**100.0%**
Under 18	27.5	28.4	26.5	27.7	29.1	60.0	1.7	25.4	21.8
Aged 18–24	10.0	8.2	8.9	8.2	4.0	6.3	0.5	8.1	19.8
Aged 25–34	13.6	12.3	13.4	14.1	4.2	5.8	1.5	9.6	21.6
Aged 35–44	16.4	16.0	17.6	18.6	5.5	7.3	2.8	12.7	18.4
Aged 45–54	13.7	14.2	15.4	16.1	6.3	6.9	4.4	14.1	11.0
Aged 55–64	8.3	8.6	8.9	8.9	5.8	4.6	5.8	10.4	6.7
Aged 65+	10.5	12.2	9.2	6.3	45.1	9.1	83.3	19.6	0.7

Note: Numbers will not add to total because people may have more than one type of health insurance coverage.
Source: Bureau of the Census, Internet site <www.census.gov/hhes/hlthins/historic/hihistt2.html>; calculations by New Strategist

Males Account for the Majority of the Injured

Females dominate most other acute conditions.

Of the acute illnesses that cause people to restrict their activity for at least half a day or to contact a physician, only 45 percent affect males. There are several reasons why males account for a minority of those experiencing acute conditions. One, females outnumber males in the U.S. population. Two, the average male is younger than the average female and consequently less vulnerable to illness. Three, males are less likely than females to seek medical attention for health problems.

Although males account for a minority of most acute conditions, they dominate injuries. Males account for 54 percent of those with sprains and strains and for 69 percent of those experiencing open wounds and lacerations. They also account for 54 percent of those with dental conditions, 51 percent of acute ear infections, and 52 percent of acute musculoskeletal conditions.

■ Males account for most injuries because they outnumber females among children and young adults, when injury is most likely.

For most acute conditions, men are in the minority

(percent of total acute conditions experienced by males, by type of condition, 1996)

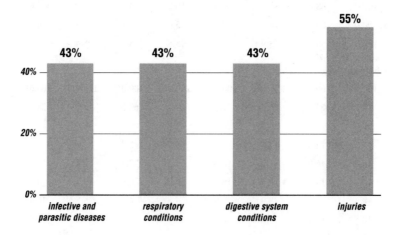

Acute Health Conditions among Males, 1996

(total number of acute conditions, number among males, and male share of total, 1996; numbers in thousands)

	total	males number	share of total
Total acute conditions	**432,001**	**193,336**	**44.8%**
Infective and parasitic diseases	**54,192**	**23,092**	**42.6**
Common childhood diseases	3,118	1,623	52.1
Intestinal virus	15,980	6,405	40.1
Viral infections	15,067	7,770	51.6
Other	20,027	7,294	36.4
Respiratory conditions	**208,623**	**90,567**	**43.4**
Common cold	62,251	28,237	45.4
Other acute upper respiratory infections	29,866	10,107	33.8
Influenza	95,049	43,868	46.2
Acute bronchitis	12,116	4,182	34.5
Pneumonia	4,791	2,337	48.8
Other respiratory conditions	4,550	1,836	40.4
Digestive system conditions	**17,646**	**7,648**	**43.3**
Dental conditions	2,970	1,598	53.8
Indigestion, nausea, and vomiting	7,963	2,548	32.0
Other digestive conditions	6,713	3,502	52.2
Injuries	**57,279**	**31,720**	**55.4**
Fractures and dislocations	8,465	4,237	50.1
Sprains and strains	12,977	6,951	53.6
Open wounds and lacerations	9,027	6,273	69.5
Contusions and superficial injuries	9,979	5,986	60.0
Other current injuries	16,832	8,273	49.2
Selected other acute conditions	**63,090**	**26,553**	**42.1**
Eye conditions	3,478	1,691	48.6
Acute ear infections	21,766	11,185	51.4
Other ear conditions	3,833	1,410	36.8
Acute urinary conditions	8,405	2,139	25.4

(continued)

(continued from previous page)

	total	males	
		number	share of total
Skin conditions	4,986	2,482	49.8%
Acute musculoskeletal conditions	8,461	4,367	51.6
Headache, excluding migraine	1,738	756	43.5
Fever, unspecified	4,708	2,523	53.6
All other acute conditions	**31,170**	**13,756**	**44.1**

Note: The acute conditions shown here are those that caused people to restrict their activity for at least half a day or caused people to contact a physician about the illness or injury.
Source: National Center for Health Statistics, Current Estimates from the National Health Interview Survey, 1996, *Series 10, No. 200, 1999; calculations by New Strategist*

Males Dominate Only a Few Chronic Conditions

They are more likely to have hearing problems.

Men account for the 59 percent majority of Americans with hearing problems. They also account for the majority of those with speech impairments and paralysis of the extremities. But for most other conditions, ranging from cataracts to diabetes, high blood pressure to asthma, the majority of those affected are female.

Females dominate chronic conditions even more than acute conditions because there are more females than males in the population and because the average female is older than the average male. Since chronic conditions affect older people more than younger, females account for an even larger majority of chronic conditions than acute conditions.

Males dominate only a handful of chronic conditions including gout, hernias, cerebrovascular disease, and emphysema. But they account for only 38 percent of people with arthritis, 21 percent of those with migraines, and 43 percent of those with high blood pressure.

■ As the men and women of the large baby-boom generation age, the management of chronic conditions will become increasingly important to the health care industry.

Men account for most of those with hearing impairments

(percent distribution of people with hearing impairments, by sex, 1996)

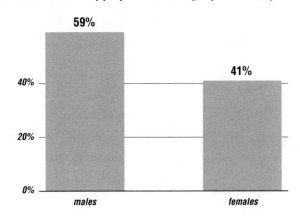

Chronic Health Conditions among Males, 1996

(total number of chronic conditions, number among males, and male share of total, 1996; numbers in thousands)

		males	
	total	*number*	*share of total*
Selected skin and musculoskeletal conditions			
Arthritis	33,638	12,774	38.0%
Gout	2,487	1,780	71.6
Intervertebral disc disorders	6,700	3,476	51.9
Bone spur or tendinitis	2,934	1,221	41.6
Disorders of bone or cartilage	1,730	405	23.4
Trouble with bunions	2,360	531	22.5
Bursitis	5,006	2,038	40.7
Sebaceous skin cyst	1,190	731	61.4
Trouble with acne	4,952	2,332	47.1
Psoriasis	2,940	1,606	54.6
Dermatitis	8,249	3,336	40.4
Trouble with dry (itching) skin	6,627	2,621	39.6
Trouble with ingrown nails	5,807	3,060	52.7
Trouble with corns and calluses	3,778	1,481	39.2
Impairments			
Visual impairment	8,280	4,893	59.1
Color blindness	2,811	2,538	90.3
Cataracts	7,022	2,451	34.9
Glaucoma	2,595	1,145	44.1
Hearing impairment	22,044	12,918	58.6
Tinnitus	7,866	4,524	57.5
Speech impairment	2,720	1,778	65.4
Absence of extremities	1,285	893	69.5
Paralysis of extremities	2,138	1,234	57.7
Deformity or orthopedic impairment	29,499	14,517	49.2
Selected digestive conditions			
Ulcer	3,709	1,679	45.3
Hernia of abdominal cavity	4,470	2,304	51.5
Gastritis or duodenitis	3,729	1,375	36.9
Frequent indigestion	6,420	3,288	51.2
Enteritis or colitis	1,686	512	30.4
Spastic colon	2,083	568	27.3
Diverticula of intestines	2,529	857	33.9
Frequent constipation	3,149	869	27.6

(continued)

(continued from previous page)

	total	males number	share of total
Selected conditions of the genitourinary, nervous, endocrine, metabolic, or blood system			
Goiter or other disorders of the thyroid	4,598	1,008	21.9%
Diabetes	7,627	3,632	47.6
Anemias	3,457	557	16.1
Epilepsy	1,335	570	42.7
Migraine	11,546	2,447	21.2
Neuralgia or neuritis	353	140	39.7
Kidney trouble	2,553	1,137	44.5
Bladder disorders	3,139	484	15.4
Diseases of prostate	2,803	2,802	100.0
Selected circulatory conditions			
Rheumatic fever	1,759	701	39.9
Heart disease	20,653	10,330	50.0
Ischemic heart disease	7,672	4,720	61.5
Heart rhythm disorders	8,716	3,592	41.2
Other selected diseases of the heart, excl. hypertension	4,265	2,017	47.3
High blood pressure (hypertension)	28,314	12,177	43.0
Cerebrovascular disease	2,999	1,785	59.5
Hardening of the arteries	1,556	880	56.6
Varicose veins of lower extremities	7,399	1,411	19.1
Hemorrhoids	8,531	3,263	38.2
Selected respiratory conditions			
Chronic bronchitis	14,150	6,049	42.7
Asthma	14,596	5,751	39.4
Hay fever	23,721	10,558	44.5
Chronic sinusitis	33,161	13,461	40.6
Deviated nasal septum	1,985	901	45.4
Chronic disease of tonsils or adenoids	2,513	909	36.2
Emphysema	1,821	956	52.5

Note: Chronic conditions are those that last at least three months or belong to a group of conditions considered to be chronic regardless of when they began.
Source: National Center for Health Statistics, Current Estimates from the National Health Interview Survey, 1996, *Series 10, No. 200, 1999; calculations by New Strategist*

Many Men Are Disabled

The majority of men aged 65 or older have a disability.

Nineteen percent of the nation's males are disabled, according to a 1997 Census Bureau survey. Eleven percent are severely disabled, and 3 percent are so disabled they need assistance.

The percentage of people who are disabled rises with age. Ten percent of boys under age 15 are disabled. Among men aged 65 or older, the 50 percent majority are disabled— although a smaller 33 percent are severely disabled. Among men aged 80 or older, the 51 percent majority are severely disabled.

The proportion of men who need assistance also rises with age. Fourteen percent of men aged 65 or older are so disabled they need assistance to manage their daily life. The proportion peaks at 28 percent among men aged 80 or older.

■ The aging of the population will inflate the number of disabled Americans in the years ahead.

Severe disabilities are common among older men

(percent of males with a severe disability, by age, 1997)

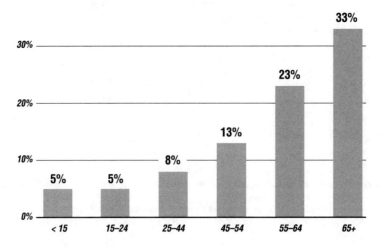

Males with Disabilities by Age, 1997

(total number of males and number and percent with a disability, by age, severity, and need for assistance, 1997; numbers in thousands)

| | | with a disability | | | | | |
| | | total | | severe | | needs assistance | |
	total	number	percent	number	percent	number	percent
Total males	**130,985**	**24,331**	**18.6%**	**14,754**	**11.3%**	**4,149**	**3.2%**
Under age 15	30,494	3,015	9.9	1,502	4.9	130	0.4
Aged 15 to 24	18,663	2,166	11.6	1,007	5.4	216	1.2
Aged 25 to 44	41,571	5,403	13.0	3,323	8.0	846	2.0
Aged 45 to 54	16,418	3,427	20.9	2,138	13.0	535	3.3
Aged 55 to 64	10,342	3,518	34.0	2,364	22.9	584	5.7
Aged 65 or older	13,498	6,801	50.4	4,421	32.8	1,838	13.6
Aged 65 to 69	4,338	1,813	41.8	1,171	27.0	333	7.7
Aged 70 to 74	3,722	1,695	45.5	1,022	27.5	392	10.5
Aged 75 to 79	2,800	1,494	53.4	881	31.5	381	13.6
Aged 80 or older	2,639	1,800	68.2	1,347	51.1	732	27.7

Note: For the definition of disability, see glossary.
Source: Bureau of the Census, Americans with Disabilities: 1997, *detailed tables for Current Population Report P70-73, 2001*

Males Account for Fewer than Half of Physician Visits

They account for only 32 percent of physician office visits for depression.

Male patients made only 41 percent of the more than 700 million physician office visits in 1999. Males account for the 53 percent majority of visits by children under age 15 because there are more boys than girls in the population. But in every other age group, males are a minority of patients. In the 15-to-44 age group, men account for only 35 to 36 percent of visits.

The male share of physician office visits differs by reason for visit. Males account for most visits for well-baby exams, ear infections, and fever—probably because these types of visits are dominated by children, the slight majority of whom are boys. Males account for fewer than 40 percent of physician visits for postoperative exams, stomach pain, depression, and headache.

■ Males are less likely than females to visit physicians in part because they are less likely to seek medical help for their problems.

Males are a minority of patients

(male share of physician office visits, by age, 1999)

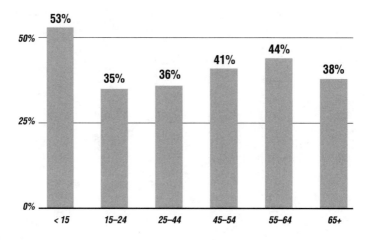

Physician Office Visits by Males by Age, 1999

(total number of physician office visits, number by males, and male share of total, by age, 1999; numbers in thousands)

	total	males number	males share of total
Total visits	**756,734**	**311,168**	**41.1%**
Under age 15	116,904	61,658	52.7
Aged 15 to 24	59,706	21,185	35.5
Aged 25 to 44	186,022	66,938	36.0
Aged 45 to 64	201,911	82,487	40.9
Aged 65 to 74	92,642	40,973	44.2
Aged 75 or older	99,548	37,926	38.1

Source: National Center for Health Statistics, National Ambulatory Medical Care Survey: 1999 Summary, *Advance Data, No. 322, 2001*

Physician Office Visits by Males by Reason for Visit, 1999

(total number of physician office visits, number by males, and male share of total, by reason for visit, 1999; numbers in thousands)

	total	males number	males share of total
Total visits	**756,734**	**311,168**	**41.1%**
General medical examination	46,039	19,915	43.3
Progress visit, not otherwise specified	33,975	16,181	47.6
Postoperative visit	22,513	8,402	37.3
Cough	20,654	9,024	43.7
Symptoms referable to throat	15,315	6,846	44.7
Well-baby examination	13,111	6,846	52.2
Vision dysfunctions	12,243	4,979	40.7
Knee symptoms	11,778	4,979	42.3
Hypertension	11,130	4,668	41.9
Earache or ear infection	11,047	5,601	50.7
Back symptoms	10,482	4,356	41.6
Skin rash	10,446	4,979	47.7
Stomach pain, cramps, and spasms	10,077	3,734	37.1
Fever	9,963	5,290	53.1
Depression	9,664	3,112	32.2
Medication, other and unspecified kinds	9,284	3,734	40.2
Low-back symptoms	9,186	4,356	47.4
Nasal congestion	9,067	4,045	44.6
Headache, pain in the head	8,599	3,112	36.2
All other reasons	454,263	186,078	41.0

Source: National Center for Health Statistics, National Ambulatory Medical Care Survey: 1999 Summary, Advance Data, *No. 322, 2001; calculations by New Strategist*

Males Are a Minority of Hospital Patients

They account for the majority of those receiving some procedures, however.

Of the nation's 84 million hospital outpatients in 1999, only 40 percent were male. Males also accounted for only 40 percent of hospital inpatients, including just 18 percent of inpatients aged 18 to 24.

The male share of hospital inpatients varies greatly by diagnosis and procedure, however. Males account for the 52 percent majority of hospital inpatients diagnosed with mental disorders, 52 percent of those with heart disease, 57 percent of those with appendicitis, and 52 percent of those with congenital anomalies. But they account for only 40 percent of inpatients with asthma and 42 percent of inpatients with bone fractures.

Males account for 68 percent of inpatients receiving heart bypass operations. They are the 51 percent majority of inpatients receiving spinal taps, and 54 percent of those receiving operations on the ear.

■ Even as hospitals have shifted more procedures to outpatient facilities, the demographics of their customers have remained the same.

Males account for a minority of both outpatients and inpatients

(percent distribution of hospital outpatients and inpatients, by sex, 1999)

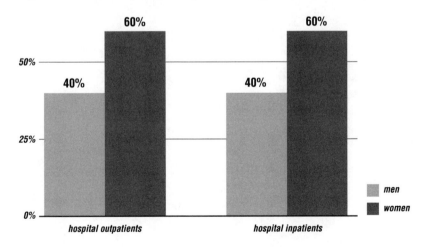

Visits to Hospital Outpatient Departments by Males by Age, 1999

(total number of hospital outpatient department visits, number by males, and male share of total, by age, 1999; numbers in thousands)

	total	males number	males share of total
Total visits	**84,623**	**33,573**	**39.7%**
Under age 15	18,551	9,594	51.7
Aged 15 to 24	10,407	3,101	29.8
Aged 25 to 44	22,134	7,807	35.3
Aged 45 to 64	20,891	8,307	39.8
Aged 65 to 74	6,969	2,799	40.2
Aged 75 or older	5,493	1,965	35.8

Source: National Center for Health Statistics, National Hospital Ambulatory Medical Care Survey: 1999 Outpatient Department Summary, *Advance Data, No. 321, 2001*

Hospital Stays by Males by Age, 1999

(total number of inpatients discharged from short-stay nonfederal hospitals, number of males discharged, male share of total, and average length of stay for males by age, 1999)

	total (000s)	males number (000s)	males share of total	males average length of stay (days)
Total discharges	**32,132**	**12,748**	**39.7%**	**5.4**
Under age 1	827	480	58.0	5.2
Aged 1 to 4	729	407	55.8	3.3
Aged 5 to 14	902	510	56.5	5.0
Aged 15 to 19	1,209	322	26.6	4.6
Aged 20 to 24	1,644	298	18.1	5.1
Aged 25 to 34	3,829	777	20.3	4.6
Aged 35 to 44	3,411	1,318	38.6	5.0
Aged 45 to 54	3,386	1,613	47.6	4.9
Aged 55 to 64	3,513	1,777	50.6	5.3
Aged 65 or older	12,683	5,245	41.4	6.1
Aged 65 to 74	4,883	2,310	47.3	5.8
Aged 75 to 84	5,227	2,172	41.6	6.2
Aged 85 or older	2,572	762	29.6	6.6

Source: National Center for Health Statistics, 1999 National Hospital Discharge Survey: Annual Summary with Detailed Diagnosis and Procedure Data, *Vital and Health Statistics, Series 13, No. 151, 2001; calculations by New Strategist*

Discharges of Males from Hospitals by Diagnosis, 1999

(total number of inpatients discharged from nonfederal hospitals, number of males discharged, and male share of total, by first-listed diagnosis, 1999; numbers in thousands)

	total	males number	males share of total
Total discharges	**32,132**	**12,748**	**39.7%**
Infectious and parasitic diseases	826	385	46.6
Septicemia	341	146	42.8
Neoplasms	1,687	655	38.8
Malignant neoplasms	1,274	596	46.8
Malignant neoplasm of large intestine and rectum	166	80	48.2
Malignant neoplasm of trachea, bronchus, and lung	164	91	55.5
Benign neoplasms	366	44	12.0
Endocrine, nutritional and metabolic diseases, and immunity disorders	1,393	577	41.4
Diabetes mellitus	545	262	48.1
Volume depletion	477	186	39.0
Diseases of the blood and blood forming organs	368	162	44.0
Mental disorders	2,018	1,048	51.9
Psychoses	1,309	640	48.9
Alcohol dependence syndrome	164	119	72.6
Diseases of the nervous system and sense organs	503	226	44.9
Diseases of the circulatory system	6,344	3,161	49.8
Heart disease	4,465	2,302	51.6
Acute myocardial infarction	829	481	58.0
Coronary atherosclerosis	1,153	703	61.0
Other ischemic heart disease	280	133	47.5
Cardiac dysrhythmias	704	329	46.7
Congestive heart failure	962	430	44.7
Cerebrovascular disease	961	434	45.2
Diseases of the respiratory system	3,689	1,742	47.2
Acute bronchitis and bronchiolitis	298	153	51.3
Pneumonia	1,378	672	48.8
Chronic bronchitis	539	228	42.3
Asthma	478	190	39.7

(continued)

(continued from previous page)

	total	males number	males share of total
Diseases of the digestive system	3,122	1,353	43.3%
Appendicitis	260	148	56.9
Noninfectious enteritis and colitis	272	107	39.3
Diverticula of intestine	239	93	38.9
Cholelithiasis	357	110	30.8
Diseases of the genitourinary system	1,719	534	31.1
Calculus of kidney and ureter	192	118	61.5
Diseases of the skin and subcutaneous tissue	518	255	49.2
Cellulitis and abscess	358	183	51.1
Diseases of the musculoskeletal system, connective tissue	1,543	675	43.7
Osteoarthrosis and allied disorders	434	169	38.9
Intervertebral disc disorders	341	179	52.5
Congenital anomalies	182	94	51.6
Certain conditions originating in the perinatal period	170	102	60.0
Symptoms, signs, and ill-defined conditions	313	146	46.6
Injury and poisoning	2,565	1,248	48.7
Fractures, all sites	1,002	419	41.8
Fracture of neck of femur	323	81	25.1
Poisonings	182	80	44.0
Supplementary classifications	4,676	386	8.3

Note: Excludes newborns.
Source: National Center for Health Statistics, 1999 National Hospital Discharge Survey: Annual Summary with Detailed Diagnosis and Procedure Data, *Vital and Health Statistics, Series 13, No. 151, 2001; calculations by New Strategist*

Discharges of Males from Hospitals by Procedure, 1999

(total number of inpatients discharged from nonfederal hospitals, number of males discharged, and male share of total, by all listed procedures, 1999; numbers in thousands)

		males	
	total	*number*	*share of total*
Total procedures	**41,315**	**16,370**	**39.6%**
Operations on the nervous system	1,048	475	45.3
Spinal tap	310	158	51.0
Operations on the endocrine system	87	20	23.0
Operations on the eye	110	59	53.6
Operations on the ear	54	32	59.3
Operations on the nose, mouth, and pharynx	284	175	61.6
Operations on the respiratory system	1,027	573	55.8
Bronchoscopy with or without biopsy	268	156	58.2
Operations on the cardiovascular system	6,133	3,498	57.0
Removal of coronary artery obstruction and insertion of stent(s)	1,069	708	66.2
Coronary artery bypass graft	571	389	68.1
Cardiac catheterization	1,271	758	59.6
Insertion, replacement, removal, revision of pacemaker	336	159	47.3
Hemodialysis	458	227	49.6
Operations on the hemic and lymphatic system	348	170	48.9
Operations on the digestive system	5,189	2,189	42.2
Endoscopy of small intestine with or without biopsy	922	402	43.6
Endoscopy of large intestine with or without biopsy	542	208	38.4
Partial excision of large intestine	251	115	45.8
Appendectomy, excluding incidental	290	158	54.5
Cholecystectomy	428	137	32.0
Lysis of peritoneal adhesions	299	56	18.7
Operations on the urinary system	966	461	47.7
Cystoscopy with or without biopsy	189	101	53.4
Operations on the male genital organs	277	277	100.0
Prostatectomy	192	192	100.0
Operations on the musculoskeletal system	3,219	1,569	48.7
Partial excision of bone	232	124	53.4
Reduction of fracture	628	285	45.4
Open reduction of fracture with internal fixation	431	179	41.5

(continued)

(continued from previous page)

	total	males number	share of total
Excision or destruction of intervertebral disc	313	167	53.4%
Total hip replacement	168	73	43.5
Total knee replacement	267	105	39.3
Operations on the integumentary system	1,351	603	44.6
Debridement of wound, infection, or burn	332	188	56.6
Miscellaneous diagnostic and therapeutic procedures	12,964	6,269	48.4
Computerized axial tomography	871	408	46.8
Arteriography and angiocardiography using contrast material	2,034	1,145	56.3
Diagnostic ultrasound	1,022	451	44.1
Respiratory therapy	1,117	560	50.1
Insertion of endotracheal tube	445	227	51.0
Injection or infusion of cancer chemotherapeutic substance	211	116	55.0

Note: Excludes newborns.
Source: National Center for Health Statistics, 1999 National Hospital Discharge Survey: Annual Summary with Detailed Diagnosis and Procedure Data, *Vital and Health Statistics, Series 13, No. 151, 2001; calculations by New Strategist*

About One-Third of Caregivers Are Men

Most male caregivers are helping someone in their own home.

Among the 9 million Americans who regularly provide unpaid care to a family member or friend with a long-term illness or disability, 3 million are men. Men account for 37 percent of those caring for someone in their own home, and for 32 percent of those caring for someone in another home.

The 49 percent minority of male caregivers are helping someone living in another household, often their own aged parents. The most common tasks they undertake are helping the person with trips outside the home (done by 67 percent of those caring for someone in another household) and helping with money management (49 percent).

The 51 percent majority of male caregivers are helping someone living in their own household, often their spouse. The most common chores for these caregivers are helping with trips outside the home (89 percent) and attending to medical needs and money management (64 percent).

■ With hospitals discharging patients sooner than they once did, the caregiving burden is increasing.

Most male caregivers are helping someone in their own home

(percent distribution of male caregivers by place of care, 1996)

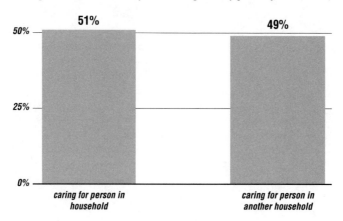

Caregiving by Men, 1996

(total number of people and men aged 15 or older, number providing regular unpaid care for a family member or friend with a long-term illness or disability; number and percent distribution of men providing care and male share of total, by type of care provided, 1996; numbers in thousands)

	total	men number	men percent distribution	men share of total
Total people	209,291	98,719	100.0%	47.2%
Total caregivers	**9,323**	**3,261**	**3.3**	**35.0**
Caring for person in household	4,472	1,667	51.1	37.3
Caring for person in another household	5,027	1,594	48.9	31.7
Caring for person in household	**4,472**	**1,667**	**100.0**	**37.3**
Helped with activities of daily living	2,518	939	56.3	37.3
Helped with medical needs	3,131	1,061	63.6	33.9
Helped with money management	3,044	1,065	63.9	35.0
Helped with trips outside the home	3,910	1,476	88.5	37.7
Caring for person in another household	**5,027**	**1,594**	**100.0**	**31.7**
Helped with activities of daily living	1,596	388	24.3	24.3
Helped with medical needs	2,032	521	32.7	25.6
Helped with money management	2,523	784	49.2	31.1
Helped with household chores	2,814	682	42.8	24.2
Helped with trips outside the home	3,627	1,063	66.7	29.3

Note: If more than one person is cared for, data are for the first person cared for; numbers will not add to total because more than one type of care may be provided.
Source: Bureau of the Census, Preliminary Estimates on Caregiving from Wave 7 of the 1996 Survey of Income and Program Participation, by John M. McNeil, No. 231, The Survey of Income and Program Participation, 1999

Few Nursing Home Residents Are Men

The male share of nursing home residents falls with age.

Among the nation's 1.5 million nursing home residents aged 65 or older, only 378,000 (26 percent) are men, according to the National Center for Health Statistics. The male share of residents declines from 43 percent of those aged 65 to 74 to just 19 percent of those aged 85 or older. Men account for few nursing home residents because, on average, they do not live as long as women. When older men become ill, most have wives at home to care for them, thereby avoiding the need to enter a nursing home.

Seventy-six percent of male nursing home residents have trouble getting around, and 66 percent are incontinent. Only 45 percent need help eating, however.

■ More help for the dependent elderly at home would limit the growth of the nursing home population and provide a higher quality of life for older Americans.

Only 19 percent of the oldest nursing home residents are men

(male share of nursing home residents aged 65 or older, by age, 1999)

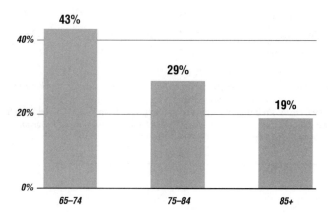

Men Living in Nursing Homes, 1999

(total number of nursing home residents aged 65 or older, number of male residents, and male share of total; percent distribution of male residents by functional status, 1999)

	total	men number	men share of total
Total residents, 65+	**1,469,500**	**377,800**	**25.7%**
Aged 65 to 74	194,800	84,100	43.2
Aged 75 to 84	517,600	149,500	28.9
Aged 85 or older	757,100	144,200	19.0

	total	dependent mobility	incontinent	dependent eating	dependent mobility, eating, and incontinent
Functional status					
Male residents, 65+	**100.0%**	**75.9%**	**66.0%**	**45.1%**	**35.0%**
Aged 65 to 74	100.0	70.5	59.6	45.0	34.8
Aged 75 to 84	100.0	76.9	68.9	44.7	35.2
Aged 85 or older	100.0	78.1	66.8	45.7	34.9

Source: National Center for Health Statistics, Health, United States, 2001; *calculations by New Strategist*

Men Account for the Majority of People with AIDS

The male share of AIDS victims is smallest among the young.

Men account for fully 83 percent of AIDS cases diagnosed in the U.S. through June 2000. They are a smaller share of cases among the young, however. Males accounted for 59 percent of AIDS cases diagnosed among 13-to-19-year-olds through 2000, versus 87 percent of those diagnosed among people aged 50 to 59. Among the 601,000 men known to have AIDS, the largest share (45 percent) were diagnosed in their thirties.

Minorities account for most men diagnosed with AIDS. Only 49 percent of men with AIDS are non-Hispanic white. Non-Hispanic blacks account for 34 percent of men diagnosed with AIDS, and Hispanics are another 15 percent. Asians and American Indians together account for only about 1 percent of AIDS victims.

■ Although men account for the great majority of people diagnosed with AIDS, the female share is growing.

Half the men with AIDS are black or Hispanic

(percent distribution of men with AIDS, by race and Hispanic origin, 2000)

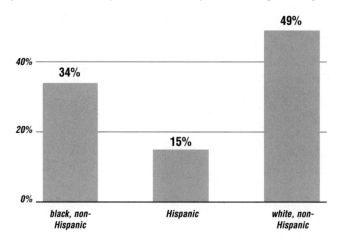

AIDS Cases among Men by Age, Race, and Hispanic Origin, through June 2000

(total cumulative number of AIDS cases among people aged 13 or older, number and percent distribution of AIDS cases among men, and male share of total, by age at diagnosis, race, and Hispanic origin, through June 2000)

	total	men number	men percent distribution	men share of total
Total cases	**720,925**	**601,471**	**100.0%**	**83.4%**
Aged 13 to 19	3,694	2,161	0.4	58.5
Aged 20 to 29	121,573	95,991	16.0	79.0
Aged 30 to 39	326,566	273,004	45.4	83.6
Aged 40 to 49	190,639	163,297	27.1	85.7
Aged 50 to 59	57,305	49,644	8.3	86.6
Aged 60 or older	21,148	17,374	2.9	82.2
Total cases	**720,925**	**601,471**	**100.0**	**83.4**
American Indian	2,203	1,804	0.3	81.9
Asian	5,455	4,792	0.8	87.8
Black, non-Hispanic	277,286	205,630	34.2	74.2
Hispanic	111,799	92,440	15.4	82.7
White, non-Hispanic	323,195	295,990	49.2	91.6

Note: American Indians include Alaska Natives; Asians include Pacific Islanders.
Source: National Center for Health Statistics, Health, United States, 2001; *calculations by New Strategist*

Heart Disease Is the Leading Killer of Men

Heart disease and cancer account for more than half of male deaths.

Thirty percent of deaths to males in 1999 were due to heart disease. Cancer was the cause of another 24 percent of deaths. Men accounted for slightly less than half of all deaths due to heart disease in 1999. They accounted for 52 percent of all deaths due to cancer.

Accidents are the fourth leading cause of death among males, with males accounting for 65 percent of all accidental deaths. Suicide is the eighth leading cause of death among males, with males accounting for fully 80 percent of suicides in 1999.

Male life expectancy stood at 74.1 years in 2000, five years less than the life expectancy of females. At age 65, men can expect to live 16.3 more years, nearly three years less than their female counterparts.

■ The death rate from heart disease has fallen over the past few decades, boosting life expectancy for men and women.

Males account for the great majority of deaths due to accidents and suicide

(percent distribution of deaths due to accidents and suicide, by sex, 1999)

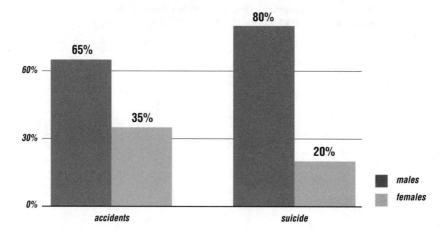

Leading Causes of Death among Males, 1999

(total number of deaths, number and percent distribution of deaths to males, and male share of total, for the ten leading causes of death among males, 1999)

	total deaths	deaths among males		
		number	percent distribution	share of total
All causes	**2,391,399**	**1,175,460**	**100.0%**	**49.2%**
1. Diseases of the heart	725,192	351,617	29.9	48.5
2. Malignant neoplasms	549,838	285,832	24.3	52.0
3. Cerebrovascular diseases	167,366	64,485	5.5	38.5
4. Accidents and adverse effects	97,860	63,535	5.4	64.9
5. Chronic lower respiratory diseases	124,181	62,415	5.3	50.3
6. Diabetes mellitus	68,399	31,150	2.7	45.5
7. Influenza and pneumonia	63,730	27,718	2.4	43.5
8. Suicide	29,199	23,458	2.0	80.3
9. Chronic liver disease and cirrhosis	26,259	17,115	1.5	65.2
10. Nephritis, nephrotic syndrome, and nephrosis	35,525	17,016	1.4	47.9
All other causes	503,850	231,119	19.7	45.9

Source: National Center for Health Statistics, Deaths: Final Data for 1999, *National Vital Statistics Report, Vol. 49, No. 8, 2001; calculations by New Strategist*

Life Expectancy by Age and Sex, 2000

(years of life remaining at selected ages by sex, and difference in male and female life expectancy, 2000)

	total	males	females	difference (male minus female)
Aged 0	76.9	74.1	79.5	–5.4
Aged 1	76.4	73.7	79.0	–5.3
Aged 5	72.5	69.8	75.1	–5.3
Aged 10	67.6	64.9	70.1	–5.2
Aged 15	62.6	60.0	65.2	–5.2
Aged 20	57.8	55.2	60.3	–5.1
Aged 25	53.1	50.6	55.4	–4.8
Aged 30	48.4	45.9	50.6	–4.7
Aged 35	43.6	41.3	45.8	–4.5
Aged 40	39.0	36.7	41.0	–4.3
Aged 45	34.4	32.2	36.3	–4.1
Aged 50	30.0	27.9	31.8	–3.9
Aged 55	25.7	23.8	27.3	–3.5
Aged 60	21.6	19.9	23.1	–3.2
Aged 65	17.9	16.3	19.2	–2.9
Aged 70	14.4	13.0	15.5	–2.5
Aged 75	11.3	10.2	12.1	–1.9
Aged 80	8.6	7.6	9.1	–1.5
Aged 85	6.3	5.6	6.7	–1.1
Aged 90	4.7	4.2	4.8	–0.6
Aged 95	3.5	3.1	3.5	–0.4
Aged 100	2.6	2.4	2.7	–0.3

Source: National Center for Health Statistics, Deaths: Preliminary Data for 2000, *National Vital Statistics Report, Vol. 49, No. 12, 2001; calculations by New Strategist*

5

Income

Men's incomes are growing more slowly than women's.

Between 1990 and 2000, the median income of men grew 8 percent, after adjusting for inflation, compared with women's 25 percent gain.

Men aged 35 to 44 are losing ground.

During the 1990s, men in their mid-thirties to mid-forties saw their median income fall 3 percent while other age groups made gains.

Black men have made the biggest income gains.

The median income of black men rose 31 percent during the 1990s, after adjusting for inflation.

Incomes peak in the 45-to-54 age group.

The median income of men aged 45 to 54 stood at $41,072 in 2000. More than one-third had an income of $50,000 or more.

Among full-time workers, men's income is 35 percent higher than women's.

The median income of men working full-time year-round stood at $39,020 in 2000. The median income of their female counterparts was $28,820.

Men with professional degrees have the highest earnings.

Among men working full-time, median earnings of those with professional degrees (such as doctors and lawyers) stood at $91,318 in 2000.

Men's Income Is Growing More Slowly than Women's

But the median income of men remains far above the median income of women.

Men's incomes have been growing slowly for the past few decades. Consequently, women's incomes are catching up to men's.

Between 1990 and 2000, men's median income grew 8 percent to $28,269, after adjusting for inflation. During the same time, women's median income grew 25 percent to $16,188. Despite the more rapid growth in women's income, men's income in 2000 was still a substantial 75 percent higher because men are more likely to work full-time. Men's incomes will remain well above women's because of their greater commitment to the labor force.

■ Because many mothers stay home to raise children, it's unlikely women's labor force participation—or income—will ever equal men's.

Men's median income rose 8 percent in the 1990s

(median income of men aged 15 or older with income, 1990 and 2000; in 2000 dollars)

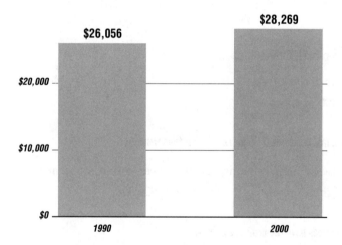

Median Income of People by Sex, 1990 to 2000

(median income of people aged 15 or older with income by sex, and index of men's income to women's, 1990 to 2000; percent change, 1990–2000; in 2000 dollars)

	men	women	index of men's income to women's
2000	$28,269	$16,188	175
1999	28,191	15,825	178
1998	27,955	15,227	184
1997	26,976	14,662	184
1996	26,054	14,009	186
1995	25,333	13,620	186
1994	25,000	13,197	189
1993	24,821	12,993	191
1992	24,681	12,928	191
1991	25,353	12,975	195
1990	26,056	12,930	202
Percent change			
1990–2000	8.5%	25.2%	–13.3%

Note: The index is calculated by dividing the median income of men by the median income of women and multiplying by 100.
Source: Bureau of the Census, Current Population Surveys, Internet site <www.census.gov/hhes/income/histinc/p08.html>; calculations by New Strategist

Falling Incomes for Men Aged 35 to 44

The youngest men made the biggest gains.

Men's median income climbed 8 percent between 1990 and 2000, but men aged 35 to 44 lost ground. The median income of men in that age group fell 3 percent during the decade, after adjusting for inflation. In 1990, the median income of men aged 35 to 44 was 47 percent greater than that of the average man. By 2000, it was only 31 percent above average.

Men under age 25 saw the biggest income gains during the 1990s, an 18 percent increase after adjusting for inflation. Behind the rise was the tight labor market created by the booming economy, which drove up wages for entry-level workers. Men aged 25 to 34 also saw an above-average increase in median income, with a 12 percent gain.

■ The rapid income gains for younger men will come to a halt if the nation experiences a prolonged economic downturn.

Older men saw little income growth during the 1990s

(percent change in median income of men aged 15 or older with income, by age, 1990 to 2000; in 2000 dollars)

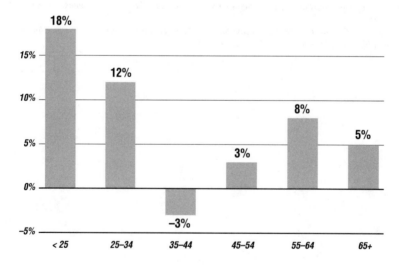

Median Income of Men by Age, 1990 to 2000

(median income of men aged 15 or older with income by age, 1990 to 2000; percent change in income, 1990–2000; index of men's income by age to total, 1990 to 2000; in 2000 dollars)

	total	< 25	25–34	35–44	45–54	55–64	65+
2000	$28,269	$9,548	$30,633	$37,088	$41,072	$34,414	$19,167
1999	28,191	8,581	30,867	37,434	42,314	34,778	19,720
1998	27,955	8,642	29,669	37,119	41,071	34,585	19,169
1997	26,976	7,991	27,815	35,150	40,257	33,337	19,011
1996	26,054	7,608	27,525	35,163	39,607	32,276	18,238
1995	25,333	7,762	26,509	35,279	39,957	32,540	18,509
1994	25,000	8,112	26,020	35,344	40,208	31,163	17,553
1993	24,821	7,562	25,791	35,689	38,997	29,569	17,623
1992	24,681	7,598	25,938	35,584	38,830	30,907	17,613
1991	25,353	7,780	26,747	36,292	39,361	31,534	17,782
1990	26,056	8,113	27,468	38,228	39,812	31,848	18,211

Percent change

1990–2000	8.5%	17.7%	11.5%	–3.0%	3.2%	8.1%	5.2%

Index of median income by age to total

2000	100	34	108	131	145	122	68
1999	100	30	109	133	150	123	70
1998	100	31	106	133	147	124	69
1997	100	30	103	130	149	124	70
1996	100	29	106	135	152	124	70
1995	100	31	105	139	158	128	73
1994	100	32	104	141	161	125	70
1993	100	30	104	144	157	119	71
1992	100	31	105	144	157	125	71
1991	100	31	105	143	155	124	70
1990	100	31	105	147	153	122	70

Note: The index is calculated by dividing the median income of men in each age group by the median income of all men and multiplying by 100.
Source: Bureau of the Census, Current Population Surveys, Internet site <www.census.gov/hhes/income/histinc/p08.html>; calculations by New Strategist

Black Men Have Experienced the Biggest Income Gains

White men saw the smallest gains during the 1990s.

Between 1990 and 2000, black men saw their median income grow 31 percent, after adjusting for inflation, rising from $16,522 to $21,659. In 1990, the median income of black men was only 63 percent as high as that of the average man. By 2000, it was 77 percent of the average.

The median income of non-Hispanic white men grew only 11 percent during the 1990s. Despite this relatively small increase, non-Hispanic white men continue to have a higher median income than men in any other racial or ethnic group, reaching $31,213 in 2000. Hispanic men have the lowest median income, just $19,829 in 2000, 30 percent below average.

■ Hispanic men's incomes are low because many are immigrants with little education and earning power.

Men in every racial and ethnic group saw incomes grow in the 1990s

(percent change in median income of men aged 15 or older with income, by race and Hispanic origin, 1990 to 2000; in 2000 dollars)

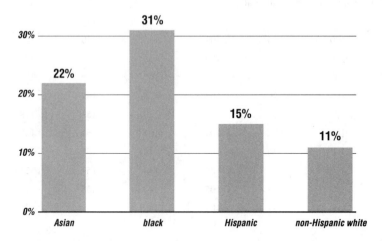

Median Income of Men by Race and Hispanic Origin, 1990 to 2000

(median income of men aged 15 or older with income by race and Hispanic origin, 1990 to 2000; percent change in income, 1990–2000; index of men's income by race/Hispanic origin group to total, 1990 to 2000; in 2000 dollars)

| | | | | | white | |
	total	Asian	black	Hispanic	total	non-Hispanic
2000	$28,269	$30,445	$21,659	$19,829	$29,696	$31,213
1999	28,191	28,663	21,270	18,847	29,524	31,622
1998	27,955	26,511	20,388	18,210	29,172	31,511
1997	26,976	26,799	19,362	17,351	27,942	29,487
1996	26,054	25,551	18,027	16,875	27,273	28,739
1995	25,333	24,884	17,972	16,663	26,830	28,611
1994	25,000	26,346	17,244	16,690	26,092	27,765
1993	24,821	25,455	17,179	16,101	25,855	27,254
1992	24,681	23,999	15,763	16,178	25,828	27,027
1991	25,353	24,311	16,055	17,115	26,500	27,464
1990	26,056	24,901	16,522	17,295	27,182	28,193

Percent change

1990–2000	8.5%	22.4%	31.1%	14.7%	9.2%	10.7%

Index of median income of race/Hispanic origin group to total

2000	100	108	77	70	105	110
1999	100	102	75	67	105	112
1998	100	95	73	65	104	113
1997	100	99	72	64	104	109
1996	100	98	69	65	105	110
1995	100	98	71	66	106	113
1994	100	105	69	67	104	111
1993	100	103	69	65	104	110
1992	100	97	64	66	105	110
1991	100	96	63	68	105	108
1990	100	96	63	66	104	108

Note: The index is calculated by dividing the median income of each race/Hispanic origin group by the median income of all men and multiplying by 100.
Source: Bureau of the Census, Current Population Surveys, Internet site <www.census.gov/hhes/income/histinc/ p02.html>; calculations by New Strategist

Men in the West Saw Little Income Growth

Men in the Midwest and South experienced the biggest gains during the 1990s.

Between 1990 and 2000, men living in the West saw their median income grow just 4 percent, after adjusting for inflation. In the Northeast, men's median income grew a larger 8 percent, while in the South and Midwest it was up 13 percent. Men in the Northeast continue to have a higher median income than men in other regions, at $30,464 in 2000.

The median income of men in the South is lower than that of men in other regions, standing at $26,699 in 2000. Southern men had a median income that was 94 percent as high as that of the average man in 2000, up from 91 percent in 1990.

■ The rapid income growth of black men is boosting the incomes of southern men, since more than half of blacks live in the South.

Men in every region made income gains in the 1990s

(percent change in median income of men aged 15 or older with income, by region, 1990 to 2000; in 2000 dollars)

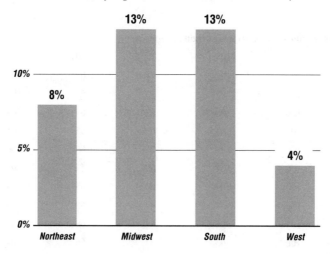

Median Income of Men by Region, 1990 to 2000

(median income of men aged 15 or older with income by region, 1990 to 2000; percent change in income, 1990–2000; index of men's income by region to total, 1990 to 2000; in 2000 dollars)

	total	Northeast	Midwest	South	West
2000	$28,269	$30,464	$29,935	$26,699	$28,009
1999	28,191	29,756	30,251	26,797	28,098
1998	27,955	29,040	29,195	26,694	27,813
1997	26,976	28,224	28,124	25,568	26,570
1996	26,054	27,637	27,773	24,305	25,574
1995	25,333	27,633	27,283	23,761	25,055
1994	25,000	27,289	25,639	23,415	25,355
1993	24,821	26,210	25,519	23,188	25,331
1992	24,681	26,654	25,304	22,431	25,337
1991	25,353	27,681	25,479	22,882	26,719
1990	26,056	28,128	26,544	23,662	26,949

Percent change

	total	Northeast	Midwest	South	West
1990–2000	8.5%	8.3%	12.8%	12.8%	3.9%

Index of median income by region to total

	total	Northeast	Midwest	South	West
2000	100	108	106	94	99
1999	100	106	107	95	100
1998	100	104	104	95	99
1997	100	105	104	95	98
1996	100	106	107	93	98
1995	100	109	108	94	99
1994	100	109	103	94	101
1993	100	106	103	93	102
1992	100	108	103	91	103
1991	100	109	100	90	105
1990	100	108	102	91	103

Note: The index is calculated by dividing the median income of men in each region by the median income of all men and multiplying by 100.
Source: Bureau of the Census, Current Population Surveys, Internet site <www.census.gov/hhes/income/histinc/p05.html>; calculations by New Strategist

Incomes Are Highest for Men Aged 45 to 54

Among full-time workers, however, income peaks in the older age groups.

In 2000, the median income of men with income stood at $28,269. Income rises with age to a peak of $41,072 in the 45-to-54 age group. Among men aged 65 or older, median income was just $19,167.

The 56 percent majority of men aged 15 or older work full-time. Among all men working full-time, median income stood at $39,020 in 2000. Income peaks at more than $48,000 for full-time workers aged 65 to 74, but only 13 percent of men in the age group work full-time.

Men under age 25 have the lowest incomes, a median of just $9,548. Only 24 percent work full-time because many are high school or college students.

■ The incomes of men aged 55 to 64 are likely to rise in the years ahead as more older men stay on the job full-time.

Men's median income peaks in middle age

(median income of men aged 15 or older with income, by age, 2000)

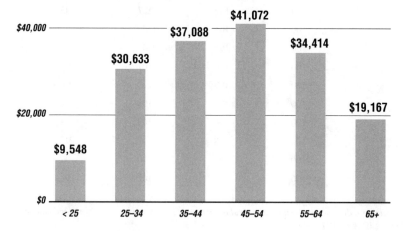

Income Distribution of Men by Age, 2000

(number and percent distribution of men aged 15 or older by income and age, median income of men with income, percent working full-time year-round, and median income of full-time workers, 2000; men in thousands as of 2001)

	total	<25	25–34	35–44	45–54	55–64	aged 65 or older		
							total	65–74	75+
Total men	**104,273**	**19,636**	**18,451**	**22,177**	**18,578**	**11,253**	**14,179**	**8,187**	**5,992**
Without income	7,290	5,152	629	493	423	353	242	128	114
With income	96,983	14,484	17,822	21,684	18,155	10,900	13,937	8,059	5,878
Under $10,000	15,994	7,434	1,500	1,669	1,528	1,263	2,600	1,356	1,243
$10,000 to $19,999	18,217	3,629	3,279	2,704	2,080	1,824	4,698	2,433	2,266
$20,000 to $29,999	16,113	1,970	3,791	3,703	2,310	1,597	2,740	1,563	1,178
$30,000 to $39,999	13,276	851	3,426	3,462	2,744	1,465	1,329	913	417
$40,000 to $49,999	9,223	254	2,062	2,648	2,361	1,093	805	534	270
$50,000 to $74,999	13,347	254	2,450	4,255	3,683	1,815	889	645	246
$75,000 to $99,999	5,140	68	697	1,578	1,625	800	371	253	117
$100,000 or more	5,674	20	615	1,666	1,826	1,042	505	366	139
Median income of men with income	$28,269	$9,548	$30,633	$37,088	$41,072	$34,414	$19,167	$21,360	$17,021
Percent working full-time	56.4%	23.9%	76.4%	80.7%	77.3%	56.6%	9.5%	13.4%	4.2%
Median income of men working full-time	$39,020	$20,824	$34,213	$41,560	$46,672	$46,753	$47,964	$48,169	$45,494

(continued)

(continued from previous page)

Total men	total	<25	25–34	35–44	45–54	55–64	aged 65 or older		
							total	65–74	75+
	100.0%	100.0%	100.0%	100.0%	100.0%	100.0%	100.0%	100.0%	100.0%
Without income	7.0	26.2	3.4	2.2	2.3	3.1	1.7	1.6	1.9
With income	93.0	73.8	96.6	97.8	97.7	96.9	98.3	98.4	98.1
Under $10,000	15.3	37.9	8.1	7.5	8.2	11.2	18.3	16.6	20.7
$10,000 to $19,999	17.5	18.5	17.8	12.2	11.2	16.2	33.1	29.7	37.8
$20,000 to $29,999	15.5	10.0	20.5	16.7	12.4	14.2	19.3	19.1	19.7
$30,000 to $39,999	12.7	4.3	18.6	15.6	14.8	13.0	9.4	11.2	7.0
$40,000 to $49,999	8.8	1.3	11.2	11.9	12.7	9.7	5.7	6.5	4.5
$50,000 to $74,999	12.8	1.3	13.3	19.2	19.8	16.1	6.3	7.9	4.1
$75,000 to $99,999	4.9	0.3	3.8	7.1	8.7	7.1	2.6	3.1	2.0
$100,000 or more	5.4	0.1	3.3	7.5	9.8	9.3	3.6	4.5	2.3

Source: Bureau of the Census, Current Population Surveys, Internet sites <http://ferret.bls.census.gov/macro/032001/perinc/new01_006.htm> and <http://ferret.bls.census.gov/macro/032001/perinc/new01_022.htm>; calculations by New Strategist

The Incomes of Non-Hispanic White Men Are Highest

Hispanic men have the lowest incomes.

Non-Hispanic white men had a median income of $31,213 in 2000. More than one in four had an income of $50,000 or more. Hispanic men, in contrast, had a median income of just $19,829 and only 9 percent had an income of $50,000 or more. The incomes of black men are slightly higher than those of Hispanics, with a median of $21,659. One in eight black men has an income of $50,000 or more.

Black men are less likely to work full-time than Hispanic or non-Hispanic white men. Only 49 percent of black men aged 15 or older have full-time jobs compared with 57 percent of non-Hispanic whites and 58 percent of Hispanics. Among men working full time, the median income of blacks is 73 percent as high as that of non-Hispanic whites. The Hispanic median is only 59 percent of the non-Hispanic white median.

■ The incomes of Hispanic men are well below those of non-Hispanic whites and blacks because many are recent immigrants with little education and earning power.

Among men, blacks have higher incomes than Hispanics

(median income of men aged 15 or older working full-time, year-round, by race and Hispanic origin, 2000)

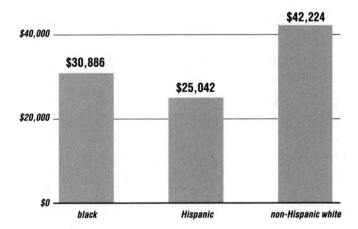

Income Distribution of Men by Race and Hispanic Origin, 2000

(number and percent distribution of men aged 15 or older by income, race, and Hispanic origin, median income of men with income, percent working full-time year-round, and median income of full-time workers, 2000; men in thousands as of 2001)

	total	black	Hispanic	white total	white non-Hispanic
Total men	**104,273**	**11,841**	**11,644**	**87,223**	**76,090**
Without income	7,290	1,717	1,391	5,009	3,690
With income	96,983	10,124	10,253	82,214	72,400
Under $10,000	15,994	2,381	2,008	12,721	10,802
$10,000 to $19,999	18,217	2,267	3,161	15,141	12,081
$20,000 to $29,999	16,113	1,883	2,107	13,514	11,507
$30,000 to $39,999	13,276	1,426	1,240	11,263	10,095
$40,000 to $49,999	9,223	758	703	8,106	7,431
$50,000 to $74,999	13,347	980	711	11,716	11,043
$75,000 to $99,999	5,140	256	167	4,540	4,381
$100,000 or more	5,674	173	157	5,210	5,062
Median income of men with income	$28,269	$21,659	$19,829	$29,696	$31,213
Percent working full-time	56.4%	49.0%	58.1%	57.3%	57.2%
Median income of men working full-time	$39,020	$30,886	$25,042	$40,350	$42,224
Total men	**100.0%**	**100.0%**	**100.0%**	**100.0%**	**100.0%**
Without income	7.0	14.5	11.9	5.7	4.8
With income	93.0	85.5	88.1	94.3	95.2
Under $10,000	15.3	20.1	17.2	14.6	14.2
$10,000 to $19,999	17.5	19.1	27.1	17.4	15.9
$20,000 to $29,999	15.5	15.9	18.1	15.5	15.1
$30,000 to $39,999	12.7	12.0	10.6	12.9	13.3
$40,000 to $49,999	8.8	6.4	6.0	9.3	9.8
$50,000 to $74,999	12.8	8.3	6.1	13.4	14.5
$75,000 to $99,999	4.9	2.2	1.4	5.2	5.8
$100,000 or more	5.4	1.5	1.3	6.0	6.7

Source: Bureau of the Census, Current Population Surveys, Internet site <http://ferret.bls.census.gov/macro/032001/perinc/new01_000 .htm>; calculations by New Strategist

Men's Incomes Are Still Far Ahead of Women's

But the income gap is shrinking as women's incomes grow faster.

Men's incomes are much higher than women's, much of the gap stemming from differing labor force patterns between the sexes. Men are more likely to work than women, and among workers men are more likely to have full-time jobs. Even among full-time workers, however, the income gap persists. In 2000, men working full-time had a median income of $39,020. This figure was 35 percent higher than the $28,820 median of women who work full-time.

The median income of women who work full-time is approaching that of men because women's incomes are growing faster. During the 1990s, the median income of men who work full-time rose 5 percent, after adjusting for inflation. The median income of their female counterparts rose a larger 9 percent during those years.

■ Although women's incomes are catching up to men's, the income gap between them will persist as long as men and women continue to make different career choices.

Men are ahead, but women are catching up

(median income of people aged 15 or older working full-time, year-round, by sex, 1990 to 2000; in 2000 dollars)

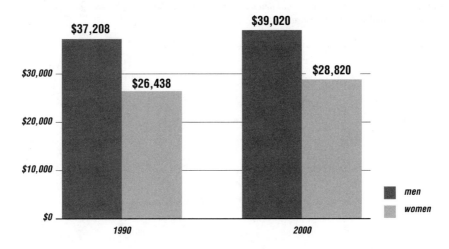

Median Income by Sex, 1990 to 2000

(median income of people aged 15 or older who work full-time year-round, by sex, and index of men's income to women's, 1990 to 2000; percent change, 1990–2000; in 2000 dollars)

	median income		index of men's income to women's
	men	women	
2000	$39,020	$28,820	135
1999	38,836	28,289	137
1998	38,253	28,338	135
1997	37,714	27,850	135
1996	36,662	27,2 58	134
1995	36,154	26,698	135
1994	36,386	26,778	136
1993	36,554	26,429	138
1992	37,202	26,657	140
1991	37,568	26,314	143
1990	37,208	26,438	141
Percent change			
1990–2000	4.9%	9.0%	–

Note: The index is calculated by dividing the median income of men by the median income of women and multiplying by 100.
Source: Bureau of the Census, Current Population Survey, Internet site <www.census.gov/hhes/income/histinc/p36.html>; calculations by New Strategist

Men's Earnings Rise with Education

Those with professional degrees earn the most

Earnings rise in lock step with education. Knowledge of this fact is behind the decades-long increase in college enrollment rates. Among men working full-time, those who dropped out of high school earned a median of $24,439 in 2000. Those with a bachelor's degree earned $53,508, while men with professional degrees earned $91,318.

Among college-educated men working full-time, nearly two-thirds had earnings of $50,000 or more. Among those with professional degrees (doctors, lawyers, etc.), more than 45 percent had earnings of $100,000 or more.

■ The proportion of men who go to college will continue to climb because of the great financial rewards of a college diploma.

The more education, the higher the earnings

(median earnings of men aged 15 or older working full-time, year-round, by educational attainment, 2000)

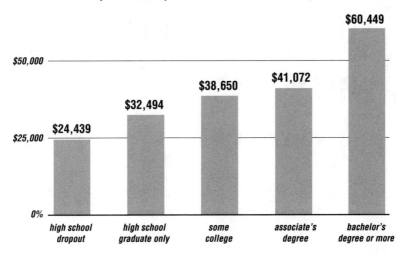

Earnings Distribution of Men Working Full-Time by Education, 2000

(number and percent distribution of men aged 25 or older working full-time year-round, by earnings and education, and median earnings, 2000; men in thousands as of 2001)

	total	less than 9th grade	9th to 12th grade, no diploma	high school graduate only	some college	associate's degree	bachelors degree or more				
							total	bachelor's degree	master's degree	professional degree	doctoral degree
Men with earnings	**54,057**	**1,968**	**3,354**	**16,833**	**9,792**	**4,725**	**17,385**	**11,393**	**3,680**	**1,274**	**1,038**
Under $10,000	1,311	103	140	570	211	75	216	151	39	13	13
$10,000 to $19,999	6,027	840	985	2,245	957	329	673	519	123	19	13
$20,000 to $29,999	9,471	549	1,047	3,929	1,864	772	1,309	1,081	168	36	23
$30,000 to $39,999	9,989	268	561	3,841	2,029	1,054	2,235	1,744	349	62	81
$40,000 to $49,999	7,453	93	307	2,559	1,594	810	2,091	1,459	447	86	99
$50,000 to $74,999	11,197	79	248	2,745	2,119	1,182	4,824	3,162	1,142	243	278
$75,000 to $99,999	4,234	12	15	599	524	329	2,754	1,620	726	232	176
$100,000 or more	4,376	22	53	348	495	175	3,284	1,659	688	584	354
Median earnings	$40,181	$20,447	$24,439	$32,494	$38,650	$41,072	$60,449	$53,508	$65,058	$91,318	$75,630
Men with earnings	**100.0%**	**100.0%**	**100.0%**	**100.0%**	**100.0%**	**100.0%**	**100.0%**	**100.0%**	**100.0%**	**100.0%**	**100.0%**
Under $10,000	2.4	5.2	4.2	3.4	2.2	1.6	1.2	1.3	1.1	1.0	1.3
$10,000 to $19,999	11.1	42.7	29.4	13.3	9.8	7.0	3.9	4.6	3.3	1.5	1.3
$20,000 to $29,999	17.5	27.9	31.2	23.3	19.0	16.3	7.5	9.5	4.6	2.8	2.2
$30,000 to $39,999	18.5	13.6	16.7	22.8	20.7	22.3	12.9	15.3	9.5	4.9	7.8
$40,000 to $49,999	13.8	4.7	9.2	15.2	16.3	17.1	12.0	12.8	12.1	6.8	9.5
$50,000 to $74,999	20.7	4.0	7.4	16.3	21.6	25.0	27.7	27.8	31.0	19.1	26.8
$75,000 to $99,999	7.8	0.6	0.4	3.6	5.4	7.0	15.8	14.2	19.7	18.2	17.0
$100,000 or more	8.1	1.1	1.6	2.1	5.1	3.7	18.9	14.6	18.7	45.8	34.1

Source: Bureau of the Census, Current Population Survey, Internet site <http://ferret.bls.census.gov/macro/032001/perinc/new03_076.htm>; calculations by New Strategist

The Highest-Paid Men Are Physicians

Among women, pharmacists have the highest wages.

Male physicians earned a weekly median of $1,553 in 2000, putting them at the top of the pay scale among men. The weekly wage of male physicians is fully 73 percent higher than that of their female counterparts ($899). Among all full-time wage and salary workers, men's median weekly earnings are 32 percent higher than women's.

Among women, pharmacists earn the most, a weekly median of $1,152 in 2000. Male pharmacists earned an even greater $1,312, 14 percent more than their female counterparts. Male lawyers earned a median of $1,439 per week in 2000, making them the second-highest-paid men.

Men earning the least are waiters ($312), cashiers ($313), and farm workers ($313). Even they earn more than the lowest paid women, however. Female food counter workers earned a median of only $245 a week in 2000.

While many assume sex discrimination explains the pay gap between men and women, a more important reason is that the average male worker is better educated and has more experience (i.e., has been on the job longer) than the average female worker. Typically, pay rises with education and experience.

■ The earnings gap between men and women will narrow in the years ahead as well-educated, career-oriented younger women gain job experience.

Median Weekly Earnings by Detailed Occupation, 2000

(median weekly earnings of full-time wage and salary workers by detailed occupation and sex, and index of men's earnings to women's, 2000)

	men	women	index of men's earnings to women's
Total employed	**$646**	**$491**	**132**
Managerial and professional specialty	**994**	**709**	**140**
Executive, administrative, and managerial	1,014	686	148
Administrators and officials, public administration	980	740	132
Financial managers	1,201	787	153
Personnel and labor relations managers	1,153	837	138
Purchasing managers	1,035	–	–
Managers, marketing, advertising, and public relations	1,250	846	148
Administrators, education and related fields	1,098	827	133
Managers, medicine and health	1,039	676	154
Managers, food serving and lodging establishments	651	475	137
Managers, properties and real estate	754	565	133
Management-related occupations	931	659	141
Accountants and auditors	953	690	138
Underwriters	–	704	–
Other financial officers	1,084	659	164
Management analysts	1,340	819	164
Personnel, training, and labor relations specialists	864	678	127
Buyers, wholesale and retail trade, except farm products	809	569	142
Construction inspectors	725	–	–
Inspectors and compliance officers, except construction	855	734	116
Professional specialty	977	725	135
Engineers, architects, and surveyors	1,122	938	120
Architects	1,126	–	–
Engineers	1,126	949	119
Aerospace engineers	1,289	–	–
Chemical engineers	1,255	–	–
Civil engineers	1,046	–	–
Electrical and electronic engineers	1,150	1,104	104
Industrial engineers	995	–	–
Mechanical engineers	1,128	–	–
Mathematical and computer scientists	1,055	901	117
Computer systems analysts and scientists	1,065	922	116
Operations and systems researchers and analysts	986	817	121
Natural scientists	1,007	726	139
Chemists, except biochemists	1,013	–	–

(continued)

(continued from previous page)

	men	women	index of men's earnings to women's
Biological and life scientists	$874	–	–
Health diagnosing occupations	1,459	$940	155
Physicians	1,553	899	173
Health assessment and treating occupations	949	778	122
Registered nurses	890	782	114
Pharmacists	1,312	1,152	114
Dietitians	–	609	–
Therapists	831	727	114
Speech therapists	–	774	–
Teachers, college and university	1,020	805	127
Teachers, except college and university	827	673	123
Teachers, prekindergarten and kindergarten	–	455	–
Teachers, elementary school	860	701	123
Teachers, secondary school	836	741	113
Teachers, special education	816	670	122
Counselors, educational and vocational	914	759	120
Librarians, archivists, and curators	–	657	–
Librarians	–	657	–
Social scientists and urban planners	963	708	136
Economists	1,148	785	146
Psychologists	893	698	128
Social, recreation, and religious workers	678	577	118
Social workers	637	589	108
Recreation workers	–	398	–
Clergy	716	–	–
Lawyers and judges	1,448	1,054	137
Lawyers	1,439	1,053	137
Writers, artists, entertainers, and athletes	789	641	123
Designers	805	609	132
Painters, sculptors, craft artists, and artist printmakers	750	–	–
Editors and reporters	795	718	111
Public relations specialists	923	670	138
Technical, sales, administrative support	**655**	**452**	**145**
Technicians and related support	761	541	141
Health technologists and technicians	620	507	122
Clinical laboratory technologists and technicians	624	572	109
Radiologic technicians	–	628	–
Licensed practical nurses	–	514	–
Engineering and related technologists and technicians	721	586	123
Electrical and electronic technicians	725	599	121

(continued)

(continued from previous page)

	men	women	index of men's earnings to women's
Drafting occupations	$722	$612	118
Surveying and mapping technicians	649	–	–
Science technicians	678	460	147
Chemical technicians	731	–	–
Technicians, except health, engineering, and science	957	655	146
Airplane pilots and navigators	1,272	–	–
Computer programmers	968	868	112
Legal assistants	703	596	118
Sales occupations	684	407	168
Supervisors and proprietors	695	485	143
Sales representatives, finance and business services	887	591	150
Insurance sales	856	551	155
Real estate sales	890	585	152
Securities and financial services sales	1,118	641	174
Advertising and related sales	870	679	128
Sales occupations, other business services	777	575	135
Sales representatives, commodities, except retail	832	665	125
Sales workers, retail and personal services	470	301	156
Sales workers, motor vehicles and boats	703	–	–
Sales workers, apparel	–	301	—
Sales workers, furniture and home furnishings	594	369	161
Sales workers, radio, television, hi-fi, and appliances	576	–	–
Sales workers, hardware and building supplies	466	395	118
Sales workers, parts	468	–	–
Sales workers, other commodities	460	319	144
Sales counter clerks	–	352	—
Cashiers	313	276	113
Street and door-to-door sales workers	–	421	–
Administrative support, including clerical	563	449	125
Supervisors	703	545	129
General office	706	532	133
Financial records processing	–	588	–
Distribution, scheduling, and adjusting clerks	692	544	127
Computer equipment operators	634	492	129
Computer operators	633	493	128
Secretaries, stenographers, and typists	–	455	–
Secretaries	–	450	–
Stenographers	–	496	–
Typists	–	467	–

(continued)

(continued from previous page)

	men	women	index of men's earnings to women's
Information clerks	$486	$400	122
Interviewers	–	441	–
Hotel clerks	–	343	–
Transportation ticket and reservation agents	598	433	138
Receptionists	–	388	–
Records processing, except financial	492	459	107
Order clerks	528	478	110
Personnel clerks, except payroll and timekeeping	–	512	–
File clerks	–	382	–
Records clerks	–	486	–
Financial records processing	544	473	115
Bookkeepers, accounting and auditing clerks	539	478	113
Payroll and timekeeping clerks	–	504	–
Billing clerks	–	428	–
Billing, posting, and calculating machine operators	–	457	–
Communications equipment operators	–	381	–
Telephone operators	–	384	–
Mail and message distributing	679	563	121
Postal clerks, except mail carriers	728	663	110
Mail carriers, postal service	739	652	113
Mail clerks, except postal service	402	367	110
Messengers	494	–	–
Material recording, scheduling, and distributing clerks	504	450	112
Dispatchers	649	450	144
Production coordinators	729	522	140
Traffic, shipping, and receiving clerks	455	416	109
Stock and inventory clerks	503	464	108
Expediters	450	413	109
Adjusters and investigators	584	477	122
Insurance adjusters, examiners, and investigators	677	503	135
Investigators and adjusters, except insurance	556	459	121
Eligibility clerks, social welfare	–	485	–
Bill and account collectors	–	473	–
Miscellaneous administrative support occupations	523	420	125
General office clerks	471	430	110
Bank tellers	–	354	–
Data-entry keyers	489	436	112
Statistical clerks	–	427	–
Teachers' aides	–	338	–

(continued)

(continued from previous page)

	men	women	index of men's earnings to women's
Service occupations	**$414**	**$316**	**131**
Private household	–	261	–
Child care workers	–	264	–
Cleaners and servants	–	259	–
Protective services	659	500	132
Supervisors	881	–	–
Police and detectives	941	–	–
Firefighting and fire prevention	803	–	–
Firefighting	805	–	–
Police and detectives	716	559	128
Police and detectives, public service	792	693	114
Sheriffs, bailiffs, and other law enforcement officers	692	–	–
Correctional institution officers	618	495	125
Guards	418	385	109
Guards and police, except public service	417	414	101
Service occupations, except private household and protective	357	314	114
Food preparation and service occupations	325	294	111
Supervisors	415	321	129
Bartenders	370	336	110
Waiters and waitresses	346	301	115
Cooks, except short order	324	290	112
Food counter, fountain, and related occupations	–	245	–
Kitchen workers, food preparation	297	289	103
Waiters' and waitresses' assistants	312	293	106
Miscellaneous food preparation occupations	293	288	102
Health service occupations	377	339	111
Dental assistants	–	417	–
Health aides, except nursing	375	350	107
Nursing aides, orderlies, and attendants	378	333	114
Cleaning and building service occupations	382	307	124
Supervisors	501	384	130
Maids and housemen	348	297	117
Janitors and cleaners	372	309	120
Pest control	487	–	–
Personal service occupations	400	321	125
Hairdressers and cosmetologists	–	339	–
Attendants, amusement and recreation facilities	428	365	117
Public transportation attendants	–	603	–
Welfare service aides	–	358	–
Early childhood teachers' assistants	–	283	–

(continued)

(continued from previous page)

	men	women	index of men's earnings to women's
Precision production, craft, and repair	**$628**	**$445**	**141**
Mechanics and repairers	649	627	104
Supervisors	814	–	—
Mechanics and repairers, except supervisors	641	621	103
Vehicle and mobile equipment mechanics and repairers	605	–	–
Automobile mechanics	538	–	–
Bus, truck, and stationary engine mechanics	632	–	–
Aircraft engine mechanics	748	–	–
Automobile body and related repairers	572	–	–
Heavy equipment mechanics	665	–	–
Industrial machinery repairers	669	–	–
Electrical and electronic equipment repairers	710	648	110
Electronic repairers, communications and industrial equipment	611	–	–
Data processing equipment repairers	692	638	108
Telephone installers and repairers	776	–	–
Heating, air conditioning, and refrigeration mechanics	622	–	–
Miscellaneous mechanics and repairers	634	–	–
Millwrights	783	–	–
Construction trades	599	475	126
Supervisors	745	–	–
Construction trades, except supervisors	579	451	128
Brickmasons and stonemasons	562	–	–
Carpet installers	493	–	–
Carpenters	533	–	–
Drywall installers	476	–	–
Electricians	693	–	–
Electrical power installers and repairers	805	–	–
Painters, construction and maintenance	484	–	–
Plumbers, pipefitters, steamfitters, and apprentices	644	–	–
Concrete and terrazzo finishers	546	–	–
Roofers	477	–	–
Structural metalworkers	716	–	–
Extractive occupations	801	–	–
Precision production occupations	645	414	156
Supervisors	726	520	140
Precision metalworking occupations	665	–	–
Tool and die makers	817	–	–
Machinists	633	–	–
Sheet-metal workers	677	–	–
Precision woodworking occupations	473	–	–
Cabinet makers and bench carpenters	478	–	–

(continued)

(continued from previous page)

	men	women	index of men's earnings to women's
Precision textile, apparel, and furnishings machine workers	$429	–	–
Precision workers, assorted materials	493	$397	124
Electrical and electronic equipment assemblers	439	390	113
Precision food production occupations	441	366	120
Butchers and meat cutters	456	355	128
Bakers	426	–	–
Precision inspectors, testers, and related workers	762	–	–
Inspectors, testers, and graders	768	–	–
Plant and system operators	721	–	–
Water and sewage treatment plant operators	622	–	–
Stationary engineers	750	–	–
Operators, fabricators, and laborers	**487**	**351**	**139**
Machine operators, assemblers, and inspectors	495	355	139
Machine operators and tenders, except precision	491	342	144
Metalworking and plastic working machine operators	519	450	115
Punching and stamping press machine operators	481	–	–
Grinding, abrading, buffing, and polishing machine operators	458	–	–
Metal and plastic processing machine operators	481	–	–
Molding and casting machine operators	506	–	–
Woodworking machine operators	429	–	–
Sawing machine operators	428	–	–
Printing machine operators	589	345	171
Printing press operators	590	–	–
Textile, apparel, and furnishings machine operators	379	304	125
Textile sewing machine operators	315	301	105
Laundering and dry cleaning machine operators	396	279	142
Machine operators, assorted materials	495	363	136
Packaging and filling machine operators	404	327	124
Mixing and blending machine operators	521	–	–
Separating, filtering, and clarifying machine operators	726	–	–
Painting and paint spraying machine operators	482	–	–
Furnace, kiln, and oven operators, except food	500	–	–
Slicing and cutting machine operators	430	–	–
Fabricators, assemblers, and hand working occupations	493	380	130
Welders and cutters	523	–	–
Assemblers	465	382	122
Production inspectors, testers, samplers, and weighers	552	368	150
Production inspectors, checkers, and examiners	592	379	156
Graders and sorters, except agricultural	357	305	117

(continued)

(continued from previous page)

	men	women	index of men's earnings to women's
Transportation and material moving occupations	$558	$407	137
Motor vehicle operators	564	399	141
Supervisors	740	–	–
Truck drivers	573	407	141
Drivers, sales workers	582	–	–
Bus drivers	506	401	126
Taxicab drivers and chauffeurs	480	–	–
Transportation occupations, except motor vehicles	821	–	–
Rail transportation	883	–	–
Locomotive operating occupations	926	–	–
Water transportation	784	–	–
Material moving equipment operators	516	424	122
Operating engineers	615	–	–
Crane and tower operators	667	–	–
Excavating and loading machine operators	581	–	–
Industrial truck and tractor equipment operators	453	–	–
Handlers, equipment cleaners, helpers, and laborers	394	320	123
Helpers, construction and extractive occupations	375	–	–
Helpers, construction trades	371	–	–
Construction laborers	445	–	–
Production helpers	396	–	–
Freight, stock, and material handlers	381	316	121
Stock handlers and baggers	339	304	112
Machine feeders and offbearers	461	–	–
Garage and service station related occupations	324	–	–
Vehicle washers and equipment cleaners	347	–	–
Hand packers and packagers	331	309	107
Laborers, except construction	407	339	120
Farming, forestry, and fishing	**347**	**294**	**118**
Farm operators and managers	578	–	–
Other agricultural and related occupations	337	291	116
Farm occupations, except managerial	316	285	111
Farm workers	313	281	111
Related agricultural occupations	361	295	122
Supervisors, related agricultural occupations	564	–	–
Groundskeepers and gardeners, except farm	343	–	–
Forestry and logging occupations	487	–	–

Note: The index is calculated by dividing men's median earnings by women's and multiplying by 100; (–) means sample is too small to make a reliable estimate.
Source: Bureau of Labor Statistics, Employment and Earnings, *January 2001; calculations by New Strategist*

Incomes of Male-Headed Families Grew Slowly

Married couples saw rapid income growth during the 1990s.

Between 1990 and 2000, the median income of male-headed families grew only 4 percent, after adjusting for inflation. The incomes of men who live alone also grew just 4 percent—less than half the increase experienced by all households. Married couples, in contrast, saw their incomes grow 15 percent, after adjusting for inflation. The median income of married couples stood at $59,184 in 2000. One in five households headed by a married couple had an income of $100,000 or more.

Male householders living with nonrelatives (cohabiting partners, for example) had a median income of more than $50,000 in 2000. Behind the high income of these households is the likelihood that there are at least two earners in the home. Men living alone had a median income of $26,723 in 2000, while male-headed families had a median income of $42,143—about the same as the national median.

■ Men's incomes have been growing slowly in part because highly paid manufacturing jobs are becoming harder to find.

Married couples are the most affluent household type

(median income of households with male heads, by household type, 2000)

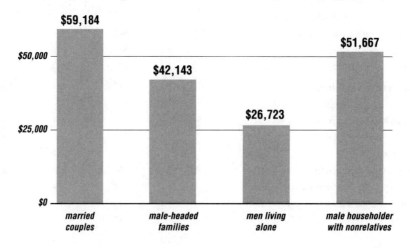

Median Income of Households Headed by Men, 1990 to 2000

(median income of households headed by men by household type, 1990 to 2000; percent change, 1990–2000; in 2000 dollars)

	total households	married couples	male family hh, no spouse present	men living alone
2000	$42,151	$59,184	$42,143	$26,723
1999	42,187	58,736	43,243	27,754
1998	41,032	57,272	41,590	27,458
1997	39,594	55,297	39,197	25,541
1996	38,798	54,502	38,980	26,290
1995	38,262	52,918	37,653	25,360
1994	37,136	51,842	35,073	24,420
1993	36,746	50,729	35,109	25,138
1992	36,965	50,636	36,572	24,107
1991	37,315	50,875	38,409	25,093
1990	38,446	51,354	40,512	25,633
Percent change				
1990–2000	9.6%	15.2%	4.0%	4.3%

Source: Bureau of the Census, Current Population Surveys, Internet site <www.census.gov/hhes/income/histinc/h09.html>; calculations by New Strategist

Income Distribution of Households Headed by Men, 2000

(number and percent distribution of households headed by men by income and household type, 2000; households in thousands as of 2001)

		families		nonfamilies	
	total	*married couples*	*male hh, no spouse present*	*men living alone*	*male hh with nonrelatives*
Total households	**106,418**	**55,611**	**4,252**	**11,536**	**3,682**
Under $10,000	9,540	1,335	267	1,896	177
$10,000 to $19,999	14,525	3,932	461	2,402	282
$20,000 to $29,999	14,053	5,533	646	2,019	466
$30,000 to $39,999	12,428	5,977	593	1,606	424
$40,000 to $49,999	10,461	5,820	519	1,052	419
$50,000 to $59,999	9,051	5,594	420	816	438
$60,000 to $69,999	7,783	5,241	406	515	335
$70,000 to $79,999	6,184	4,478	234	373	251
$80,000 to $89,999	4,659	3,523	174	218	175
$90,000 to $99,999	3,473	2,642	122	167	158
$100,000 or more	14,262	11,537	410	473	556
Median income	$42,151	$59,184	$42,143	$26,723	$51,667
Total households	**100.0%**	**100.0%**	**100.0%**	**100.0%**	**100.0%**
Under $10,000	9.0	2.4	6.3	16.4	4.8
$10,000 to $19,999	13.6	7.1	10.8	20.8	7.7
$20,000 to $29,999	13.2	9.9	15.2	17.5	12.7
$30,000 to $39,999	11.7	10.7	13.9	13.9	11.5
$40,000 to $49,999	9.8	10.5	12.2	9.1	11.4
$50,000 to $59,999	8.5	10.1	9.9	7.1	11.9
$60,000 to $69,999	7.3	9.4	9.5	4.5	9.1
$70,000 to $79,999	5.8	8.1	5.5	3.2	6.8
$80,000 to $89,999	4.4	6.3	4.1	1.9	4.8
$90,000 to $99,999	3.3	4.8	2.9	1.4	4.3
$100,000 or more	13.4	20.7	9.6	4.1	15.1

Source: Bureau of the Census, Current Population Surveys, Internet site <http://ferret.bls.census.gov/macro/ 032001/hhinc/new01_001 .htm>; calculations by New Strategist

Married Couples Are the Nation's Income Elite

Dual-earner couples make the most money.

Married couples account for 81 percent of households with incomes of $100,000 or more. Most couples achieve this affluence only because both husband and wife are in the labor force. Among all couples, median household income stood at $59,184 in 2000. Among couples in which both husband and wife work, median income stood at $71,432. If both husband and wife worked full-time, median income was a substantial $78,604. Nearly one-third had incomes of $100,000 or more.

Most husbands earn more than their wives. The 53 percent majority earn at least $10,000 more. But 22 percent of wives earned more than their husbands in 2000, up from only 16 percent two decades ago.

■ The dual-income couples of the baby-boom generation are behind the record level of affluence in the United States today. As boomers retire, affluence will recede.

Single-earner couples make much less

(median income of households headed by married couples,
by work status of husband and wife, 2000)

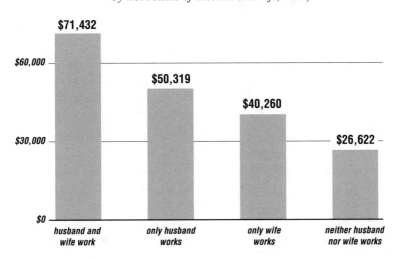

Income Distribution of Married Couples by Age of Householder, 2000

(number and percent distribution of married-couple households by income and age of householder, 2000; households in thousands as of 2001)

	total	< age 25	25–34	35–44	45–54	55–64	65+
Total married-couple households	**55,611**	**1,480**	**9,148**	**14,222**	**13,122**	**8,177**	**9,462**
Under $10,000	1,335	71	221	215	193	323	310
$10,000 to $19,999	3,932	237	466	529	414	546	1,739
$20,000 to $29,999	5,533	311	840	890	685	749	2,060
$30,000 to $39,999	5,977	239	1,213	1,228	902	799	1,592
$40,000 to $49,999	5,820	224	1,118	1,456	1,131	884	1,006
$50,000 to $59,999	5,594	163	1,241	1,501	1,266	766	656
$60,000 to $69,999	5,241	80	1,036	1,612	1,321	697	493
$70,000 to $79,999	4,478	52	775	1,454	1,220	623	353
$80,000 to $89,999	3,523	37	525	1,143	1,063	504	251
$90,000 to $99,999	2,642	20	428	828	838	365	162
$100,000 or more	11,537	46	1,282	3,364	4,088	1,918	840
Median income	$59,184	$34,614	$55,506	$67,704	$75,217	$60,236	$33,235
Total married-couple households	**100.0%**	**100.0%**	**100.0%**	**100.0%**	**100.0%**	**100.0%**	**100.0%**
Under $10,000	2.4	4.8	2.4	1.5	1.5	4.0	3.3
$10,000 to $19,999	7.1	16.0	5.1	3.7	3.2	6.7	18.4
$20,000 to $29,999	9.9	21.0	9.2	6.3	5.2	9.2	21.8
$30,000 to $39,999	10.7	16.1	13.3	8.6	6.9	9.8	16.8
$40,000 to $49,999	10.5	15.1	12.2	10.2	8.6	10.8	10.6
$50,000 to $59,999	10.1	11.0	13.6	10.6	9.6	9.4	6.9
$60,000 to $69,999	9.4	5.4	11.3	11.3	10.1	8.5	5.2
$70,000 to $79,999	8.1	3.5	8.5	10.2	9.3	7.6	3.7
$80,000 to $89,999	6.3	2.5	5.7	8.0	8.1	6.2	2.7
$90,000 to $99,999	4.8	1.4	4.7	5.8	6.4	4.5	1.7
$100,000 or more	20.7	3.1	14.0	23.7	31.2	23.5	8.9

Source: Bureau of the Census, Current Population Surveys, Internet site <http://ferret.bls.census.gov/macro/032001/hhinc/new02_011 .htm>; calculations by New Strategist

Income Distribution of Married Couples by Work Status of Husband and Wife, 2000

(number and percent distribution of married-couple families by income and work experience of husband and wife, 2000; families in thousands as of 2001)

	total	husband and wife work		husband works, wife does not		wife works, husband does not		neither husband nor wife works
		total	both work full-time	total	husband works full-time	total	wife works full-time	
Total married-couple householders	**55,611**	**33,454**	**17,956**	**11,037**	**8,887**	**3,116**	**1,783**	**8,003**
Under $10,000	1,335	186	31	290	110	133	33	727
$10,000 to $19,999	3,932	657	121	1,017	671	340	129	1,920
$20,000 to $29,999	5,533	1,624	416	1,398	995	553	292	1,958
$30,000 to $39,999	5,977	2,679	971	1,517	1,229	518	285	1,261
$40,000 to $49,999	5,820	3,382	1,511	1,247	1,000	465	312	726
$50,000 to $59,999	5,594	3,762	1,944	1,089	928	283	193	461
$60,000 to $69,999	5,241	3,838	2,213	884	775	240	151	281
$70,000 to $79,999	4,478	3,353	2,006	796	705	141	84	189
$80,000 to $89,999	3,523	2,829	1,760	461	388	109	88	124
$90,000 to $99,999	2,642	2,161	1,333	341	309	66	48	72
$100,000 or more	11,537	8,984	5,651	2,000	1,775	267	167	287
Median income	$59,184	$71,432	$78,604	$50,319	$53,577	$40,260	$44,011	$26,622
Total married-couple householders	**100.0%**	**100.0%**	**100.0%**	**100.0%**	**100.0%**	**100.0%**	**100.0%**	**100.0%**
Under $10,000	2.4	0.6	0.2	2.6	1.2	4.3	1.9	9.1
$10,000 to $19,999	7.1	2.0	0.7	9.2	7.6	10.9	7.2	24.0
$20,000 to $29,999	9.9	4.9	2.3	12.7	11.2	17.7	16.4	24.5
$30,000 to $39,999	10.7	8.0	5.4	13.7	13.8	16.6	16.0	15.8
$40,000 to $49,999	10.5	10.1	8.4	11.3	11.3	14.9	17.5	9.1
$50,000 to $59,999	10.1	11.2	10.8	9.9	10.4	9.1	10.8	5.8
$60,000 to $69,999	9.4	11.5	12.3	8.0	8.7	7.7	8.5	3.5
$70,000 to $79,999	8.1	10.0	11.2	7.2	7.9	4.5	4.7	2.4
$80,000 to $89,999	6.3	8.5	9.8	4.2	4.4	3.5	4.9	1.5
$90,000 to $99,999	4.8	6.5	7.4	3.1	3.5	2.1	2.7	0.9
$100,000 or more	20.7	26.9	31.5	18.1	20.0	8.6	9.4	3.6

Source: Bureau of the Census, Current Population Surveys, Internet site <http://ferret.bls.census.gov/macro/032001/faminc/new04_000 .htm>; calculations by New Strategist

Earnings Difference between Husbands and Wives, 2000

(number and percent distribution of married-couple family groups by earnings difference between husbands and wives, 2000; numbers in thousands)

	number	percent distribution
Total married couples	**56,497**	**100.0%**
Husband earns at least $50,000 more than wife	8,735	15.5
Husband earns $30,000–$49,999 more than wife	7,944	14.1
Husband earns $10,000–$29,999 more than wife	13,195	23.4
Husband earns $5,000–$9,999 more than wife	3,354	5.9
Husband earns within $4,999 of wife's earnings	14,860	26.3
Wife earns $5,000–$9,999 more than husband	2,133	3.8
Wife earns $10,000–$29,999 more than husband	4,123	7.3
Wife earns $30,000–$49,999 more than husband	1,410	2.5
Wife earns at least $50,000 more than husband	742	1.3

Source: Bureau of the Census, America's Families and Living Arrangements: March 2000, *detailed tables for Current Population Report P20-537, Internet site <www.census.gov/population/www/socdemo/hh-fam/ p20-537_00.html>; calculations by New Strategist*

Wives Who Earn More than Their Husbands, 1981 to 2000

(number of married couples in which both husband and wife have earnings, number in which wives earn more than husbands, and percent of wives earning more than husbands, 1981 to 2000; couples in thousands as of the following year)

	husbands and wives with earnings	wives earning more than husbands	
		number	percent
2000	33,355	7,489	22.5%
1999	33,344	7,420	22.3
1998	32,783	7,435	22.7
1997	32,745	7,446	22.7
1996	32,390	7,327	22.6
1995	32,030	7,028	21.9
1994	32,093	7,218	22.5
1993	31,267	6,960	22.3
1992	31,224	6,979	22.4
1991	31,003	6,499	21.0
1987	29,079	5,266	18.1
1983	26,120	4,800	18.4
1981	25,744	4,088	15.9

Source: Bureau of the Census, Current Population Surveys, Internet site <www.census.gov/hhes/income/histinc/f22.html>

Male-Headed Families Have Average Incomes

But families headed by men aged 45 to 54 have above-average incomes.

Male-headed families had a median income of $42,143 in 2000, almost equal to the $42,151 national median. Families headed by men under age 25 have the lowest incomes, with a median of $38,286. Male family heads aged 45 to 54 have the highest incomes, a median of $48,976 in 2000, well above the national median. Thirteen percent of male family heads in the 45-to-54 age group had an income of $100,000 or more.

Male-headed families include not only single parents, but also men living with adult relatives such as grown children, siblings, or aged parents. Families headed by young men are likely to include children, while those headed by middle-aged or older men are likely to include related adults. Many of the latter have two or more earners in the home, which boosts incomes.

■ The incomes of male-headed families should continue their slow rise, keeping pace with the incomes of men.

Most male-headed families have incomes above $40,000

(income distribution of male-headed families, 2000)

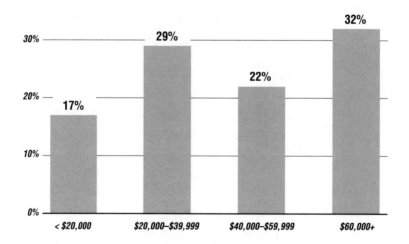

Income Distribution of Male-Headed Families by Age of Householder, 2000

(number and percent distribution of male-headed family households by income and age of householder, 2000; households in thousands as of 2001)

	total	< 25	25–34	35–44	45–54	55–64	65+
Total male-headed families	**4,252**	**706**	**864**	**1,043**	**843**	**379**	**417**
Under $10,000	267	53	39	66	44	35	28
$10,000 to $19,999	461	79	102	92	86	48	55
$20,000 to $29,999	646	127	143	145	85	60	86
$30,000 to $39,999	593	116	117	176	108	31	44
$40,000 to $49,999	519	72	111	148	106	30	51
$50,000 to $59,999	420	63	102	112	66	36	39
$60,000 to $69,999	406	76	72	85	83	52	37
$70,000 to $79,999	234	30	36	63	63	23	17
$80,000 to $89,999	174	15	22	60	50	9	17
$90,000 to $99,999	122	8	24	18	43	16	14
$100,000 or more	410	65	94	76	106	42	26
Median income	$42,143	$38,286	$42,003	$41,941	$48,976	$46,203	$38,631
Total male-headed families	**100.0%**	**100.0%**	**100.0%**	**100.0%**	**100.0%**	**100.0%**	**100.0%**
Under $10,000	6.3	7.5	4.5	6.3	5.2	9.2	6.7
$10,000 to $19,999	10.8	11.2	11.8	8.8	10.2	12.7	13.2
$20,000 to $29,999	15.2	18.0	16.6	13.9	10.1	15.8	20.6
$30,000 to $39,999	13.9	16.4	13.5	16.9	12.8	8.2	10.6
$40,000 to $49,999	12.2	10.2	12.8	14.2	12.6	7.9	12.2
$50,000 to $59,999	9.9	8.9	11.8	10.7	7.8	9.5	9.4
$60,000 to $69,999	9.5	10.8	8.3	8.1	9.8	13.7	8.9
$70,000 to $79,999	5.5	4.2	4.2	6.0	7.5	6.1	4.1
$80,000 to $89,999	4.1	2.1	2.5	5.8	5.9	2.4	4.1
$90,000 to $99,999	2.9	1.1	2.8	1.7	5.1	4.2	3.4
$100,000 or more	9.6	9.2	10.9	7.3	12.6	11.1	6.2

Source: Bureau of the Census, Current Population Survey, Internet site <http://ferret.bls.census.gov/macro/032001/hhinc/new02_016 .htm>; calculations by New Strategist

Low Incomes for Older Men Who Live Alone

Middle-aged men who live alone have much higher incomes.

The median income of the nearly 12 million men who live alone stood at $26,723 in 2000. But incomes for this household type vary greatly by age, with older men having much lower incomes than those in middle age.

Among men aged 65 or older who live alone, median income was only $17,374 in 2000. Most are widowers dependent on Social Security to make ends meet. In contrast, among men aged 25 to 54 who live alone, median income was above $30,000 in 2000. More than one in four of those aged 35 to 54 had an income of $50,000 or more.

■ The incomes of men who live alone are likely to remain stable in the years ahead, along with men's earning power.

Incomes peak in middle age for men living alone

(median income of men living alone, by age, 2000)

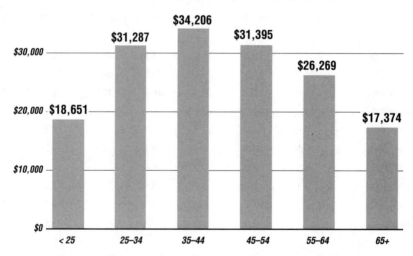

Income Distribution of Men Living Alone by Age of Householder, 2000

(number and percent distribution of men living alone by income and age of householder, 2000; households in thousands as of 2001)

	total	< 25	25–34	35–44	45–54	55–64	65+
Total men living alone	**11,536**	**692**	**2,174**	**2,549**	**2,313**	**1,357**	**2,451**
Under $10,000	1,896	144	170	286	409	261	623
$10,000 to $19,999	2,402	232	363	389	360	271	787
$20,000 to $29,999	2,019	136	479	410	307	220	470
$30,000 to $39,999	1,606	111	384	377	338	192	202
$40,000 to $49,999	1,052	26	229	314	277	105	100
$50,000 to $59,999	816	9	190	243	226	78	72
$60,000 to $69,999	515	9	137	169	96	48	55
$70,000 to $79,999	373	5	76	136	69	64	24
$80,000 to $89,999	218	11	39	51	66	34	17
$90,000 to $99,999	167	2	28	47	45	19	24
$100,000 or more	473	6	75	128	121	65	78
Median income	$26,723	$18,651	$31,287	$34,206	$31,395	$26,269	$17,374
Total men living alone	**100.0%**	**100.0%**	**100.0%**	**100.0%**	**100.0%**	**100.0%**	**100.0%**
Under $10,000	16.4	20.8	7.8	11.2	17.7	19.2	25.4
$10,000 to $19,999	20.8	33.5	16.7	15.3	15.6	20.0	32.1
$20,000 to $29,999	17.5	19.7	22.0	16.1	13.3	16.2	19.2
$30,000 to $39,999	13.9	16.0	17.7	14.8	14.6	14.1	8.2
$40,000 to $49,999	9.1	3.8	10.5	12.3	12.0	7.7	4.1
$50,000 to $59,999	7.1	1.3	8.7	9.5	9.8	5.7	2.9
$60,000 to $69,999	4.5	1.3	6.3	6.6	4.2	3.5	2.2
$70,000 to $79,999	3.2	0.7	3.5	5.3	3.0	4.7	1.0
$80,000 to $89,999	1.9	1.6	1.8	2.0	2.9	2.5	0.7
$90,000 to $99,999	1.4	0.3	1.3	1.8	1.9	1.4	1.0
$100,000 or more	4.1	0.9	3.4	5.0	5.2	4.8	3.2

Source: Bureau of the Census, Current Population Survey, Internet site <http://ferret.bls.census.gov/macro/ 032001/hhinc/new02_036 .htm>; calculations by New Strategist

Fewer Men Are Poor

Men account for fewer than half of the nation's poor.

In 2000, males accounted for only 43 percent of the poverty population—a figure almost unchanged since 1990. The poverty rate among men and boys fell from 12 to 10 percent during those years. Among males in 2000, 20 percent of blacks, 19 percent of Hispanics, and 6 percent of non-Hispanic whites were poor. The poverty rate reaches a high of 30 percent among black males under age 18.

The strong economy of the late 1990s reduced poverty somewhat among male-headed families. For those with children under age 18, the poverty rate fell from 19 percent in 1990 to 16 percent in 2000. The number of poor male-headed families with children rose 35 percent during those years, however, as male-headed families became more common.

■ Single-parent families will always be vulnerable to poverty because they are likely to have only one or even no earners in the home.

Male-headed families with children are slightly less likely to be poor

(poverty rate among male-headed families with children under age 18, 1990 and 2000)

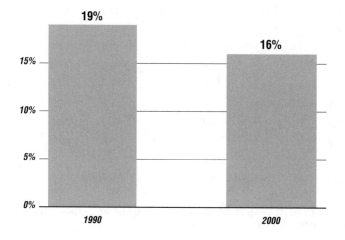

Males in Poverty, 1990 to 2000

(number of people below poverty level, number and percent of males below poverty level, and male share of poor, 1990 to 2000; males in thousands as of the following year)

| | | males in poverty | | |
	total poor	number	percent	share of poor
2000	31,054	13,417	9.9%	43.2%
1999	32,258	13,813	10.3	42.8
1998	34,476	14,712	11.1	42.7
1997	35,574	15,187	11.6	42.7
1996	36,529	15,611	12.0	42.7
1995	36,425	15,683	12.2	43.1
1994	38,060	16,316	12.8	42.9
1993	39,265	16,900	13.3	43.0
1992	38,014	16,222	12.9	42.7
1991	35,708	15,082	12.3	42.2
1990	33,584	14,211	11.7	42.3

Source: Bureau of the Census, Current Population Surveys, Internet sites <www.census.gov/hhes/poverty/histpov/hstpov7.html> and <http://ferret.bls.census.gov/macro/032001/pov/new01_001.htm>; calculations by New Strategist

Males in Poverty by Age, Race, and Hispanic Origin, 2000

(number and percent of males below poverty level by age, race, and Hispanic origin, 2000; males in thousands as of 2001)

	total	black	Hispanic	white total	white non-Hispanic
Number in poverty					
Total males	**13,417**	**3,267**	**3,287**	**9,241**	**6,148**
Under age 18	5,836	1,758	1,690	3,674	2,106
Aged 18 to 24	1,568	346	378	1,111	754
Aged 25 to 34	1,421	273	458	1,032	591
Aged 35 to 44	1,520	330	328	1,103	795
Aged 45 to 54	1,122	234	175	800	632
Aged 55 to 59	477	90	45	357	314
Aged 60 to 64	411	45	78	348	275
Aged 65 or older	1,063	190	137	816	681
Aged 65 to 74	575	87	100	459	361
Aged 75 or older	488	103	36	357	320
Poverty rate					
Total males	**9.9%**	**19.6%**	**19.5%**	**8.3%**	**6.5%**
Under age 18	15.8	30.5	27.7	12.7	9.1
Aged 18 to 24	11.6	18.5	17.9	10.2	8.5
Aged 25 to 34	7.7	11.8	16.0	6.9	4.8
Aged 35 to 44	6.9	12.5	12.8	6.0	5.0
Aged 45 to 54	6.0	12.1	11.3	5.1	4.4
Aged 55 to 59	7.4	15.3	9.0	6.4	6.2
Aged 60 to 64	8.5	10.1	19.5	8.3	7.2
Aged 65 or older	7.5	17.1	17.6	6.5	5.8
Aged 65 to 74	7.0	13.3	20.1	6.3	5.3
Aged 75 or older	8.2	22.4	13.1	6.7	6.3

Source: Bureau of the Census, Current Population Survey, Internet site <http://ferret.bls.census.gov/macro/032001/pov/new01_001.htm>

Families in Poverty by Family Type, 1990 to 2000

(total number of married couples and male-headed families, and number and percent below poverty level by presence of children under age 18 at home, 1990 to 2000; percent change in numbers and rates, 1990–2000; families in thousands as of the following year)

| | married couples | | | male householder, no spouse present | | |
| | total | in poverty | | total | in poverty | |
		number	percent		number	percent
With and without children < 18						
2000	55,611	2,638	4.7%	4,252	488	11.5%
1999	55,315	2,673	4.8	4,028	472	11.7
1998	54,778	2,879	5.3	3,977	476	12.0
1997	54,321	2,821	5.2	3,911	507	13.0
1996	53,604	3,010	5.6	3,847	531	13.8
1995	53,570	2,982	5.6	3,513	493	14.0
1994	53,865	3,272	6.1	3,228	549	17.0
1993	53,181	3,481	6.5	2,914	488	16.8
1992	53,090	3,385	6.4	3,065	484	15.8
1991	52,457	3,158	6.0	3,025	392	13.0
1990	52,147	2,981	5.7	2,907	349	12.0
Percent change						
1990–2000	6.6%	–11.5%	–17.5%	46.3%	39.8%	–4.2%
With children < 18						
2000	26,563	1,604	6.0%	2,254	363	16.1%
1999	26,373	1,662	6.3	2,169	350	16.2
1998	26,226	1,822	6.9	2,107	350	16.6
1997	26,430	1,863	7.1	2,175	407	18.7
1996	26,184	1,964	7.5	2,063	412	20.0
1995	26,034	1,961	7.5	1,934	381	19.7
1994	26,367	2,197	8.3	1,750	395	22.6
1993	26,121	2,363	9.0	1,577	354	22.5
1992	25,907	2,237	8.6	1,569	353	22.5
1991	25,357	2,106	8.3	1,513	297	19.6
1990	25,410	1,990	7.8	1,386	260	18.8
Percent change						
1990–2000	4.5%	–8.4%	–11.5%	52.1%	34.6%	–11.7%

Source: Bureau of the Census, Current Population Surveys, Internet sites <www.census.gov/hhes/poverty/histpov/hstpov4.html> and <http://ferret.bls.census.gov/macro/032001/pov/new16a_000.htm>; calculations by New Strategist

6

Labor Force

The labor force participation rate of men is still falling.

Seventy-five percent of men aged 16 or older are in the labor force, down 1 percentage point since 1990.

More than 80 percent of Hispanic men are in the labor force.

The figure is lower for whites and blacks. Seventy-five percent of white men are in the labor force, as are 69 percent of blacks.

Dual earners are in the majority.

Fifty-six percent of married couples are dual earners, while 21 percent have only the husband in the labor force.

Job tenure has fallen for men.

The decline has been greatest for men aged 55 to 64, falling from 13 to 10 years between 1991 and 2000.

Many men work in blue-collar occupations.

Thirty-eight percent of employed men are precision production, craft, and repair workers or operators, fabricators, and laborers.

Men's labor force participation will continue to decline.

Between 2000 and 2010, the labor force participation rate will increase only among men aged 65 to 74.

Labor Force Participation of Men Continues to Fall

Rates are up for the oldest men, however.

In 2000, 75 percent of men aged 16 or older were in the labor force, down 1 percentage point since 1990. Only the oldest men—those aged 65 or older—were more likely to work in 2000 than in 1990.

The labor force participation rate fell nearly 3 percentage points for men aged 16 to 19 during the 1990s, from 56 to 53 percent. Behind the decline is the greater propensity of young men to enter college rather than go to work following high school. Among men aged 35 to 54, labor force participation fell about 2 percentage points. Women's rising labor force participation rate may explain the decline. As more women work, men are freer to drop out of the labor force temporarily to attend school or care for the family. Among men aged 65 or older, labor force participation rose from 16 to 18 percent during the 1990s. Behind the rise is the tight labor market, which lured some retirees back to work.

■ The labor force participation of men aged 65 or older should rise during the next decade as a growing number of men discover they do not have enough savings to retire.

Men's labor force participation rate fell in all but one age group

(percentage point change in labor force participation rate of men, by age, 1990–2000)

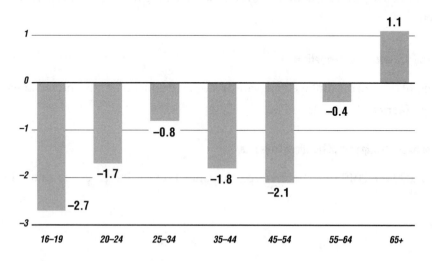

Men's Labor Force Participation by Age, 1990 and 2000

(labor force participation rate of men aged 16 or older, by age, 1990 and 2000; percentage point change, 1990–2000)

	2000	1990	percentage point change 1990–2000
Total men	**74.7%**	**76.1%**	**–1.4**
Aged 16 to 19	53.0	55.7	–2.7
Aged 20 to 24	82.6	84.3	–1.7
Aged 25 to 34	93.4	94.2	–0.8
Aged 35 to 44	92.6	94.4	–1.8
Aged 45 to 54	88.6	90.7	–2.1
Aged 55 to 64	67.3	67.7	–0.4
Aged 65 or older	17.5	16.4	1.1

Note: The labor force includes both the employed and the unemployed.
Source: Bureau of Labor Statistics, Employment and Earnings, *January 2001 and January 1991; calculations by New Strategist*

Unemployment Is Highest among Young Men

Few middle-aged or older men are unemployed.

In 2000, the nation was enjoying the lowest unemployment rate in decades. Nevertheless, unemployment among teenagers was in the double digits. Seventeen percent of men aged 16 to 17 were unemployed in 2000, as were 12 percent of those aged 18 or 19. Unemployment was less than 3 percent among men aged 30 to 64.

Labor force participation peaks at 94 percent among men aged 30 to 34. At this age, most men are focusing on their career as they shoulder the financial responsibilities of marriage and children. Men's labor-force participation falls below 90 percent in the 50-to-54 age group and continues to slide with age. Just 77 percent of men aged 55 to 59 are working, a proportion that drops to 55 percent among those aged 60 to 64. Only 30 percent of men aged 65 to 69 are in the labor force.

■ Unemployment is highest among the young because many are in low-paying entry-level positions where job turnover is high.

More than 9 out of 10 men aged 25 to 44 are in the labor force

(labor force participation rate of men aged 16 or older, by age, 2000)

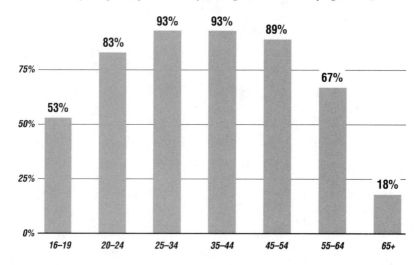

Employment Status of Men by Age, 2000

(employment status of men aged 16 or older by ten- and five-year age groups, 2000; numbers in thousands)

	civilian noninstitutional population	civilian labor force				
		total	percent of population	employed	unemployed	
					number	percent
Total men	**100,731**	**75,247**	**74.7%**	**72,293**	**2,954**	**3.9%**
Aged 16 to 19	8,151	4,317	53.0	3,713	604	14.0
Aged 20 to 24	9,154	7,558	82.6	7,009	549	7.3
Aged 25 to 34	18,289	17,073	93.4	16,494	579	3.4
Aged 35 to 44	21,951	20,334	92.6	19,770	564	2.8
Aged 45 to 54	18,004	15,951	88.6	15,561	391	2.4
Aged 55 to 64	11,257	7,574	67.3	7,389	185	2.4
Aged 65 or older	13,925	2,439	17.5	2,357	82	3.4
Aged 16 to 17	4,108	1,688	41.1	1,405	283	16.8
Aged 18 to 19	4,043	2,629	65.0	2,308	321	12.2
Aged 20 to 24	9,154	7,558	82.6	7,009	549	7.3
Aged 25 to 29	8,746	8,085	92.4	7,766	318	3.9
Aged 30 to 34	9,543	8,988	94.2	8,728	260	2.9
Aged 35 to 39	10,851	10,112	93.2	9,824	289	2.9
Aged 40 to 44	11,100	10,222	92.1	9,946	275	2.7
Aged 45 to 49	9,707	8,749	90.1	8,539	210	2.4
Aged 50 to 54	8,297	7,202	86.8	7,022	181	2.5
Aged 55 to 59	6,298	4,856	77.1	4,744	113	2.3
Aged 60 to 64	4,959	2,718	54.8	2,646	72	2.7
Aged 65 to 69	4,274	1,288	30.1	1,246	43	3.3
Aged 70 to 74	3,801	682	17.9	655	27	3.9
Aged 75 or older	5,850	469	8.0	456	13	2.7

Note: The civilian labor force includes both the employed and the unemployed. The civilian population includes both those in the labor force and those not in the labor force.
Source: Bureau of Labor Statistics, Employment and Earnings, *January 2001*

Hispanic Men Are Most Likely to Work

Black men are least likely to be in the labor force.

Eighty-one percent of Hispanic men are in the labor force compared with 75 percent of white men and just 69 percent of black men.

By age, labor force participation rates do not differ much between Hispanic and white men. But because Hispanic men are younger, on average, than white men—and therefore less likely to be retired—their overall labor force participation rate is higher. Among both Hispanics and whites, labor force participation peaks at 94 percent in the 25-to-34 age group.

The labor force participation rate of black men is lower than that of whites and Hispanics at every age. Only 39 percent of black men aged 16 to 19 are in the labor force, for example, compared to more than half of Hispanic and white men. Among men aged 55 to 64, only 57 percent of blacks are working or looking for work compared to more than two-thirds of Hispanics and whites.

■ The labor force participation rate of black men is lower than that of Hispanics or whites in part because black men are more likely to become discouraged in the job search and give up looking for work.

More than 80 percent of Hispanic men are in the labor force

(labor force participation rate of men aged 16 or older, by race and Hispanic origin, 2000)

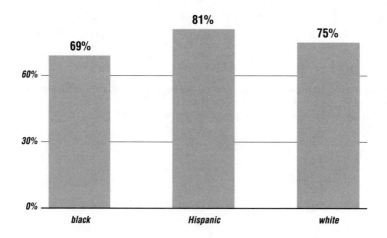

Men's Labor Force Participation by Age, Race, and Hispanic Origin, 2000

(labor force participation rate of men aged 16 or older by age, race, and Hispanic origin, 2000)

	total	black	Hispanic	white
Total men	**74.7%**	**69.0%**	**80.6%**	**75.4%**
Aged 16 to 19	53.0	39.0	50.9	56.6
Aged 20 to 24	82.6	73.4	89.2	85.0
Aged 25 to 34	93.4	87.7	94.0	94.4
Aged 35 to 44	92.6	85.3	93.3	93.7
Aged 45 to 54	88.6	79.1	87.5	89.8
Aged 55 to 64	67.3	57.1	69.4	68.2
Aged 65 or older	17.5	14.2	18.2	17.7

Note: The labor force includes both the employed and the unemployed.
Source: Bureau of Labor Statistics, Employment and Earnings, *January 2001*

Men Account for One-Third of Part-Time Workers

They are the 58 percent majority of full-time workers.

Ninety percent of working men have full-time jobs. The proportion of men who work full-time rises from a low of 40 percent among those aged 16 to 19 to a high of 96 percent among those aged 25 to 54.

The men most likely to work part-time are teenagers. Sixty percent of employed men aged 16 to 19 work part-time. Many are high school students. Among working men aged 20 to 24, a substantial 19 percent are part-timers. Many are attending college. Only 4 percent of men aged 25 to 54 work part-time.

Men account for 53 percent of all employed workers, but they are only 32 percent of part-timers. In the 16-to-19 age group, however, men are nearly half (47 percent) of part-timers. Among part-time workers aged 55 or older, men account for a large 41 percent share.

■ Part-time work is desirable for some because it allows for a more flexible schedule. Men are most likely to want flexibility when they are students or retirees.

Few men aged 25 to 54 work part-time

(percent of employed men who work part-time, by age, 2000)

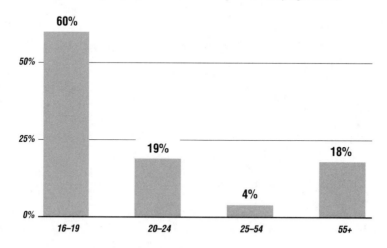

Men Working Full- or Part-Time by Age, 2000

(total number of people aged 16 or older employed full- or part-time, number and percent distribution of men employed full- or part-time, and male share of full- and part-time workers, by age, 2000; numbers in thousands)

	total	full-time	part-time
Total workers	**135,208**	**112,291**	**22,917**
Aged 16 to 19	7,275	2,521	4,754
Aged 20 to 24	13,321	10,020	3,301
Aged 25 to 54	96,916	86,419	10,497
Aged 55 or older	17,696	13,331	4,365
Male workers	**72,293**	**64,938**	**7,355**
Aged 16 to 19	3,713	1,480	2,233
Aged 20 to 24	7,009	5,659	1,350
Aged 25 to 54	51,826	49,847	1,979
Aged 55 or older	9,746	7,952	1,794

Percent distribution of male workers by full- and part-time status

Male workers	**100.0%**	**89.8%**	**10.2%**
Aged 16 to 19	100.0	39.9	60.1
Aged 20 to 24	100.0	80.7	19.3
Aged 25 to 54	100.0	96.2	3.8
Aged 55 or older	100.0	81.6	18.4

Male share of total workers by full- and part-time status

Total workers	**53.5%**	**57.8%**	**32.1%**
Aged 16 to 19	51.0	58.7	47.0
Aged 20 to 24	52.6	56.5	40.9
Aged 25 to 54	53.5	57.7	18.9
Aged 55 or older	55.1	59.7	41.1

Source: Bureau of Labor Statistics, Employment and Earnings, *January 2001; calculations by New Strategist*

Working Parents Are the Norm

Few families can afford a stay-at-home mother.

In 2000, 64 percent of married couples with children under age 18 were dual earners. The proportion stands at 70 percent among couples with school-aged children and at a smaller 57 percent among those with preschoolers.

Traditional couples, in which the husband works while the wife stays home, are in the minority but still substantial in number. The husband is the only one employed in 7 million couples with children under age 18 (or 29 percent). Among couples with preschoolers, the father is the only one employed in an even larger 38 percent.

Overall, 95 percent of men with children under age 18 are in the labor force, a proportion that does not vary much by age of child. Fully 89 to 91 percent of fathers have full-time jobs.

■ Working parents now being the norm, schools, churches, and other community organizations must reinvent themselves to meet the needs of today's families.

Most married couples with children are dual earners

(percent of married couples with children under age 18 in which both parents or only the father work, by age of children at home, 2000)

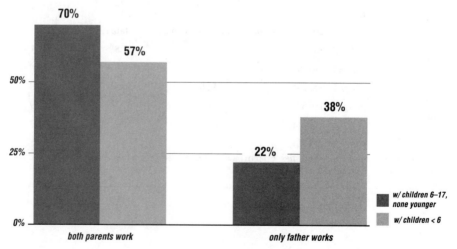

Labor Force Status of Families with Children under Age 18, 2000

(number and percent distribution of married-couple and male-headed families by employment status of parent and age of youngest own child under age 18 at home, by family type, 2000; numbers in thousands)

	total	aged 6 to 17, none younger	under age 6
		with children under age 18	
Married couples	**24,915**	**13,628**	**11,287**
One or both parents employed	24,282	13,248	11,034
Mother employed	17,012	10,247	6,765
Both parents employed	15,996	9,575	6,421
Mother employed, not father	1,016	672	344
Father employed, not mother	7,270	3,001	4,269
Neither parent employed	633	380	254
Male-headed families	**1,812**	**1,086**	**726**
Father employed	1,568	929	639
Father not employed	244	157	87
Married couples	**100.0%**	**100.0%**	**100.0%**
One or both parents employed	97.5	97.2	97.8
Mother employed	68.3	75.2	59.9
Both parents employed	64.2	70.3	56.9
Mother employed, not father	4.1	4.9	3.0
Father employed, not mother	29.2	22.0	37.8
Neither parent employed	2.5	2.8	2.3
Male-headed families	**100.0**	**100.0**	**100.0**
Father employed	86.5	85.6	88.0
Father not employed	13.5	14.4	12.0

Source: Bureau of Labor Statistics, Current Population Survey, Internet site <www.bls.gov/news.release/famee.t04.htm>

Labor Force Status of Men by Presence of Children at Home, 2000

(number and percent distribution of men aged 16 or older by presence of children under age 18 at home and labor force status, 2000; numbers in thousands)

	total		percent in labor force			not in
	number	*percent*	*total*	*full-time*	*part-time*	*labor force*
Total men	**99,498**	**100.0%**	**74.7%**	**64.4%**	**7.4%**	**25.3%**
No children under age 18	71,825	100.0	67.0	54.5	9.3	33.0
With children under age 18	27,673	100.0	94.7	90.1	2.5	5.3
With children 6 to 17 only	15,165	100.0	93.5	89.1	2.4	6.5
With children under age 6	12,508	100.0	96.1	91.2	2.7	3.9

Source: Bureau of Labor Statistics, Current Population Survey, Internet site <www.bls.gov/news.release/ famee.t05.htm>; calculations by New Strategist

The Majority of Couples Are Dual Earners

In 56 percent of the nation's married couples, both husband and wife are in the labor force.

In nearly every age group, the majority of couples are dual earners. The dual-earner share hits a peak of 73 percent among couples aged 40 to 44. Only among couples aged 55 or older are dual earners in the minority.

Twenty-one percent of the nation's married couples are traditional, only the husband being in the labor force. The traditional arrangement is most common among very young couples. It accounts for the near majority of the few married couples under age 20 and for 33 percent of those aged 20 to 24.

In 16 percent of couples—most of them retirees—neither spouse is in the labor force. Neither husband nor wife work in 19 percent of couples aged 55 to 64. The proportion rises to 72 percent among couples aged 65 or older.

■ As boomers age, a growing share of couples will have neither spouse in the labor force.

About one in five couples is traditional

(percent distribution of married couples by labor force status of husband and wife, 2000)

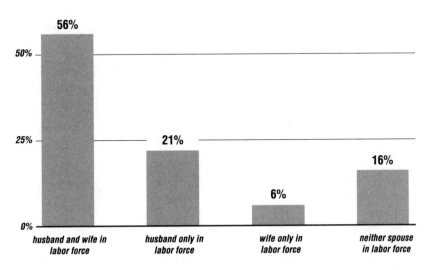

Labor Force Status of Married Couples, 2000

(number and percent distribution of married couples by age of householder and labor force status of husband and wife, 2000; numbers in thousands)

| | total | husband and/or wife in labor force | | | neither husband nor wife in labor force |
		both	husband only	wife only	
Married couples	**55,311**	**31,095**	**11,815**	**3,301**	**9,098**
Under age 20	96	49	47	–	–
Aged 20 to 24	1,354	848	448	39	21
Aged 25 to 29	3,775	2,656	1,021	55	44
Aged 30 to 34	5,615	3,876	1,556	119	64
Aged 35 to 39	6,886	4,850	1,802	162	72
Aged 40 to 44	7,218	5,241	1,612	255	110
Aged 45 to 54	12,792	9,046	2,499	772	475
Aged 55 to 64	8,138	3,739	1,782	1,086	1,530
Aged 65 or older	9,437	790	1,049	814	6,783
Married couples	**100.0%**	**56.2%**	**21.4%**	**6.0%**	**16.4%**
Under age 20	100.0	51.0	49.0	–	–
Aged 20 to 24	100.0	62.6	33.1	2.9	1.6
Aged 25 to 29	100.0	70.4	27.0	1.5	1.2
Aged 30 to 34	100.0	69.0	27.7	2.1	1.1
Aged 35 to 39	100.0	70.4	26.2	2.4	1.0
Aged 40 to 44	100.0	72.6	22.3	3.5	1.5
Aged 45 to 54	100.0	70.7	19.5	6.0	3.7
Aged 55 to 64	100.0	45.9	21.9	13.3	18.8
Aged 65 or older	100.0	8.4	11.1	8.6	71.9

Note: (–) means sample is too small to make a reliable estimate.
Source: Bureau of the Census, Household and Family Characteristics: March 2000 (Update), *detailed tables for Current Population Report P20-537, Internet site <www.census.gov/population/socdemo/hh-fam/p20-537/2000/tabFG1.txt>; calculations by New Strategist*

Job Tenure Has Fallen for Men

The decline is greatest for older men.

Job tenure continued to decline for men during the 1990s, according to the Bureau of Labor Statistics. The number of years working men aged 25 or older have been with their current employer fell from 5.4 years in 1991 to 5.0 years in 2000. The decline has been greatest for older men. Among men aged 55 to 64, job tenure fell the most—from 13 to 10 years—during the decade.

Long-term jobs are becoming less common for men of all ages. The proportion of working men who have been with their current employer for 10 or more years fell 2 percentage points between 1991 and 2000, from 36 to 34 percent. The decline was steepest for men aged 55 to 59, falling from 61 percent in 1991 to 54 percent in 2000.

■ Job tenure can decline because of layoffs or increased job hopping. Since older men are experiencing the biggest decline, layoffs may be the primary reason.

Job tenure peaks in middle age

(median number of years male workers have been with their current employer, by age, 2000)

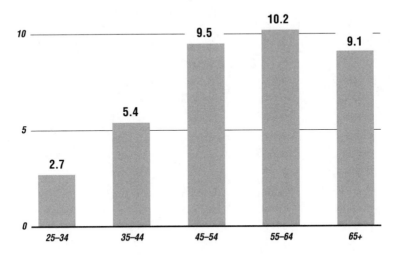

Job Tenure of Men by Age, 1991 and 2000

(median number of years male workers aged 25 or older have been with their current employer by age; 1991 and 2000; change in years, 1991–2000)

	2000	1991	change in years 1991–2000
Total male workers	5.0	5.4	–0.4
Aged 25 to 34	2.7	3.1	–0.4
Aged 35 to 44	5.4	6.5	–1.1
Aged 45 to 54	9.5	11.2	–1.7
Aged 55 to 64	10.2	13.4	–3.2
Aged 65 or older	9.1	7.0	2.1

Source: Bureau of Labor Statistics, Current Population Surveys, Internet site <www.bls.gov/news.release/ tenure.t01.htm>; calculations by New Strategist

Long-Term Employment of Men by Age, 1991 and 2000

(percent of men aged 25 or older employed as wage and salary workers who have been with their current employer for ten or more years, by age, 1991 and 2000; percentage point change in share, 1991–2000)

	2000	1991	percentage point change 1991–2000
Total male workers	**33.6%**	**35.9%**	**–2.3**
Aged 25 to 29	3.0	5.7	–2.7
Aged 30 to 34	15.3	21.1	–5.8
Aged 35 to 39	29.5	35.6	–6.1
Aged 40 to 44	40.4	46.3	–5.9
Aged 45 to 49	49.0	53.5	–4.5
Aged 50 to 54	51.6	58.5	–6.9
Aged 55 to 59	53.7	61.0	–7.3
Aged 60 to 64	52.5	57.5	–5.0
Aged 65 or older	48.9	42.6	6.3

Source: Bureau of Labor Statistics, Current Population Survey, Internet site <www.bls.gov/news.release/ tenure.t02.htm>; calculations by New Strategist

Men Dominate Most Occupations

Blue-collar jobs are overwhelmingly filled by men.

Although white collar employment has been growing much faster than blue collar for decades, a large share of men continue to work in blue-collar occupations. Thirty-eight percent of men are precision production, craft and repair workers or operators, fabricators, and laborers. Twenty-eight percent are managers or professionals, while 20 percent are technical, sales, or administrative support workers. Men account for fully 91 percent of all precision production, craft, and repair workers and for 76 percent of operators, fabricators, and laborers.

Men account for a small share of workers in many white-collar occupations. They are only 22 percent of the health care managers, for example, and 33 percent of administrators in education. They account for only 7 percent of registered nurses and 1 percent of secretaries. In other occupations, men are in the overwhelming majority, such as truck driving (95 percent) and firefighting (97 percent). Men account for 90 percent of engineers, 72 percent of physicians, and 70 percent of lawyers.

■ The earnings gap between the sexes stems partly from the different occupational choices of men and women. Men are more likely than women to choose demanding occupations, which pay more, because they have the support of a wife managing home and family.

Men make different occupational choices than women

(male share of workers by selected occupation, 2000)

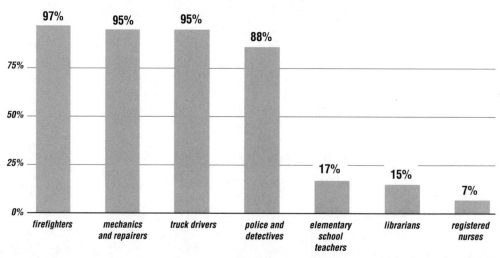

firefighters	97%
mechanics and repairers	95%
truck drivers	95%
police and detectives	88%
elementary school teachers	17%
librarians	15%
registered nurses	7%

Male Workers by Occupation, 2000

(total number of employed workers aged 16 or older in the civilian labor force, number and percent distribution of employed men, and male share of total workers, by occupation, 2000; numbers in thousands)

		men		
	total	number	percent distribution	male share of total
Total employed	**135,208**	**72,293**	**100.0%**	**53.5%**
Managerial and professional specialty	40,887	20,543	28.4	50.2
Executive, administrative, and managerial	19,774	10,814	15.0	54.7
Professional specialty	21,113	9,728	13.5	46.1
Technical, sales, and administrative support	39,442	14,288	19.8	36.2
Technicians and related support	4,385	2,118	2.9	48.3
Sales occupations	16,340	8,231	11.4	50.4
Administrative support, including clerical	18,717	3,939	5.4	21.0
Service occupations	18,278	7,245	10.0	39.6
Private household	792	35	0.0	4.4
Protective service	2,399	1,944	2.7	81.0
Service, except private household and protective	15,087	5,265	7.3	34.9
Precision production, craft, and repair	14,882	13,532	18.7	90.9
Operators, fabricators, and laborers	18,319	13,988	19.3	76.4
Machine operators, assemblers, and inspectors	7,319	4,622	6.4	63.2
Transportation and material moving occupations	5,557	5,003	6.9	90.0
Handlers, equipment cleaners, helpers, and laborers	5,443	4,363	6.0	80.2
Farming, forestry, and fishing	3,399	2,698	3.7	79.4

Source: Bureau of Labor Statistics, Employment and Earnings, *January 2001; calculations by New Strategist*

Men's Share of Employed by Detailed Occupation, 2000

(total number of employed people aged 16 or older in the civilian labor force and men's share of total employed, by selected occupation, 2000; numbers in thousands)

	total	percent men
Total employed	**135,208**	**53.5%**
Managerial and professional specialty	**40,887**	**50.2**
Executive, administrative, and managerial	19,774	54.7
Officials and administrators, public administration	651	47.3
Administrators, protective services	62	72.2
Financial managers	784	49.9
Personnel and labor relations managers	226	38.2
Purchasing managers	123	58.7
Managers, marketing, advertising, and public relations	755	62.4
Administrators, education and related fields	848	33.0
Managers, medicine and health	752	22.1
Postmasters and mail superintendents	55	41.5
Managers, food serving and lodging establishments	1,446	53.2
Managers, properties and real estate	552	49.1
Funeral directors	58	81.7
Management-related occupations	4,932	43.5
Accountants and auditors	1,592	43.3
Underwriters	104	28.1
Other financial officers	837	48.7
Management analysts	426	61.5
Personnel, training, and labor relations specialists	628	33.4
Buyers, wholesale and retail trade, except farm products	224	48.7
Construction inspectors	72	90.5
Inspectors and compliance officers, except construction	255	59.9
Professional specialty	21,113	46.1
Engineers, architects, and surveyors	2,326	88.9
Architects	215	76.5
Engineers	2,093	90.1
Aerospace engineers	78	90.3
Chemical engineers	85	89.6
Civil engineers	288	90.3
Electrical and electronic engineers	725	90.2
Industrial engineers	244	84.7
Mechanical engineers	342	93.7
Mathematical and computer scientists	2,074	68.6
Computer systems analysts and scientists	1,797	70.8
Operations and systems researchers and analysts	227	54.5

(continued)

(continued from previous page)

	total	percent men
Natural scientists	566	66.5%
Chemists, except biochemists	153	69.7
Agricultural and food scientists	53	71.8
Biological and life scientists	114	54.6
Medical scientists	84	50.5
Health diagnosing occupations	1,038	72.9
Physicians	719	72.1
Dentists	168	81.3
Veterinarians	55	69.4
Health assessment and treating occupations	2,966	14.3
Registered nurses	2,111	7.2
Pharmacists	208	53.5
Dietitians	97	10.1
Therapists	478	25.3
Respiratory therapists	78	37.6
Occupational therapists	55	8.6
Physical therapists	144	38.9
Speech therapists	102	6.5
Physicians' assistants	72	42.4
Teachers, except college and university	5,353	24.6
Prekindergarten and kindergarten	626	1.5
Elementary school	2,177	16.7
Secondary school	1,319	42.1
Special education	362	17.4
Counselors, educational and vocational	258	29.8
Librarians, archivists, and curators	263	15.6
Librarians	232	14.8
Social scientists and urban planners	450	41.1
Economists	139	46.7
Psychologists	265	35.4
Social, recreation, and religious workers	1,492	43.6
Social workers	828	27.6
Recreation workers	126	29.0
Clergy	369	86.2
Lawyers and judges	926	70.3
Lawyers	881	70.4
Writers, artists, entertainers, and athletes	2,439	50.0
Authors	138	45.9
Technical writers	70	35.8
Designers	738	42.8
Musicians and composers	161	65.9
Actors and directors	139	58.5

(continued)

	total	percent men
Painters, sculptors, craft artists, and artist printmakers	238	53.5%
Photographers	148	67.4
Editors and reporters	288	44.2
Public relations specialists	205	38.9
Announcers	54	89.3
Athletes	90	80.2
Technical, sales, and administrative support	**39,442**	**36.2**
Technicians and related support	4,385	48.3
Health technologists and technicians	1,724	19.5
Clinical laboratory technologists and technicians	342	25.0
Dental hygienists	112	1.5
Radiologic technicians	161	30.8
Licensed practical nurses	374	6.4
Engineering and related technologists and technicians	1,002	79.6
Electrical and electronic technicians	468	83.1
Drafting occupations	219	76.6
Surveying and mapping technicians	79	92.6
Science technicians	270	58.6
Biological technicians	108	40.5
Chemical technicians	71	78.8
Technicians, except health, engineering, and science	1,389	59.5
Airplane pilots and navigators	129	96.3
Computer programmers	699	73.5
Legal assistants	387	15.6
Sales occupations	16,340	50.4
Supervisors and proprietors	4,937	59.7
Sales representatives, finance and business services	2,934	55.5
Insurance sales	577	57.5
Real estate sales	787	45.7
Securities and financial services sales	600	68.7
Advertising and related sales	165	38.1
Sales occupations, other business services	805	57.3
Sales representatives, commodities, except retail	1,581	72.5
Sales representatives, mining, manufacturing, and wholesale	1,549	72.1
Sales workers, retail and personal services	6,782	36.5
Sales workers, motor vehicles and boats	329	89.0
Sales workers, apparel	411	22.9
Sales workers, shoes	114	44.6
Sales workers, furniture and home furnishings	185	49.3
Sales workers, radio, television, hi-fi, and appliances	258	73.0
Sales workers, hardware and building supplies	328	77.8
Sales workers, parts	186	91.1

(continued)

(continued from previous page)

	total	percent men
Sales workers, other commodities	1,428	33.6%
Sales counter clerks	185	32.0
Cashiers	2,939	22.5
Street and door-to-door sales workers	311	24.0
News vendors	110	55.3
Sales-related occupations	107	30.9
Demonstrators, promoters, and models	71	26.4
Administrative support occupations, including clerical	18,717	21.0
Supervisors, administrative support	710	39.7
Supervisors, general office	404	28.8
Supervisors, financial records processing	73	19.1
Supervisors, distribution, scheduling, and adjusting clerks	217	65.8
Computer equipment operators	323	51.4
Computer operators	321	51.3
Secretaries, stenographers, and typists	3,328	2.0
Secretaries	2,623	1.1
Stenographers	154	5.3
Typists	551	5.4
Information clerks	2,071	12.0
Interviewers	212	21.1
Hotel clerks	130	23.7
Transportation ticket and reservation agents	287	28.1
Receptionists	1,017	3.3
Records processing, except financial	1,119	18.5
Order clerks	305	22.9
Personnel clerks, except payroll and timekeeping	84	17.5
Library clerks	152	13.0
File clerks	338	19.8
Records clerks	227	14.1
Financial records processing	2,269	8.2
Bookkeepers, accounting, and auditing clerks	1,719	7.8
Payroll and timekeeping clerks	174	8.7
Billing clerks	198	7.8
Billing, posting, and calculating machine operators	134	8.3
Duplicating, mail, and other office machine operators	55	45.8
Communications equipment operators	167	15.7
Telephone operators	156	16.1
Mail and message distributing	978	58.8
Postal clerks, except mail carriers	304	45.6
Mail carriers, postal service	340	69.4
Mail clerks, except postal service	178	46.0
Messengers	157	76.1

(continued)

(continued from previous page)

	total	*percent men*
Material recording, scheduling, and distributing clerks	2,052	53.3%
Dispatchers	269	48.3
Production coordinators	227	41.5
Traffic, shipping, and receiving clerks	661	66.2
Stock and inventory clerks	460	55.1
Weighers, measurers, and checkers and samplers	64	48.1
Expediters	310	33.5
Adjusters and investigators	1,818	24.5
Insurance adjusters, examiners, and investigators	451	26.1
Investigators and adjusters, except insurance	1,097	24.0
Eligibility clerks, social welfare	94	10.8
Bill and account collectors	176	30.6
Miscellaneous administrative support	3,826	16.1
General office clerks	864	16.4
Bank tellers	431	10.0
Data-entry keyers	749	16.5
Statistical clerks	104	11.5
Teachers' aides	710	9.0
Service occupations	**18,278**	**39.6**
Private household	792	4.5
Child care workers	275	2.5
Cleaners and servants	500	5.2
Protective service	2,399	81.0
Supervisors	201	84.9
Police and detectives	116	85.7
Guards	53	76.5
Firefighting and fire prevention	248	96.2
Firefighting	233	97.0
Police and detectives	1,060	83.5
Police and detectives, public service	560	87.9
Sheriffs, bailiffs, and other law enforcement officers	156	80.8
Correctional institution officers	344	77.5
Guards	889	73.0
Guards and police, except public services	745	79.9
Service occupations, except private household and protective service	15,087	34.9
Food preparation and service occupations	6,327	42.3
Supervisors, food preparation and service	434	31.4
Bartenders	365	48.2
Waiters and waitresses	1,440	23.3
Cooks	2,076	56.7
Food counter, fountain, and related occupations	357	32.1
Kitchen workers, food preparation	317	28.9

(continued)

(continued from previous page)

	total	percent men
Waiters' and waitresses' assistants	670	48.6%
Miscellaneous food preparation	668	47.9
Health service occupations	2,557	10.5
Dental assistants	218	3.6
Health aides, except nursing	356	17.4
Nursing aides, orderlies, and attendants	1,983	10.1
Cleaning and building service occupations	3,127	55.0
Supervisors	166	62.0
Maids and housemen	650	18.7
Janitors and cleaners	2,233	63.7
Pest control occupations	71	95.0
Personal service occupations	3,077	19.5
Supervisors	119	36.8
Barbers	108	74.7
Hairdressers and cosmetologists	820	8.8
Attendants, amusement and recreation facilities	246	60.6
Public transportation attendants	127	19.1
Welfare service aides	99	12.8
Family child care providers	457	2.3
Early childhood teachers' assistants	480	4.8
Precision production, craft, and repair	**14,882**	**90.9**
Mechanics and repairers	4,875	94.9
Supervisors	223	91.1
Mechanics and repairers, except supervisors	4,652	95.0
Vehicle and mobile equipment mechanics and repairers	1,787	98.4
Automobile mechanics	860	98.8
Bus, truck, and stationary engine mechanics	345	99.1
Aircraft engine mechanics	126	93.9
Small engine repairers	60	98.3
Automobile body and related repairers	186	98.7
Heavy equipment mechanics	162	99.2
Industrial machinery repairers	524	95.8
Electrical and electronic equipment repairers	999	88.5
Electronic repairers, communications and industrial equipment	192	90.7
Data processing equipment repairers	342	84.6
Telephone line installers and repairers	53	96.9
Telephone installers and repairers	295	86.9
Heating, air conditioning, and refrigeration mechanics	371	98.8
Miscellaneous mechanics and repairers	949	93.7
Office machine repairers	53	90.2
Millwrights	78	97.6

(continued)

(continued from previous page)

	total	percent men
Construction trades	6,120	97.4%
Supervisors	967	97.8
Construction trades, except supervisors	5,153	97.3
Brickmasons and stonemasons	242	99.3
Tile setters, hard and soft	94	98.7
Carpet installers	125	98.7
Carpenters	1,467	98.3
Drywall installers	206	94.4
Electricians	860	97.3
Electrical power installers and repairers	132	98.6
Painters, construction and maintenance	624	94.2
Plumbers, pipefitters, and steamfitters	540	98.7
Concrete and terrazzo finishers	99	98.9
Insulation workers	58	93.9
Roofers	215	98.4
Structural metalworkers	79	97.7
Extractive occupations	128	98.1
Precision production occupations	3,759	75.0
Supervisors	1,129	80.3
Precision metalworking	865	92.5
Tool and die makers	121	97.3
Machinists	488	93.7
Sheet-metal workers	121	95.8
Precision woodworking occupations	127	89.0
Cabinet makers and bench carpenters	89	99.2
Precision textile, apparel, and furnishings machine workers	192	45.8
Dressmakers	77	7.3
Upholsterers	64	79.2
Precision workers, assorted materials	554	47.4
Optical goods workers	77	41.5
Electrical and electronic equipment assemblers	336	37.6
Precision food production occupations	481	60.1
Butchers and meat cutters	265	72.7
Bakers	154	54.4
Food batchmakers	62	20.5
Precision inspectors, testers, and related workers	148	75.6
Inspectors, testers, and graders	136	75.5
Plant and system operators	264	94.6
Water and sewage treatment plant operators	69	94.5
Stationary engineers	118	93.3

(continued)

(continued from previous page)

	total	percent men
Operators, fabricators, and laborers	**18,319**	**76.4%**
Machine operators, assemblers, and inspectors	7,319	63.1
Machine operators and tenders, except precision	4,546	63.4
Metalworking and plastic working machine operators	349	81.6
Punching and stamping press machine operators	94	74.3
Grinding, abrading, buffing, and polishing machine operators	98	84.8
Metal and plastic processing machine operators	150	76.5
Molding and casting machine operators	84	66.0
Woodworking machine operators	137	85.2
Sawing machine operators	78	87.4
Printing machine operators	369	76.3
Printing press operators	292	82.4
Textile, apparel, and furnishings machine operators	854	30.8
Textile sewing machine operators	425	21.6
Pressing machine operators	81	33.4
Laundering and dry cleaning machine operators	214	43.1
Machine operators, assorted materials	2,665	67.8
Packaging and filling machine operators	345	39.3
Mixing and blending machine operators	112	91.9
Separating, filtering, and clarifying machine operators	62	96.3
Painting and paint spraying machine operators	187	87.6
Furnace, kiln, and oven operators, except food	53	94.2
Slicing and cutting machine operators	149	70.9
Photographic process machine operators	103	37.4
Fabricators, assemblers, and handworking occupations	2,070	66.5
Welders and cutters	594	95.1
Assemblers	1,299	55.4
Production inspectors, testers, samplers, and weighers	703	51.5
Production inspectors, checkers, and examiners	497	52.0
Production testers	64	70.4
Graders and sorters, except agricultural	134	41.1
Transportation and material moving occupations	5,557	90.0
Motor vehicle operators	4,222	88.5
Supervisors	77	81.4
Truck drivers	3,088	95.3
Drivers, sales workers	167	89.5
Bus drivers	539	50.4
Taxicab drivers and chauffeurs	280	89.2
Parking lot attendants	60	83.8
Transportation occupations, except motor vehicles	183	96.5
Rail transportation	127	95.8
Locomotive operating occupations	63	98.3

(continued)

(continued from previous page)

	total	*percent men*
Water transportation	56	98.2%
Material moving equipment operators	1,152	94.6
Operating engineers	253	98.3
Crane and tower operators	70	99.1
Excavating and loading machine operators	98	97.1
Grader, dozer, and scraper operators	52	94.5
Industrial truck and tractor equipment operators	569	93.0
Handlers, equipment cleaners, helpers, and laborers	5,443	80.2
Helpers, construction and extractive occupations	120	94.1
Helpers, construction trades	111	95.8
Construction laborers	1,015	96.2
Production helpers	75	76.2
Freight, stock, and material handlers	2,015	77.6
Garbage collectors	54	96.2
Stock handlers and baggers	1,125	70.0
Machine feeders and offbearers	82	69.7
Freight, stock, and material handlers, n.e.c.	739	88.4
Garage and service station related occupations	184	92.3
Vehicle washers and equipment cleaners	313	86.2
Hand packers and packagers	366	36.8
Laborers, except construction	1,307	79.2
Farming, forestry, and fishing	**3,399**	**79.4**
Farm operators and managers	1,125	74.6
Farmers, except horticultural	879	72.7
Horticultural specialty farmers	69	87.2
Managers, farms, except horticultural	149	77.7
Other agricultural and related occupations	2,115	81.1
Farm occupations, except managerial	847	80.5
Farm workers	768	81.3
Related agricultural occupations	1,268	81.5
Supervisors	174	90.7
Groundskeepers and gardeners, except farm	870	92.6
Animal caretakers, except farm	148	29.3
Graders and sorters, agricultural products	68	31.7
Forestry and logging occupations	109	91.6
Timber cutting and logging occupations	66	96.0
Fishers, hunters, and trappers	51	88.1

Source: Bureau of Labor Statistics, Employment and Earnings, *January 2001; calculations by New Strategist*

Thirty Percent of Men Work in Manufacturing or Construction

Men account for the great majority of workers in both industries.

Men account for 53 percent of all workers, but the proportion varies greatly by industry. In some industries, workers are overwhelmingly male while in others men account for a minority of the employed.

Men account for 90 percent of construction workers, for example, and 67 percent of workers in the manufacturing industry. They are the 49 percent minority of workers in retail trade, however, and only 38 percent of workers in the service industries, which include fields from health and education to advertising and marketing.

By occupation and industry, 14 percent of men are managers or professionals in the service industries. Nine percent are technical, sales, or administrative support workers in wholesale or retail trade. Eight percent are precision production, craft, and repair workers in the construction industry, and 7 percent are operators, fabricators, or laborers in the manufacturing industry.

■ Although employment in the service industries is growing among men, a larger share continue to work in construction and manufacturing.

Men dominate most industries

(male share of workers by industry, 2000)

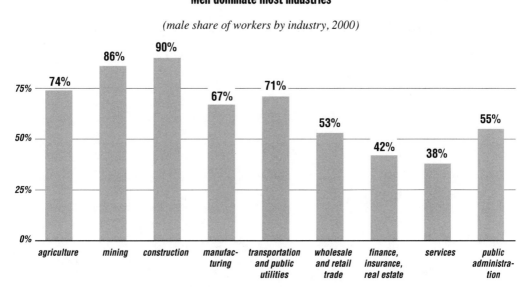

Male Employment by Industry, 2000

(total number of employed people aged 16 or older, number and percent distribution of employed men, and male share of total employed, by industry, 2000; numbers in thousands)

	total	number	percent distribution	share of total
		men		
Total employed	**135,208**	**72,294**	**100.0%**	**53.5%**
Agriculture	3,305	2,434	3.4	73.6
Mining	521	450	0.6	86.4
Construction	9,433	8,520	11.8	90.3
Manufacturing	19,940	13,458	18.6	67.5
Durable goods	12,168	8,775	12.1	72.1
Nondurable goods	7,772	4,682	6.5	60.2
Transportation and public utilities	9,740	6,945	9.6	71.3
Wholesale and retail trade	27,832	14,705	20.3	52.8
Wholesale trade	5,421	3,775	5.2	69.6
Retail trade	22,411	10,930	15.1	48.8
Finance, insurance, and real estate	8,727	3,624	5.0	41.5
Services	49,695	18,845	26.1	37.9
Private household	894	71	0.1	7.9
Other service industries	48,801	18,775	26.0	38.5
Professional services	32,784	9,838	13.6	30.0
Public Administration	6,015	3,313	4.6	55.1

Source: Bureau of Labor Statistics, Employment and Earnings, *January 2001; calculations by New Strategist*

Employment of Men by Industry and Occupation, 2000

(number and percent distribution of employed men aged 16 or older by industry and occupation, 2000; numbers in thousands)

	total	managerial, prof. specialty	technical, sales, admin. support	service	precision prod., craft, repair	operators, fabricators, laborers	farming, forestry, fishing
Total employed men	**72,294**	**20,544**	**14,287**	**7,244**	**13,532**	**13,987**	**2,698**
Agriculture	2,434	125	35	9	51	81	2,132
Mining	450	103	27	5	191	125	–
Construction	8,520	1,191	172	17	5,425	1,701	15
Manufacturing	13,458	3,456	1,548	200	3,120	5,052	82
Transportation/public utilities	6,945	1,332	1,445	157	1,241	2,753	16
Wholesale/retail trade	14,705	1,779	6,360	2,479	1,252	2,794	40
Finance/insurance/real estate	3,624	1,428	1,776	202	144	31	42
Services	18,845	9,902	2,512	2,805	1,927	1,353	345
Public administration	3,313	1,228	412	1,370	181	97	26

Percent distribution by industry and occupation

	total	managerial, prof. specialty	technical, sales, admin. support	service	precision prod., craft, repair	operators, fabricators, laborers	farming, forestry, fishing
Total employed men	**100.0%**	**28.4%**	**19.8%**	**10.0%**	**18.7%**	**19.3%**	**3.7%**
Agriculture	3.4	0.2	0.0	0.0	0.1	0.1	2.9
Mining	0.6	0.1	0.0	0.0	0.3	0.2	–
Construction	11.8	1.6	0.2	0.0	7.5	2.4	0.0
Manufacturing	18.6	4.8	2.1	0.3	4.3	7.0	0.1
Transportation/public utilities	9.6	1.8	2.0	0.2	1.7	3.8	0.0
Wholesale/retail trade	20.3	2.5	8.8	3.4	1.7	3.9	0.1
Finance/insurance/real estate	5.0	2.0	2.5	0.3	0.2	0.0	0.1
Services	26.1	13.7	3.5	3.9	2.7	1.9	0.5
Public administration	4.6	1.7	0.6	1.9	0.3	0.1	0.0

Note: (–) means sample is too small to make a reliable estimate.
Source: Bureau of Labor Statistics, Employment and Earnings, *January 2001; calculations by New Strategist*

Many Older Men Are Self-Employed

Few younger men work for themselves.

Among male workers in nonagricultural industries, 8 percent were self-employed in 2000, according to the Bureau of Labor Statistics. The BLS counts as self-employed only those whose longest job in the previous 12 months was self-employment. It does not include people who run their own business on the side.

The proportion of male workers who are self-employed rises with age. Among those under age 25, fewer than 2 percent are self-employed. The share rises to 12 percent among men aged 55 to 64, and to a substantial 20 percent among working men aged 65 or older.

Self-employment rises with age because older workers have the skills and experience necessary to sell themselves successfully in the marketplace. In addition, self-employment gives older workers the flexible schedules they want as they supplement their income in retirement.

■ As boomer men age, the number of self-employed should grow substantially.

More than 3 million men aged 35 to 54 are self-employed

(number of men in nonagricultural industries who are self-employed, by age, 2000; numbers in thousands)

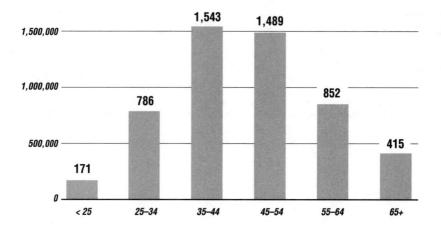

Self-Employed Men by Age, 2000

(total number of men aged 16 or older employed in nonagricultural industries, and number and percent whose longest job was self-employment, by age, 2000; numbers in thousands)

| | total | self-employed | |
		number	percent
Total employed men	**69,859**	**5,256**	**7.5%**
Aged 16 to 19	3,533	33	0.9
Aged 20 to 24	6,769	138	2.0
Aged 25 to 34	16,013	786	4.9
Aged 35 to 44	19,201	1,543	8.0
Aged 45 to 54	15,141	1,489	9.8
Aged 55 to 64	7,087	852	12.0
Aged 65 or older	2,116	415	19.6

Source: Bureau of Labor Statistics, Employment and Earnings, *January 2001; calculations by New Strategist*

Alternative Work Arrangements Attract Older Men

One in four men aged 65 or older has an alternative work arrangement.

Among the nation's 71 million employed men, 11 percent have what the Bureau of Labor Statistics calls an "alternative" work arrangement. The BLS defines alternative workers as independent contractors, on-call workers, employees of temporary-help agencies, or workers provided by contract firms. These workers are considered alternative because they are not employees of the organization for whom they perform their services, nor do they necessarily work regular schedules.

Alternative work arrangements are most common among older men. Fifteen percent of men aged 55 to 64 are alternative workers, as are 25 percent of those aged 65 or older. Most of them are independent contractors, a category that includes freelancers, consultants, real estate agents, and others who obtain customers on their own for whom they provide a product or service. Many independent contractors are self-employed.

Fewer than 2 percent of men are on-call workers, such as substitute teachers. Fewer than 1 percent are temps or workers provided by contract firms.

■ Independent contracting will grow in popularity as baby-boom men age.

More than 7 million men have alternative work arrangements

(number of employed men with alternative work arrangements, by age, 2001; numbers in thousands)

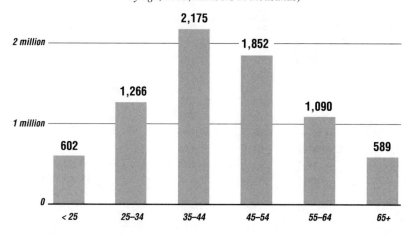

Men with Alternative Work Arrangements by Age, 2001

(number and percent distribution of employed men aged 16 or older by age and work arrangement, 2001; numbers in thousands)

	employed	total in traditional arrange- ments	alternative workers				
			total	indepen- dent contractors	on-call workers	temporary help agency workers	workers provided by contract firms
Total men	**71,376**	**63,803**	**7,573**	**5,537**	**1,109**	**480**	**447**
Aged 16 to 19	3,320	3,155	165	61	82	15	7
Aged 20 to 24	6,778	6,341	437	120	178	82	57
Aged 25 to 34	16,235	14,969	1,266	776	245	130	115
Aged 35 to 44	19,668	17,493	2,175	1,632	251	154	138
Aged 45 to 54	15,567	13,715	1,852	1,545	180	51	76
Aged 55 to 64	7,449	6,359	1,090	911	98	42	39
Aged 65 or older	2,358	1,769	589	491	76	7	15

Percent distribution by work arrangement

Total men	**100.0%**	**89.4%**	**10.6%**	**7.8%**	**1.6%**	**0.7%**	**0.6%**
Aged 16 to 19	100.0	95.0	5.0	1.8	2.5	0.5	0.2
Aged 20 to 24	100.0	93.6	6.4	1.8	2.6	1.2	0.8
Aged 25 to 34	100.0	92.2	7.8	4.8	1.5	0.8	0.7
Aged 35 to 44	100.0	88.9	11.1	8.3	1.3	0.8	0.7
Aged 45 to 54	100.0	88.1	11.9	9.9	1.2	0.3	0.5
Aged 55 to 64	100.0	85.4	14.6	12.2	1.3	0.6	0.5
Aged 65 or older	100.0	75.0	25.0	20.8	3.2	0.3	0.6

Note: Numbers may not add to total because the total employed includes day laborers, an alternative arrangement not shown separately, and because a small number of workers were both on call and provided by contract firms. Independent contractors are workers who obtain customers on their own to provide a product or service, including the self-employed. On-call workers are in a pool of workers who are called to work only as needed, such as substitute teachers and construction workers supplied by a union hiring hall. Temporary help agency workers are those who said they are paid by a temporary help agency. Workers provided by contract firms are those employed by a company that provides employees or their services under contract, such as security, landscaping, and computer program- ming.
Source: Bureau of Labor Statistics, Current Population Survey, Internet site <www.bls.gov/news.release/ conemp.t05.htm>; calculations by New Strategist

Older Men Are More Likely to Be Union Members

Union representation is highest among men aged 45 to 64.

Union membership has been slipping for decades as employment in service industries, where unions have been slow to organize, outpaced employment in manufacturing. Only 16 percent of the nation's 63 million male wage and salary workers are represented by unions. An even smaller 15 percent are union members.

Union representation and membership rises with age, peaking in the 45-to-54 age group. Only 7 percent of 16-to-24-year-old male workers are represented by unions. The figure rises to a peak of 23 percent among those aged 45 to 54.

■ As many companies offer sweetened benefit packages to attract and retain workers, the demand for union representation has weakened.

Ten million men are represented by unions

(number of male wage and salary workers represented by unions, by age, 2000; numbers in thousands)

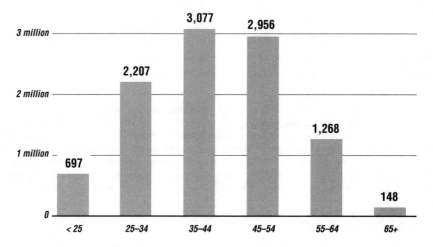

Union Membership of Men by Age, 2000

(number and percent of men aged 16 or older employed as wage and salary workers by age and union affiliation, 2000; numbers in thousands)

	total employed	represented by unions		members of unions	
		number	percent	number	percent
Total men	**62,853**	**10,355**	**16.5%**	**9,578**	**15.2%**
Aged 16 to 24	10,440	697	6.7	618	5.9
Aged 25 to 34	15,197	2,207	14.5	2,030	13.4
Aged 35 to 44	17,028	3,077	18.1	2,871	16.9
Aged 45 to 54	12,898	2,956	22.9	2,739	21.2
Aged 55 to 64	5,770	1,268	22.0	1,191	20.6
Aged 65 or older	1,519	148	9.8	129	8.5

Note: Workers represented by unions are either members of a labor union or similar employee association or workers who report no union affiliation but whose jobs are covered by a union or an employee association contract. Members of unions are union members as well as members of employee associations similar to unions.
Source: Bureau of Labor Statistics, Employment and Earnings, *January 2001*

Among New Workers, Men Will Be Outnumbered by Women

Men will account for most of those leaving the labor force.

Between 2000 and 2010, new entrants to the labor force will be almost evenly divided between men and women, with women having a slight edge. Because the average male worker is older than the average female worker, men will leave the labor force in greater numbers than women during the coming decade. Consequently, men will account for a smaller 52 percent of the labor force in 2010 than the 53 percent in 2000.

In 2000, the labor force numbered 141 million. By 2010 it will grow to 158 million. Twenty million men will enter the workforce during the decade, while 13 million will leave. By 2010, the labor force will include 82 million men and 76 million women.

■ The majority of men and women being in the labor force, balancing work and family has become a worker's issue rather than a woman's issue.

The number of men in the labor force will grow by 7 million

(number of people in the labor force by sex, 2000 and 2010; numbers in thousands)

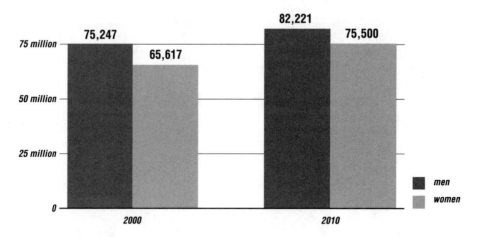

Workers Entering and Leaving the Labor Force by Sex, 2000 to 2010

(number and percent distribution of people aged 16 or older in the civilian labor force by sex, 2000 and 2010; projected entrants, leavers, and stayers by sex, 2000 to 2010; numbers in thousands)

	total labor force, 2000	2000–2010 entrants	2000–2010 leavers	2000–2010 stayers	total labor force, 2010
Total workers	**140,864**	**41,048**	**24,191**	**116,673**	**157,721**
Men	75,247	20,379	13,406	61,842	82,221
Women	65,617	20,669	10,785	54,931	75,500
Total workers	**100.0%**	**100.0%**	**100.0%**	**100.0%**	**100.0%**
Men	53.4	49.6	55.4	53.0	52.1
Women	46.6	50.4	44.6	47.0	47.9

Source: Bureau of Labor Statistics, Monthly Labor Review, *November 2001*

Men's Labor Force Participation Will Continue to Decline

The labor force participation rate of some men will rise, however.

The labor force participation rate of men is projected to decline slightly between 2000 and 2010, from 75 to 73 percent. Even among men aged 55 to 64, the Bureau of Labor Statistics projects a small 0.3 percent decline in labor force participation, a continuation of the trend toward early retirement. The story is different among men aged 65 to 74, however. The labor force participation of men in this age group is projected to rise more than 3 percentage points, from 24 to 28 percent during the decade.

The number of workers aged 55 to 64 will grow the fastest between 2000 and 2010. The number of working men in this age group is projected to increase 47 percent during the decade as boomers enter the cohort. In contrast, the number of working men aged 35 to 44 is projected to decline 12 percent as the small generation X (the baby-bust generation) enters the age group.

■ As boomer men enter the 55-to-64 age group during the next ten years, those who can afford to do so will opt for early retirement.

Many boomer men will be retired by 2010

(labor force participation rate of men, by age, 2010)

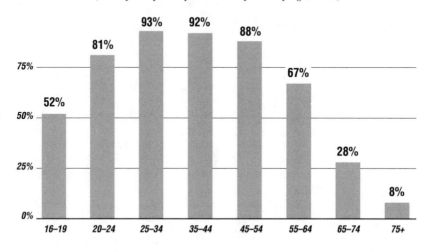

Men in the Labor Force by Age, 2000 and 2010

(number and percent of men aged 16 or older in the labor force by age, 2000 and 2010; percent change in number and percentage point change in rate, 2000–2010; numbers in thousands)

	2000	2010	percent change
Number of men	**75,247**	**82,221**	**9.3%**
Aged 16 to 19	4,317	4,741	9.8
Aged 20 to 24	7,558	8,650	14.4
Aged 25 to 34	17,073	17,902	4.9
Aged 35 to 44	20,334	17,809	−12.4
Aged 45 to 54	15,951	18,855	18.2
Aged 55 to 64	7,574	11,148	47.2
Aged 65 or older	2,439	3,115	27.8
Aged 65 to 74	1,970	2,610	32.5
Aged 75 or older	469	506	7.9

	2000	2010	percentage point change
Percent of men	**74.7%**	**73.2%**	**−1.5**
Aged 16 to 19	53.0	52.3	−0.7
Aged 20 to 24	82.6	81.2	−1.4
Aged 25 to 34	93.4	93.1	−0.3
Aged 35 to 44	92.6	92.3	−0.3
Aged 45 to 54	88.6	87.8	−0.8
Aged 55 to 64	67.3	67.0	−0.3
Aged 65 or older	17.5	19.5	2.0
Aged 65 to 74	24.4	27.7	3.4
Aged 75 or older	8.0	7.7	−0.3

Source: Bureau of Labor Statistics, Monthly Labor Review, *November 2001*

7

Living Arrangements

Most men are married.

Among blacks, however, only 39 percent are married. This compares with 59 percent of non-Hispanic whites, 56 percent of Asians, and 53 percent of Hispanics.

Male-headed single-parent families are a tiny share of households.

Among the nation's 105 million households in 2000, only 1.8 million were male-headed families with children under age 18.

Few men live alone.

The proportion of men living alone peaks among those aged 75 or older at just 21 percent compared with 49 percent of their female counterparts.

For most families, the nest is slow to empty.

While only 46 percent of the nation's married couples have children under age 18 living under their roof, the 56 percent majority have children of any age at home.

Husbands and wives are alike in many ways.

Most married couples are within three years of one another in age, are of the same race, and have equal educational attainment.

Most Men Are Married

The married are a minority only among men under age 30.

The 56 percent majority of men are currently married, while 31 percent have never married, 10 percent are divorced, and 3 percent are widowed. These proportions vary greatly by age.

The median age at first marriage for men is 26.8 years. The never-married share of men falls from 84 percent in the 20-to-24 age group to just 30 percent in the 30-to-34 age group. The proportion of men who are currently married tops 50 percent in the 30-to-34 age group. It rises with age to more than 70 percent for men spanning the ages from 45 to 74. Even among men aged 75 or older, the 69 percent majority are married.

Divorce is most common among men in their forties. Sixteen to 17 percent of men in the age group are currently divorced. Many divorced men have remarried, so these figures underestimate the proportion who have ever been divorced.

Few men are widowers. The proportion is in the single digits until aged 70 or older. Among men aged 75 or older, 23 percent are currently widowed—well below the 60 percent among their female counterparts. These numbers differ because men tend to marry slightly younger women, have a higher mortality rate than women at every age, and are more likely to remarry when widowed.

■ As men's life expectancy increases, fewer women will be widows.

Nearly one-third of men, most of them young, have never married

(percent distribution of men aged 15 or older, by marital status, 2000)

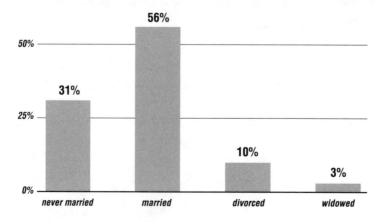

Marital Status of Men by Age, 2000: Total Men

(number and percent distribution of men aged 15 or older by age and marital status, 2000; numbers in thousands)

	total	never married	married	divorced	widowed
Total men	**103,114**	**32,253**	**57,866**	**10,390**	**2,604**
Under age 20	10,295	10,140	72	80	3
Aged 20 to 24	9,208	7,710	1,327	171	–
Aged 25 to 29	8,942	4,625	3,797	512	9
Aged 30 to 34	9,621	2,899	5,791	917	15
Aged 35 to 39	11,032	2,241	7,171	1,577	42
Aged 40 to 44	11,103	1,740	7,526	1,783	54
Aged 45 to 49	9,654	1,156	6,836	1,611	53
Aged 50 to 54	8,235	541	6,446	1,144	104
Aged 55 to 59	6,105	347	4,652	948	158
Aged 60 to 64	5,032	265	3,969	627	171
Aged 65 or older	13,886	590	10,283	1,022	1,994
Aged 65 to 69	4,376	227	3,412	453	285
Aged 70 to 74	3,673	121	2,860	311	382
Aged 75 or older	5,837	242	4,011	258	1,327
Total men	**100.0%**	**31.3%**	**56.1%**	**10.1%**	**2.5%**
Under age 20	100.0	98.5	0.7	0.8	0.0
Aged 20 to 24	100.0	83.7	14.4	1.9	–
Aged 25 to 29	100.0	51.7	42.5	5.7	0.1
Aged 30 to 34	100.0	30.1	60.2	9.5	0.2
Aged 35 to 39	100.0	20.3	65.0	14.3	0.4
Aged 40 to 44	100.0	15.7	67.8	16.1	0.5
Aged 45 to 49	100.0	12.0	70.8	16.7	0.5
Aged 50 to 54	100.0	6.6	78.3	13.9	1.3
Aged 55 to 59	100.0	5.7	76.2	15.5	2.6
Aged 60 to 64	100.0	5.3	78.9	12.5	3.4
Aged 65 or older	100.0	4.2	74.1	7.4	14.4
Aged 65 to 69	100.0	5.2	78.0	10.4	6.5
Aged 70 to 74	100.0	3.3	77.9	8.5	10.4
Aged 75 or older	100.0	4.1	68.7	4.4	22.7

Note: Divorced includes separated; (–) means sample is too small to make a reliable estimate.
Source: Bureau of the Census, Marital Status and Living Arrangements: March 2000 (Update), detailed tables for Current Population Report, P20-537, 2001; Internet site <www.census.gov/population/socdemo/hh-fam/p20-537/2000/tabA1.txt>

Black Men Are Least Likely to Be Married

The never-married outnumber the married among black men.

Only 39 percent of black men aged 15 or older are currently married. Among black men aged 35 or older, however, the majority are married. Non-Hispanic white men are most likely to be married, at 59 percent. Fifty-six percent of Asian and 53 percent of Hispanic men are married.

Forty-five percent of black men have never married. In contrast, among non-Hispanic white men, only 28 percent have never married. Among Asian and Hispanic men, the figure is 38 percent.

Asian men are far less likely to be currently divorced (5 percent) than other men. The figure is 8 to 10 percent among Hispanics and non-Hispanic whites and 14 percent among blacks. Fully 27 percent of black men aged 45 to 49 are currently divorced.

Older black men are more likely to be widowers than other men their age. Among black men aged 75 or older, 34 percent are widowed compared with 25 percent of their Hispanic counterparts, 22 percent of non-Hispanic whites, and only 18 percent of Asians.

■ Differences in marital status by race and Hispanic origin give rise to differences in lifestyles, wants, and needs.

Most Asian, Hispanic, and non-Hispanic white men are married

(percent of men who are currently married, by race and Hispanic origin, 2000)

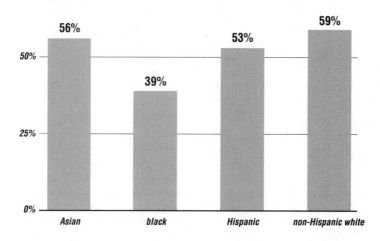

Marital Status of Men by Age, 2000: Asian Men

(number and percent distribution of Asian men aged 15 or older by age and marital status, 2000; numbers in thousands)

	total	never married	married	divorced	widowed
Asian men	**4,041**	**1,528**	**2,281**	**183**	**49**
Under age 20	483	483	–	–	–
Aged 20 to 24	419	372	47	–	–
Aged 25 to 29	475	315	146	14	–
Aged 30 to 34	457	135	302	19	2
Aged 35 to 39	434	100	292	40	3
Aged 40 to 44	394	58	304	31	–
Aged 45 to 49	339	29	297	13	–
Aged 50 to 54	339	11	305	22	–
Aged 55 to 59	177	3	164	11	–
Aged 60 to 64	146	9	110	17	9
Aged 65 or older	379	14	313	16	36
Aged 65 to 69	147	2	133	7	5
Aged 70 to 74	93	4	83	0	6
Aged 75 or older	139	8	97	9	25
Asian men	**100.0%**	**37.8%**	**56.4%**	**4.5%**	**1.2%**
Under age 20	100.0	100.0	–	–	–
Aged 20 to 24	100.0	88.8	11.2	–	–
Aged 25 to 29	100.0	66.3	30.7	2.9	–
Aged 30 to 34	100.0	29.5	66.1	4.2	0.4
Aged 35 to 39	100.0	23.0	67.3	9.2	0.7
Aged 40 to 44	100.0	14.7	77.2	7.9	–
Aged 45 to 49	100.0	8.6	87.6	3.8	–
Aged 50 to 54	100.0	3.2	90.0	6.5	–
Aged 55 to 59	100.0	1.7	92.7	6.2	–
Aged 60 to 64	100.0	6.2	75.3	11.6	6.2
Aged 65 or older	100.0	3.7	82.6	4.2	9.5
Aged 65 to 69	100.0	1.4	90.5	4.8	3.4
Aged 70 to 74	100.0	4.3	89.2	0.0	6.5
Aged 75 or older	100.0	5.8	69.8	6.5	18.0

Note: Divorced includes separated; (–) means sample is too small to make a reliable estimate.
Source: Bureau of the Census, Marital Status and Living Arrangements: March 2000 (Update), *detailed tables for Current Population Report, P20-537, 2001; Internet site <www.census.gov/population/socdemo/hh-fam/ p20-537/2000/tabA1.txt>*

Marital Status of Men by Age, 2000: Black Men

(number and percent distribution of black men aged 15 or older by age and marital status, 2000; numbers in thousands)

	total	never married	married	divorced	widowed
Black men	**11,687**	**5,246**	**4,501**	**1,612**	**328**
Under age 20	1,534	1,511	1	22	–
Aged 20 to 24	1,274	1,158	90	27	–
Aged 25 to 29	1,102	698	323	82	–
Aged 30 to 34	1,203	554	469	180	–
Aged 35 to 39	1,337	416	672	239	9
Aged 40 to 44	1,290	338	667	274	10
Aged 45 to 49	1,065	253	515	284	13
Aged 50 to 54	806	123	515	151	18
Aged 55 to 59	556	53	350	126	28
Aged 60 to 64	424	42	282	80	21
Aged 65 or older	1,095	99	616	148	230
Aged 65 to 69	376	49	213	82	30
Aged 70 to 74	285	17	172	42	54
Aged 75 or older	434	33	231	24	146
Black men	**100.0%**	**44.9%**	**38.5%**	**13.8%**	**2.8%**
Under age 20	100.0	98.5	0.1	1.4	–
Aged 20 to 24	100.0	90.9	7.1	2.1	–
Aged 25 to 29	100.0	63.3	29.3	7.4	–
Aged 30 to 34	100.0	46.1	39.0	15.0	–
Aged 35 to 39	100.0	31.1	50.3	17.9	0.7
Aged 40 to 44	100.0	26.2	51.7	21.2	0.8
Aged 45 to 49	100.0	23.8	48.4	26.7	1.2
Aged 50 to 54	100.0	15.3	63.9	18.7	2.2
Aged 55 to 59	100.0	9.5	62.9	22.7	5.0
Aged 60 to 64	100.0	9.9	66.5	18.9	5.0
Aged 65 or older	100.0	9.0	56.3	13.5	21.0
Aged 65 to 69	100.0	13.0	56.6	21.8	8.0
Aged 70 to 74	100.0	6.0	60.4	14.7	18.9
Aged 75 or older	100.0	7.6	53.2	5.5	33.6

Note: Divorced includes separated; (–) means sample is too small to make a reliable estimate.
Source: Bureau of the Census, Marital Status and Living Arrangements: March 2000 (Update), *detailed tables for Current Population Report, P20-537, 2001; Internet site <www.census.gov/population/socdemo/hh-fam/ p20-537/2000/tabA1.txt>*

Marital Status of Men by Age, 2000: Hispanic Men

(number and percent distribution of Hispanic men aged 15 or older by age and marital status, 2000; numbers in thousands)

	total	never married	married	divorced	widowed
Hispanic men	**11,327**	**4,249**	**5,952**	**957**	**170**
Under age 20	1,509	1,478	21	10	–
Aged 20 to 24	1,453	1,105	319	30	–
Aged 25 to 29	1,416	594	746	77	–
Aged 30 to 34	1,439	414	920	101	4
Aged 35 to 39	1,422	298	978	139	6
Aged 40 to 44	1,058	134	790	132	3
Aged 45 to 49	810	107	579	119	4
Aged 50 to 54	679	43	510	121	5
Aged 55 to 59	461	27	325	86	23
Aged 60 to 64	359	21	259	62	16
Aged 65 or older	720	27	504	83	107
Aged 65 to 69	273	11	199	43	21
Aged 70 to 74	196	9	134	28	24
Aged 75 or older	251	7	171	12	62
Hispanic men	**100.0%**	**37.5%**	**52.5%**	**8.4%**	**1.5%**
Under age 20	100.0	97.9	1.4	0.7	–
Aged 20 to 24	100.0	76.0	22.0	2.1	–
Aged 25 to 29	100.0	41.9	52.7	5.4	–
Aged 30 to 34	100.0	28.8	63.9	7.0	0.3
Aged 35 to 39	100.0	21.0	68.8	9.8	0.4
Aged 40 to 44	100.0	12.7	74.7	12.5	0.3
Aged 45 to 49	100.0	13.2	71.5	14.7	0.5
Aged 50 to 54	100.0	6.3	75.1	17.8	0.7
Aged 55 to 59	100.0	5.9	70.5	18.7	5.0
Aged 60 to 64	100.0	5.8	72.1	17.3	4.5
Aged 65 or older	100.0	3.8	70.0	11.5	14.9
Aged 65 to 69	100.0	4.0	72.9	15.8	7.7
Aged 70 to 74	100.0	4.6	68.4	14.3	12.2
Aged 75 or older	100.0	2.8	68.1	4.8	24.7

Note: Divorced includes separated; (–) means sample is too small to make a reliable estimate.
Source: Bureau of the Census, Marital Status and Living Arrangements: March 2000 (Update), detailed tables for Current Population Report, P20-537, 2001; Internet site <www.census.gov/population/socdemo/hh-fam/ p20-537/2000/tabA1.txt>

Marital Status of Men by Age, 2000: White Men

(number and percent distribution of white men aged 15 or older by age and marital status, 2000; numbers in thousands)

	total	never married	married	divorced	widowed
White men	**86,443**	**25,113**	**50,651**	**8,483**	**2,196**
Under age 20	8,118	7,986	71	58	3
Aged 20 to 24	7,424	6,119	1,166	139	–
Aged 25 to 29	7,274	3,556	3,299	410	9
Aged 30 to 34	7,870	2,188	4,965	703	13
Aged 35 to 39	9,189	1,693	6,174	1,291	31
Aged 40 to 44	9,305	1,330	6,476	1,455	45
Aged 45 to 49	8,172	865	5,968	1,299	40
Aged 50 to 54	7,032	402	5,583	964	83
Aged 55 to 59	5,309	287	4,093	803	125
Aged 60 to 64	4,415	214	3,547	518	135
Aged 65 or older	12,335	471	9,308	843	1,714
Aged 65 to 69	3,818	175	3,040	357	246
Aged 70 to 74	3,275	98	2,600	262	315
Aged 75 or older	5,242	198	3,668	224	1,153
White men	**100.0%**	**29.1%**	**58.6%**	**9.8%**	**2.5%**
Under age 20	100.0	98.4	0.9	0.7	0.0
Aged 20 to 24	100.0	82.4	15.7	1.9	–
Aged 25 to 29	100.0	48.9	45.4	5.6	0.1
Aged 30 to 34	100.0	27.8	63.1	8.9	0.2
Aged 35 to 39	100.0	18.4	67.2	14.0	0.3
Aged 40 to 44	100.0	14.3	69.6	15.6	0.5
Aged 45 to 49	100.0	10.6	73.0	15.9	0.5
Aged 50 to 54	100.0	5.7	79.4	13.7	1.2
Aged 55 to 59	100.0	5.4	77.1	15.1	2.4
Aged 60 to 64	100.0	4.8	80.3	11.7	3.1
Aged 65 or older	100.0	3.8	75.5	6.8	13.9
Aged 65 to 69	100.0	4.6	79.6	9.4	6.4
Aged 70 to 74	100.0	3.0	79.4	8.0	9.6
Aged 75 or older	100.0	3.8	70.0	4.3	22.0

Note: Divorced includes separated; (–) means sample is too small to make a reliable estimate.
Source: Bureau of the Census, Marital Status and Living Arrangements: March 2000 (Update), *detailed tables for Current Population Report, P20-537, 2001; Internet site <www.census.gov/population/socdemo/hh-fam/ p20-537/2000/tabA1.txt>*

Marital Status of Men by Age, 2000: Non-Hispanic White Men

(number and percent distribution of non-Hispanic white men aged 15 or older by age and marital status, 2000; numbers in thousands)

	total	never married	married	divorced	widowed
Non-Hispanic white men	**75,692**	**21,109**	**44,957**	**7,596**	**2,030**
Under age 20	6,685	6,583	49	49	3
Aged 20 to 24	6,030	5,057	858	115	–
Aged 25 to 29	5,940	3,010	2,586	335	9
Aged 30 to 34	6,514	1,799	4,091	615	9
Aged 35 to 39	7,847	1,432	5,227	1,164	24
Aged 40 to 44	8,313	1,203	5,732	1,336	42
Aged 45 to 49	7,400	763	5,413	1,188	36
Aged 50 to 54	6,384	363	5,094	850	78
Aged 55 to 59	4,868	260	3,786	718	104
Aged 60 to 64	4,069	193	3,298	460	119
Aged 65 or older	11,643	445	8,824	767	1,608
Aged 65 to 69	3,559	165	2,852	318	225
Aged 70 to 74	3,086	89	2,470	236	291
Aged 75 or older	4,998	191	3,502	213	1,092
Non-Hispanic white men	**100.0%**	**27.9%**	**59.4%**	**10.0%**	**2.7%**
Under age 20	100.0	98.5	0.7	0.7	0.0
Aged 20 to 24	100.0	83.9	14.2	1.9	–
Aged 25 to 29	100.0	50.7	43.5	5.6	0.2
Aged 30 to 34	100.0	27.6	62.8	9.4	0.1
Aged 35 to 39	100.0	18.2	66.6	14.8	0.3
Aged 40 to 44	100.0	14.5	69.0	16.1	0.5
Aged 45 to 49	100.0	10.3	73.1	16.1	0.5
Aged 50 to 54	100.0	5.7	79.8	13.3	1.2
Aged 55 to 59	100.0	5.3	77.8	14.7	2.1
Aged 60 to 64	100.0	4.7	81.1	11.3	2.9
Aged 65 or older	100.0	3.8	75.8	6.6	13.8
Aged 65 to 69	100.0	4.6	80.1	8.9	6.3
Aged 70 to 74	100.0	2.9	80.0	7.6	9.4
Aged 75 or older	100.0	3.8	70.1	4.3	21.8

Note: Divorced includes separated; (–) means sample is too small to make a reliable estimate.
Source: Bureau of the Census, Marital Status and Living Arrangements: March 2000 (Update), detailed tables for Current Population Report, P20-537, 2001; Internet site <www.census.gov/population/socdemo/hh-fam/p20-537/2000/tabA1.txt>

Divorce Is Highest among Fiftysomething Men

Men in their forties are almost as likely to have divorced.

More than one-third of men aged 40 to 59 have experienced divorce, according to a Census Bureau study of marriage and divorce. The analysis, published in 2002 and based on data through 1996, is the first Census Bureau study on marriage and divorce in ten years. Among men in their fifties in 1996, 36 percent had ever divorced. The figure was a slightly smaller 34 percent among men aged 40 to 49, the oldest members of the baby-boom generation.

Among men aged 60 or older, divorce is less common. Only 18 percent of men in their seventies have ever divorced. The figure was 27 percent among men aged 60 to 69. Divorce is less common among men under age 40, in part because they have not had as much time to get divorced. Among men aged 35 to 39, for example, 24 percent have been through a divorce.

The majority of men aged 30 and older have married only once and are still married. The percentage of men who have married twice peaks at 22 percent in the 50-to-59 age group. Seven percent of men in their fifties have married three times.

■ Based on age-specific divorce rates, the Census Bureau projects that half of men aged 45 or younger in 1996 will eventually experience divorce.

Divorce is less common among older men

(percent of men who have ever divorced, by age, 1996)

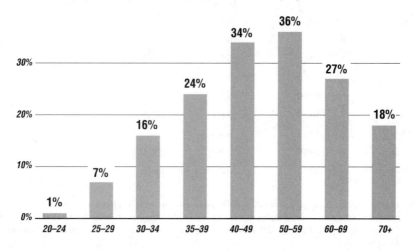

Marital History of Men by Age, 1996

(percent distribution of men aged 15 or older by marital history and age, as of 1996; numbers in thousands)

	total	15–19	20–24	25–29	30–34	35–39	40–49	50–59	60–69	70+
Total men, number	99,005	9,680	8,658	9,445	10,568	11,138	19,381	12,157	9,038	8,940
Total men, percent	100.0%	100.0%	100.0%	100.0%	100.0%	100.0%	100.0%	100.0%	100.0%	100.0%
Never married	30.6	99.0	81.7	48.6	28.7	19.2	12.0	5.3	5.2	4.4
Ever married	69.4	1.0	18.3	51.4	71.3	80.8	88.0	94.7	94.8	95.6
Married once	53.8	1.0	17.8	48.8	62.2	64.9	63.3	65.5	70.5	73.9
Still married	44.4	0.8	16.2	41.8	53.0	54.0	51.6	54.5	59.1	55.5
Married twice	12.6	0.0	0.5	2.4	8.4	13.8	20.0	22.1	18.7	17.0
Still married	10.1	0.0	0.4	2.0	7.1	11.1	16.0	17.5	15.4	12.6
Married three or more times	3.1	0.0	0.0	0.2	0.7	2.1	4.8	7.0	5.6	4.7
Still married	2.3	0.0	0.0	0.2	0.5	1.8	3.8	5.1	4.4	3.2
Ever divorced	20.4	0.0	1.3	7.3	16.1	24.3	34.1	35.7	26.8	18.0
Currently divorced	8.2	0.0	0.9	5.2	8.1	10.8	13.9	13.1	9.2	4.5
Ever widowed	3.9	0.0	0.0	0.2	0.2	0.3	1.2	3.5	9.2	25.1
Currently widowed	2.6	0.0	0.0	0.1	0.2	0.1	0.6	1.9	5.1	18.6

Source: Bureau of the Census, Number, Timing, and Duration of Marriages and Divorces: 1996, Current Population Report P70-80, 2002

Few Children Live with Their Father Only

Five times as many children live with Mom.

The proportion of children who live with only one parent—most with their mother—stood at 27 percent in 2000. Overall, 16 million children (22 percent) live with only their mother, while just 3 million (4 percent) live with only their father. Another 4 percent of children live with neither parent.

Asian children are most likely to live with both parents (81 percent). The majority of non-Hispanic white and Hispanic children also live in two-parent homes (77 and 64 percent, respectively). Among black children, single parents are the norm. Fifty-three percent of black children live in single-parent families, almost all with their mother. Only 38 percent of black children live in two-parent homes. Black children are more likely than others to live with neither parent—9 percent of black children do not live with a parent compared with 3 to 5 percent of children from other racial and ethnic groups.

■ Although few children live with only their father, the number of men heading single-parent families grew rapidly during the 1990s.

Most children still live in two-parent families

(percent distribution of children under age 18 by living arrangement, 2000)

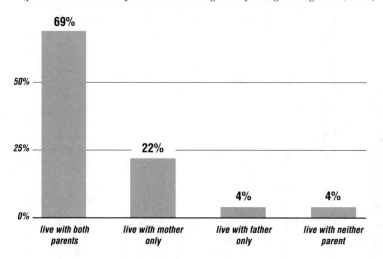

Living Arrangements of Children by Race and Hispanic Origin, 2000

(number and percent distribution of children under age 18 by living arrangement, race, and Hispanic origin of child, 2000; numbers in thousands)

	total	Asian	black	Hispanic	white total	white non-Hispanic
Total children	72,012	3,047	11,412	11,613	56,455	45,407
Both parents	49,795	2,454	4,286	7,561	42,497	35,188
One parent	19,220	504	6,080	3,425	12,192	9,046
Mother only	16,162	428	5,596	2,919	9,765	7,095
Father only	3,058	76	484	506	2,427	1,951
Neither parent	2,981	88	1,046	626	1,752	1,161
Total children	100.0%	100.0%	100.0%	100.0%	100.0%	100.0%
Both parents	69.1	80.5	37.6	65.1	75.3	77.5
One parent	26.7	16.5	53.3	29.5	21.6	19.9
Mother only	22.4	14.0	49.0	25.1	17.3	15.6
Father only	4.2	2.5	4.2	4.4	4.3	4.3
Neither parent	4.1	2.9	9.2	5.4	3.1	2.6

Note: Numbers by race and Hispanic origin will not add to total because Hispanics may be of any race and not all races are shown. Numbers by living arrangement will not add to total because group quarters is not shown.
Source: Bureau of the Census, America's Families and Living Arrangements: March 2000, *detailed tables for Current Population Report P20-537, Internet site <www.census.gov/population/www/socdemo/hh-fam/p20-537_00.html>; calculations by New Strategist*

Most Men Are Married Householders

Many younger men live with their parents.

Among the nation's 103 million men aged 15 or older, 72 percent head households as husbands, male family heads, single-person householders, or as householders living with nonrelatives. Fifty-four percent of men aged 15 or older are married householders, the most common living arrangement. Living with mom and dad ranks second, with 17 percent of men living at home. Eleven percent live alone.

Living arrangements vary greatly by age. The proportion of men who live with their parents falls from 85 percent among 15-to-19-year-olds to 48 percent among 20-to-24-year-olds. The proportion is a substantial 18 percent among men aged 25 to 29, falling below 10 percent among those aged 30 or older. Conversely, the proportion of men who are married householders rises from just 12 percent among men aged 20 to 24 to a peak of 76 percent among men aged 65 to 74. In the oldest age group, the proportion of men who are married householders falls slightly to 66 percent, while 21 percent live alone.

■ Among young adults, men are more likely than women to live with their parents because men marry at an older age.

Most men are married householders

(percent distribution of men aged 15 or older by living arrangement, 2000)

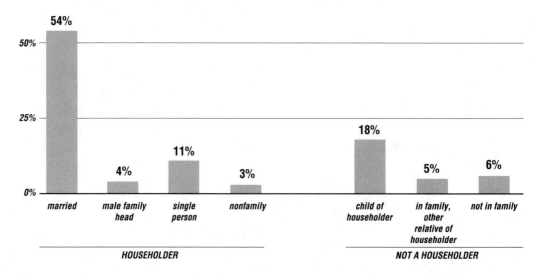

Men by Living Arrangement and Age, 2000

(number and percent distribution of men aged 15 or older by living arrangement and age, 2000; numbers in thousands)

	total	15–19	20–24	25–29	30–34	35–39	40–44	45–54	55–64	65–74	75+
Total men	103,114	10,296	9,208	8,940	9,620	11,031	11,104	17,889	11,138	8,048	5,836
Householder	**73,980**	**388**	**2,627**	**5,701**	**7,601**	**9,020**	**9,417**	**16,110**	**10,222**	**7,520**	**5,372**
Married-couple householder or spouse	55,311	47	1,121	3,493	5,476	6,828	7,246	12,815	8,338	6,096	3,850
Male family householder	4,028	162	398	426	460	537	565	713	351	203	213
Living alone	11,181	62	494	1,079	1,200	1,240	1,329	2,146	1,276	1,108	1,247
Living with nonrelatives	3,460	117	614	703	465	415	277	436	257	113	62
Not a householder	**29,134**	**9,908**	**6,581**	**3,239**	**2,019**	**2,011**	**1,687**	**1,779**	**916**	**528**	**464**
Child of householder	18,026	8,746	4,446	1,566	819	901	689	604	206	49	–
In family, other relative of householder	4,792	744	787	525	406	355	349	546	423	296	361
Not in family	6,316	418	1,348	1,148	794	755	649	629	287	183	103

(continued)

(continued from previous page)

	total	15–19	20–24	25–29	30–34	35–39	40–44	45–54	55–64	65–74	75+
Total men	100.0%	100.0%	100.0%	100.0%	100.0%	100.0%	100.0%	100.0%	100.0%	100.0%	100.0%
Householder	**71.7**	**3.8**	**28.5**	**63.8**	**79.0**	**81.8**	**84.8**	**90.1**	**91.8**	**93.4**	**92.0**
Married-couple householder or spouse	53.6	0.5	12.2	39.1	56.9	61.9	65.3	71.6	74.9	75.7	66.0
Male family householder	3.9	1.6	4.3	4.8	4.8	4.9	5.1	4.0	3.2	2.5	3.6
Living alone	10.8	0.6	5.4	12.1	12.5	11.2	12.0	12.0	11.5	13.8	21.4
Living with nonrelatives	3.4	1.1	6.7	7.9	4.8	3.8	2.5	2.4	2.3	1.4	1.1
Not a householder	**28.3**	**96.2**	**71.5**	**36.2**	**21.0**	**18.2**	**15.2**	**9.9**	**8.2**	**6.6**	**8.0**
Child of householder	17.5	84.9	48.3	17.5	8.5	8.2	6.2	3.4	1.8	0.6	–
In family, other relative of householder	4.6	7.2	8.5	5.9	4.2	3.2	3.1	3.1	3.8	3.7	6.2
Not in family	6.1	4.1	14.6	12.8	8.3	6.8	5.8	3.5	2.6	2.3	1.8

Note: (–) means sample is too small to make a reliable estimate.
Source: Bureau of the Census, America's Families and Living Arrangements: March 2000, detailed tables for Current Population Report P20-537, Internet site <www.census.gov/population/www/socdemo/hh-fam/p20-537_00.html>; calculations by New Strategist

Two-Thirds of Men Who Live Alone Are under Age 55

Men account for the majority of people living alone in some age groups, however.

Twenty-seven million Americans lived alone in 2000, only 42 percent of them men. Men account for the majority of people aged 25 to 44 who live alone, however. In the older age groups, few of those living alone are men. Among people aged 65 or older who live alone, men account for only 24 percent.

Overall, 11 percent of men live by themselves. The proportion of men who live alone ranges from 12 to 14 percent from ages 25 through 74. The figure is a slightly higher 21 percent among men aged 75 or older, but less than the 49 percent of women in the age group who live alone. These figures differ because most women marry slightly older men and men at every age have a higher mortality rate than women, making widowhood more common for women than men.

■ Among people who live alone, men have very different wants and needs than women because they are much younger and more likely to be in the labor force.

Nearly half the men who live alone are under age 45

(percent distribution of men who live alone, by age, 2000)

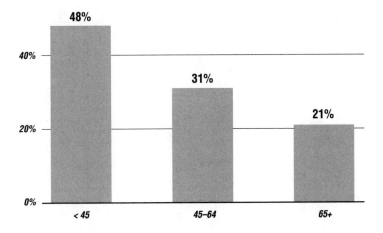

Men Who Live Alone by Age, 2000

(total number of people aged 15 or older living alone, number and percent distribution of men living alone, percent of men who live alone, and male share of total people who live alone, 2000; numbers in thousands)

	total	men			
		number	percent distribution	percent living alone	share of total
Total living alone	**26,724**	**11,181**	**100.0%**	**10.8%**	**41.8%**
Under age 20	128	62	0.6	0.6	48.4
Aged 20 to 24	1,016	494	4.4	5.4	48.6
Aged 25 to 29	1,927	1,079	9.7	12.1	56.0
Aged 30 to 34	1,921	1,200	10.7	12.5	62.5
Aged 35 to 39	1,976	1,240	11.1	11.2	62.8
Aged 40 to 44	2,133	1,329	11.9	12.0	62.3
Aged 45 to 54	4,304	2,146	19.2	12.0	49.9
Aged 55 to 64	3,538	1,276	11.4	11.5	36.1
Aged 65 or older	9,783	2,355	21.1	17.0	24.1
Aged 65 to 74	4,091	1,108	9.9	13.8	27.1
Aged 75 or older	5,692	1,247	11.2	21.4	21.9

Source: Bureau of the Census, America's Families and Living Arrangements: March 2000, *detailed tables for Current Population Report P20-537, Internet site <www.census.gov/population/www/socdemo/hh-fam/p20-537_00.html>; calculations by New Strategist*

Married Couples' Share of Households Is Shrinking

They accounted for only 53 percent of households in 2000.

The proportion of households headed by married couples fell from 56 to 53 percent between 1990 and 2000. That's because the number of married couples is growing much more slowly than other household types. Between 1990 and 2000, the number of couples increased just 6 percent. Couples with children under age 18 at home grew only 3 percent during those years.

Only 4 percent of households are families headed by men. The number of male-headed families grew rapidly during the 1990s, however, rising by 40 percent to just over 4 million in 2000. Male-headed families with children under age 18 were the fastest growing household type during the decade, increasing 55 percent. Despite the rapid growth, there were only 1.8 million of such households in 2000 compared to 7.6 million female-headed single-parent families.

The number of men living alone grew 24 percent between 1990 and 2000 compared to a smaller 11 percent rise in the number of women living alone. Behind the slower growth in female-headed single-person households is their older age. Most are headed by women aged 55 or older, an age group whose growth slowed during the 1990s as the small generation born during the Depression entered its sixties and seventies.

■ During the past few decades, households have become more diverse for women than for men.

Male-headed families grew faster than other household types during the 1990s

(percent change in number of households by household type, 1990 to 2000)

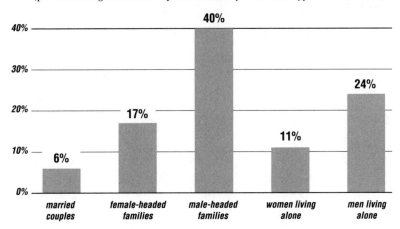

Households by Type, 1990 and 2000

(number and percent distribution of households by household type, 1990 and 2000, percent change in number, 1990–2000; numbers in thousands)

| | 2000 | | 1990 | | percent change |
	number	percent distribution	number	percent distribution	in number 1990–2000
Total households	**104,705**	**100.0%**	**93,347**	**100.0%**	**12.2%**
Family households	**72,025**	**68.8**	**66,090**	**70.8**	**9.0**
Married couples	55,311	52.8	52,317	56.0	5.7
With children < 18	25,248	24.1	24,537	26.3	2.9
Without children < 18	30,062	28.7	27,780	29.8	8.2
Female householder, no spouse present	12,687	12.1	10,890	11.7	16.5
With children < 18	7,571	7.2	6,599	7.1	14.7
Without children < 18	5,116	4.9	4,291	4.6	19.2
Male householder, no spouse present	4,028	3.8	2,884	3.1	39.7
With children < 18	1,786	1.7	1,153	1.2	54.9
Without children < 18	2,242	2.1	1,731	1.9	29.5
Nonfamily households	**32,680**	**31.2**	**27,257**	**29.2**	**19.9**
Female householder	18,039	17.2	15,651	16.8	15.3
Living alone	15,543	14.8	13,950	14.9	11.4
Male householder	14,641	14.0	11,606	12.4	26.2
Living alone	11,181	10.7	9,049	9.7	23.6

Source: Bureau of the Census, America's Families and Living Arrangements: March 2000, *detailed tables for Current Population Report P20-537, Internet site <www.census.gov/population/www/socdemo/hh-fam/p20-537_00.html>; and* Marital Status and Living Arrangements: March 1990, *Current Population Reports P20-450, 1991; calculations by New Strategist*

Household Diversity Is Greatest among the Young and the Old

In middle age, married couples head most households.

Married couples headed slightly more than half (53 percent) of American households in 2000. Couples account for a minority of households headed by people under age 25 but become the majority in the 30-to-34 age group. The married-couple share of households remains above 50 percent until age 75.

Households headed by people under age 30 are the most diverse as young adults make the transition from living with their parents to living on their own. Eighteen percent of households headed by people under age 20 are male-headed families. The share drops to just 8 percent among householders aged 20 to 24. From 20 to 22 percent of households headed by people under age 30 are male-headed nonfamily households.

Household diversity is also great among householders aged 75 or older. Only 34 percent of households headed by people aged 75 or older are married couples while a larger 43 percent are headed by women living alone. Men are unlikely to live alone in old age because most die while married or remarry if widowed. Only 12 percent of householders aged 75 or older are men living alone.

■ In contrast to older women, most older men have a spouse to care for them if they become ill or infirm.

Households of the young are different from those of the middle aged

(percent distribution of households headed by people aged 20 to 24, 45 to 54, and 75 or older, by household type, 2000)

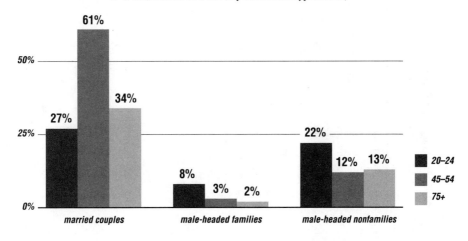

Households by Type and Age of Householder, 2000

(number and percent distribution of households by household type and age of householder, 2000; numbers in thousands)

	total	under 20	20-24	25-29	30-34	35-39	40-44	45-54	55-64	65-74	75 or older
Total households	104,705	914	4,946	8,520	10,107	11,728	12,227	20,927	13,592	11,325	10,419
Family households	**72,025**	**553**	**2,800**	**5,489**	**7,518**	**9,100**	**9,606**	**15,803**	**9,569**	**7,025**	**4,562**
Married couples	55,311	96	1,354	3,775	5,615	6,886	7,218	12,792	8,138	5,929	3,508
With children < 18	25,248	55	779	2,439	4,391	5,796	5,609	5,401	671	88	19
Without children < 18	30,062	40	576	1,335	1,224	1,091	1,609	7,391	7,468	5,840	3,489
Female householder, no spouse present	12,687	295	1,047	1,289	1,443	1,676	1,823	2,299	1,080	894	841
With children < 18	7,571	151	891	1,169	1,356	1,529	1,433	911	119	5	6
Without children < 18	5,116	143	156	119	87	147	390	1,388	960	889	835
Male householder, no spouse present	4,028	162	398	426	460	537	565	713	351	203	213
With children < 18	1,786	9	114	235	295	376	361	305	74	15	–
Without children < 18	2,242	153	284	190	165	161	204	408	276	188	213
Nonfamily households	**32,680**	**361**	**2,146**	**3,031**	**2,589**	**2,629**	**2,621**	**5,123**	**4,023**	**4,300**	**5,857**
Female householder	18,039	183	1,038	1,249	923	974	1,015	2,541	2,490	3,079	4,547
Living alone	15,543	66	522	848	720	736	804	2,158	2,262	2,983	4,444
Male householder	14,641	178	1,108	1,782	1,666	1,655	1,606	2,583	1,533	1,221	1,309
Living alone	11,181	62	494	1,079	1,200	1,240	1,329	2,146	1,276	1,108	1,247

(continued)

(continued from previous page)

	total	under 20	20-24	25-29	30-34	35-39	40-44	45-54	55-64	65-74	75 or older
Total households	100.0%	100.0%	100.0%	100.0%	100.0%	100.0%	100.0%	100.0%	100.0%	100.0%	100.0%
Family households	**68.8**	**60.5**	**56.6**	**64.4**	**74.4**	**77.6**	**78.6**	**75.5**	**70.4**	**62.0**	**43.8**
Married couples	52.8	10.5	27.4	44.3	55.6	58.7	59.0	61.1	59.9	52.4	33.7
With children < 18	24.1	6.0	15.8	28.6	43.4	49.4	45.9	25.8	4.9	0.8	0.2
Without children < 18	28.7	4.4	11.6	15.7	12.1	9.3	13.2	35.3	54.9	51.6	33.5
Female householder, no spouse present	12.1	32.3	21.2	15.1	14.3	14.3	14.9	11.0	7.9	7.9	8.1
With children < 18	7.2	16.5	18.0	13.7	13.4	13.0	11.7	4.4	0.9	0.0	0.1
Without children < 18	4.9	15.6	3.2	1.4	0.9	1.3	3.2	6.6	7.1	7.8	8.0
Male householder, no spouse present	3.8	17.7	8.0	5.0	4.6	4.6	4.6	3.4	2.6	1.8	2.0
With children < 18	1.7	1.0	2.3	2.8	2.9	3.2	3.0	1.5	0.5	0.1	–
Without children < 18	2.1	16.7	5.7	2.2	1.6	1.4	1.7	1.9	2.0	1.7	2.0
Nonfamily households	**31.2**	**39.5**	**43.4**	**35.6**	**25.6**	**22.4**	**21.4**	**24.5**	**29.6**	**38.0**	**56.2**
Female householder	17.2	20.0	21.0	14.7	9.1	8.3	8.3	12.1	18.3	27.2	43.6
Living alone	14.8	7.2	10.6	10.0	7.1	6.3	6.6	10.3	16.6	26.3	42.7
Male householder	14.0	19.5	22.4	20.9	16.5	14.1	13.1	12.3	11.3	10.8	12.6
Living alone	10.7	6.8	10.0	12.7	11.9	10.6	10.9	10.3	9.4	9.8	12.0

Note: (–) means sample is too small to make a reliable estimate.
Source: Bureau of the Census, America's Families and Living Arrangements: March 2000, detailed tables for Current Population Report P20-537, Internet site <www
.census .gov/population/www/socdemo/hh-fam/p20-537_00.html>; calculations by New Strategist

Households Vary Sharply by Race and Ethnicity

Black households are more diverse than white or Hispanic households.

Married couples head only about one-third of black households, while 30 percent of black households are female-headed families. In contrast, married couples head the majority of Asian, Hispanic, and non-Hispanic white households.

Hispanic households are more likely to be nuclear families (husband, wife, and children) than Asian, black, and non-Hispanic white households. In 2000, married couples with children under age 18 at home headed 37 percent of Hispanic households. This compares with 34 percent of Asian, 23 percent of non-Hispanic white, and just 16 percent of black households. Although there are more black than Hispanic households, Hispanic married couples with children outnumber their black counterparts by more than 1 million.

The proportion of households that are single-parent families headed by men varies little by race or ethnicity. The figure ranges from a low of 1 percent among Asian households to a high of 3 percent among Hispanics. Fewer than 2 million of the nation's 105 million households are single-parent families headed by men.

Men who live alone account for 11 percent of all households. The figure ranges from a low of 7 percent among households headed by Hispanics to a high of 12 percent among black households.

■ The diversity of household types by race and ethnicity means that Asians, blacks, Hispanics, and non-Hispanic whites often have different needs.

Nuclear families are most common among Hispanic households

(percent of households headed by married couples with children under age 18, by race and Hispanic origin of householder, 2000)

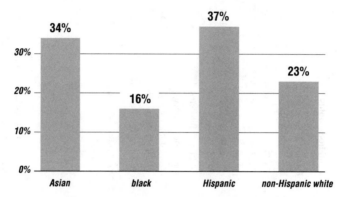

Households by Type, Race, and Hispanic Origin, 2000

(number and percent distribution of households by type, race, and Hispanic origin, 2000)

					white	
	total	*Asian*	*black*	*Hispanic*	*total*	*non-Hispanic*
Total households	104,705	3,337	12,849	9,319	87,671	78,819
Family households	**72,025**	**2,506**	**8,664**	**7,561**	**60,251**	**53,066**
Married couples	55,311	1,996	4,144	5,133	48,790	43,865
With children <18	25,248	1,145	2,093	3,423	21,809	18,516
Without children <18	30,062	852	2,050	1,710	26,981	25,349
Female householder, no spouse present	12,687	331	3,814	1,769	8,380	6,732
With children <18	7,571	170	2,409	1,145	4,869	3,815
Without children <18	5,116	162	1,405	625	3,511	2,917
Male householder, no spouse present	4,028	179	706	658	3,081	2,468
With children <18	1,786	40	280	246	1,429	1,202
Without children <18	2,242	138	427	412	1,652	1,267
Nonfamily households	**32,680**	**831**	**4,185**	**1,758**	**27,420**	**25,753**
Female householder	18,039	399	2,309	783	15,215	14,475
Living alone	15,543	311	2,025	630	13,109	12,508
Male householder	14,641	432	1,876	974	12,204	11,278
Living alone	11,181	313	1,580	666	9,198	8,562
Total households	**100.0%**	**100.0%**	**100.0%**	**100.0%**	**100.0%**	**100.0%**
Family households	**68.8**	**75.1**	**67.4**	**81.1**	**68.7**	**67.3**
Married couples	52.8	59.8	32.3	55.1	55.7	55.7
With children <18	24.1	34.3	16.3	36.7	24.9	23.5
Without children <18	28.7	25.5	16.0	18.3	30.8	32.2
Female householder, no spouse present	12.1	9.9	29.7	19.0	9.6	8.5
With children <18	7.2	5.1	18.7	12.3	5.6	4.8
Without children <18	4.9	4.9	10.9	6.7	4.0	3.7
Male householder, no spouse present	3.8	5.4	5.5	7.1	3.5	3.1
With children <18	1.7	1.2	2.2	2.6	1.6	1.5
Without children <18	2.1	4.1	3.3	4.4	1.9	1.6
Nonfamily households	**31.2**	**24.9**	**32.6**	**18.9**	**31.3**	**32.7**
Female householder	17.2	12.0	18.0	8.4	17.4	18.4
Living alone	14.8	9.3	15.8	6.8	15.0	15.9
Male householder	14.0	12.9	14.6	10.5	13.9	14.3
Living alone	10.7	9.4	12.3	7.1	10.5	10.9

Source: Bureau of the Census, America's Families and Living Arrangements: March 2000, *detailed tables for Current Population Report P20-537, Internet site <www.census.gov/population/www/socdemo/hh-fam/p20-537_00.html>; calculations by New Strategist*

Only One-Third of Households include Children under Age 18

The proportion peaks at 66 percent among households headed by 35-to-39-year-olds.

Overall, just 33 percent of American households include children under age 18, a proportion that, together with family size, has fallen over the past few decades. Even among married couples, only a 46 percent minority have children under age 18 at home. Among couples under age 45, however, most have children at home.

Only 44 percent of male-headed families have children under age 18 at home. But the majority of male families headed by a 25-to-44-year-old include children. Male family householders without children under age 18 are living with grown children or other relatives such as siblings. The 60 percent majority of female-headed families include children under age 18.

■ Because fewer households include children, the political power of children is diminishing.

Most male-headed families do not include children under age 18

(percent of households that include children under age 18, by household type, 2000)

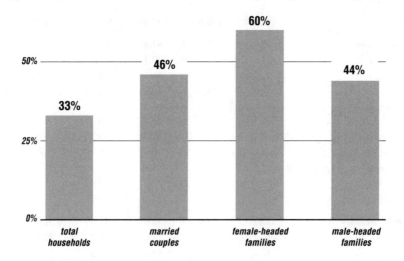

Households with Children by Age of Householder and Type of Household, 2000

(number and percent of households with own children under age 18, by age of householder and type of household, 2000; numbers in thousands)

	total households		married-couple families		female-headed families		male-headed families	
	total	*with children*	*total*	*with children*	*total*	*with children*	*total*	*with children*
Total households	**104,705**	**34,605**	**55,311**	**25,248**	**12,687**	**7,571**	**4,028**	**1,786**
Under age 20	914	216	96	55	295	151	162	9
Aged 20 to 24	4,946	1,784	1,354	779	1,047	891	398	114
Aged 25 to 29	8,520	3,844	3,775	2,439	1,289	1,169	426	235
Aged 30 to 34	10,107	6,042	5,615	4,391	1,443	1,356	460	295
Aged 35 to 39	11,728	7,701	6,886	5,796	1,676	1,529	537	376
Aged 40 to 44	12,227	7,403	7,218	5,609	1,823	1,433	565	361
Aged 45 to 54	20,927	6,617	12,792	5,401	2,299	911	713	305
Aged 55 to 64	13,592	865	8,138	671	1,080	119	351	74
Aged 65 or older	21,744	133	9,437	107	1,735	11	416	15
Total households	**100.0%**	**33.0%**	**100.0%**	**45.6%**	**100.0%**	**59.7%**	**100.0%**	**44.3%**
Under age 20	100.0	23.6	100.0	57.3	100.0	51.2	100.0	5.6
Aged 20 to 24	100.0	36.1	100.0	57.5	100.0	85.1	100.0	28.6
Aged 25 to 29	100.0	45.1	100.0	64.6	100.0	90.7	100.0	55.2
Aged 30 to 34	100.0	59.8	100.0	78.2	100.0	94.0	100.0	64.1
Aged 35 to 39	100.0	65.7	100.0	84.2	100.0	91.2	100.0	70.0
Aged 40 to 44	100.0	60.5	100.0	77.7	100.0	78.6	100.0	63.9
Aged 45 to 54	100.0	31.6	100.0	42.2	100.0	39.6	100.0	42.8
Aged 55 to 64	100.0	6.4	100.0	8.2	100.0	11.0	100.0	21.1
Aged 65 or older	100.0	0.6	100.0	1.1	100.0	0.6	100.0	3.6

Source: Bureau of the Census, America's Families and Living Arrangements: March 2000, *detailed tables for Current Population Report P20-537, Internet site <www.census.gov/population/www/socdemo/hh-fam/p20-537_00.html>; calculations by New Strategist*

Most Families Find Nest Slow to Empty

Many older couples still have children living at home.

Although only 46 percent of married couples have children under age 18 at home, the 56 percent majority have children of any age at home because many children choose to live with their parents well into adulthood. Similarly, while 44 percent of male-headed families have children under age 18 at home, a much larger 65 percent have children of any age at home.

Among married couples, about one-fifth have teens, one-fifth have children aged 6 to 11, and one-fifth have preschoolers at home. Only 4 percent of couples have infants. Those most likely to have teens at home are couples aged 40 to 44, at 49 percent. The majority of couples under age 35 have preschoolers at home, and as many as 18 percent of couples aged 20 to 24 have infants.

Among male-headed families, those headed by 40-to-44-year-olds are most likely to include teenagers, at 40 percent. Of those headed by 25-to-29-year-olds, 42 percent include preschoolers and 10 percent, infants.

Among older couples, a substantial share still have children at home. The proportion does not fall below the majority until the 55-to-64 age group. The majority of families headed by a male householder aged 25 or older have children of any age at home.

■ Parenting responsibilities continue to be important even among older householders because many still have children living under their roof.

Many older couples have children at home

(percent of married couples with children of any age at home, by age of householder, 2000)

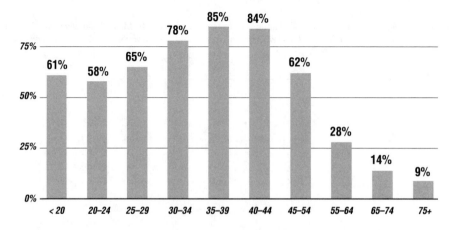

Married Couples by Age of Householder and Age of Children, 2000

(number and percent distribution of married couples by presence of own children at home, by age of householder and age of children, 2000; numbers in thousands)

| | total | with children at home | | | | | |
		of any age	under 18	12 to 17	6 to 11	under 6	under 1
Total couples	**55,311**	**31,065**	**25,248**	**11,567**	**12,501**	**11,393**	**2,264**
Under age 20	96	59	55	5	1	52	14
Aged 20 to 24	1,354	779	779	9	100	754	244
Aged 25 to 29	3,775	2,441	2,439	133	974	2,113	573
Aged 30 to 34	5,615	4,399	4,391	721	2,234	3,355	744
Aged 35 to 39	6,886	5,887	5,796	2,366	3,674	2,964	450
Aged 40 to 44	7,218	6,076	5,609	3,532	3,254	1,463	175
Aged 45 to 54	12,792	7,969	5,401	4,192	2,029	612	56
Aged 55 to 64	8,138	2,300	671	534	198	70	7
Aged 65 to 74	5,929	843	88	66	25	6	–
Aged 75 or older	3,508	312	19	8	12	5	–
Total couples	**100.0%**	**56.2%**	**45.6%**	**20.9%**	**22.6%**	**20.6%**	**4.1%**
Under age 20	100.0	61.5	57.3	5.2	1.0	54.2	14.6
Aged 20 to 24	100.0	57.5	57.5	0.7	7.4	55.7	18.0
Aged 25 to 29	100.0	64.7	64.6	3.5	25.8	56.0	15.2
Aged 30 to 34	100.0	78.3	78.2	12.8	39.8	59.8	13.3
Aged 35 to 39	100.0	85.5	84.2	34.4	53.4	43.0	6.5
Aged 40 to 44	100.0	84.2	77.7	48.9	45.1	20.3	2.4
Aged 45 to 54	100.0	62.3	42.2	32.8	15.9	4.8	0.4
Aged 55 to 64	100.0	28.3	8.2	6.6	2.4	0.9	0.1
Aged 65 to 74	100.0	14.2	1.5	1.1	0.4	0.1	–
Aged 75 or older	100.0	8.9	0.5	0.2	0.3	0.1	–

Note: Numbers will not add to total because households may contain children in more than one age group; (–) means sample is too small to make a reliable estimate.
Source: Bureau of the Census, America's Families and Living Arrangements: March 2000, *detailed tables for Current Population Report P20-537, Internet site <www.census.gov/population/www/socdemo/hh-fam/p20-537_00.html>; calculations by New Strategist*

Male-Headed Families by Age of Householder and Age of Children, 2000

(number and percent distribution of male-headed families by presence of own children at home, by age of householder and age of children, 2000; numbers in thousands)

	total	with children at home					
		of any age	under 18	12 to 17	6 to 11	under 6	under 1
Total male-headed families	**4,028**	**2,630**	**1,786**	**739**	**688**	**706**	**174**
Under age 20	162	11	9	2	–	7	4
Aged 20 to 24	398	115	114	7	10	104	38
Aged 25 to 29	426	239	235	5	82	179	43
Aged 30 to 34	460	298	295	24	165	168	41
Aged 35 to 39	537	389	376	173	172	135	33
Aged 40 to 44	565	442	361	227	146	66	5
Aged 45 to 54	713	545	305	233	86	31	5
Aged 55 to 64	351	257	74	55	23	12	4
Aged 65 to 74	203	154	15	12	5	3	–
Aged 75 or older	213	180	–	–	–	–	–
Total male-headed families	**100.0%**	**65.3%**	**44.3%**	**18.3%**	**17.1%**	**17.5%**	**4.3%**
Under age 20	100.0	6.8	5.6	1.2	–	4.3	2.5
Aged 20 to 24	100.0	28.9	28.6	1.8	2.5	26.1	9.5
Aged 25 to 29	100.0	56.1	55.2	1.2	19.2	42.0	10.1
Aged 30 to 34	100.0	64.8	64.1	5.2	35.9	36.5	8.9
Aged 35 to 39	100.0	72.4	70.0	32.2	32.0	25.1	6.1
Aged 40 to 44	100.0	78.2	63.9	40.2	25.8	11.7	0.9
Aged 45 to 54	100.0	76.4	42.8	32.7	12.1	4.3	0.7
Aged 55 to 64	100.0	73.2	21.1	15.7	6.6	3.4	1.1
Aged 65 to 74	100.0	75.9	7.4	5.9	2.5	1.5	–
Aged 75 or older	100.0	84.5	–	–	–	–	–

Note: Numbers will not add to total because households may contain children in more than one age group; (–) means sample is too small to make a reliable estimate.
Source: Bureau of the Census, America's Families and Living Arrangements: March 2000, detailed tables for Current Population Report P20-537, Internet site <www.census.gov/population/www/socdemo/hh-fam/p20-537_00.html>; calculations by New Strategist

Married Couples Are Much Better Educated than Single Parents

Most couples with children at home have at least some college experience.

Sixty percent of married couples with children under age 18 at home have at least some college experience, and 32 percent are college graduates. They are by far the best educated family heads. Only 52 percent of married couples without children at home have college experience. The educational level of couples without children at home is lower because most are older, and older Americans are less educated than middle-aged and younger adults.

Single parents are far less educated than married couples. Only 17 percent of male family heads are college graduates. The proportion is an even lower 12 percent among female family heads. Forty-five percent of men who head single-parent families have at least some college experience, as do 44 percent of their female counterparts.

■ The greater educational level of married couples, combined with their dual earnings, guarantees much higher incomes for couples than for single-parent families.

College experience is the norm for married couples

(percent of householders with at least some college experience, by type of household, 2000)

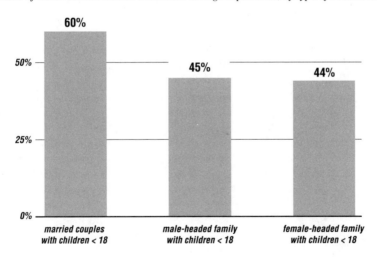

Families by Educational Attainment of Householder and Presence of Children, 2000

(number and percent distribution of families by educational attainment of householder, family type, and presence of own children under age 18 at home, 2000; numbers in thousands)

	married-couple families		female-headed families		male-headed families	
	with children	without children	with children	without children	with children	without children
Total families	**25,248**	**30,062**	**7,571**	**5,116**	**1,786**	**2,242**
Not a high school graduate	2,873	4,517	1,506	1,514	358	544
High school graduate or more	7,314	9,799	2,729	1,709	618	806
Some college	7,062	7,466	2,402	1,264	505	519
Bachelor's degree or more	8,000	8,281	935	629	306	374
Total families	**100.0%**	**100.0%**	**100.0%**	**100.0%**	**100.0%**	**100.0%**
Not a high school graduate	11.4	15.0	19.9	29.6	20.0	24.3
High school graduate or more	29.0	32.6	36.0	33.4	34.6	36.0
Some college	28.0	24.8	31.7	24.7	28.3	23.1
Bachelor's degree or more	31.7	27.5	12.3	12.3	17.1	16.7

Source: Bureau of the Census, America's Families and Living Arrangements: March 2000, *detailed tables for Current Population Report P20-537, Internet site <www.census.gov/population/www/socdemo/hh-fam/p20-537_00.html>; calculations by New Strategist*

Husbands and Wives Are Alike in Many Ways

Most couples are close in age, of the same race and ethnicity, and share the same educational level.

Men usually marry slightly younger women, but most husbands and wives are close in age. Thirty-two percent are within one year of each other in age, and in another 22 percent the husband is only two to three years older than the wife.

Both husband and wife are white in 87 percent of the nation's married couples. In 7 percent both are black, and in 3 percent both are Asian. No single interracial combination accounts for more than 1 percent of couples. Interethnic combinations are more common. In nearly 3 percent of couples, one spouse is Hispanic and the other is non-Hispanic white.

The 54 percent majority of married couples share the same educational level. In 25 percent of couples the husband is more educated than the wife, and in a slightly smaller 21 percent the wife is more educated than the husband.

■ The similarities between husbands and wives mean that high earners tend to marry one another, boosting incomes for some.

Most husbands and wives share the same educational level

(percent distribution of married couples by education of husband and wife, 2000)

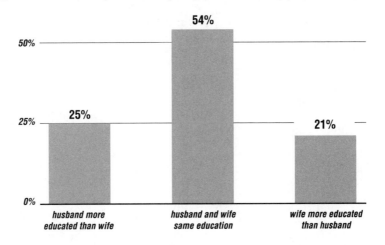

Age Difference between Husbands and Wives, 2000

(number and percent distribution of married-couple family groups by age difference between husband and wife, 2000; numbers in thousands)

	number	percent distribution
Total married couples	**56,497**	**100.0%**
Husband 20 or more years older than wife	414	0.7
Husband 15–19 years older than wife	870	1.5
Husband 10–14 years older than wife	2,817	5.0
Husband 6–9 years older than wife	6,948	12.3
Husband 4–5 years older than wife	7,841	13.9
Husband 2–3 years older than wife	12,674	22.4
Husband and wife within 1 year	17,982	31.8
Wife 2–3 years older than husband	3,399	6.0
Wife 4–5 years older than husband	1,687	3.0
Wife 6–9 years older than husband	1,199	2.1
Wife 10–14 years older than husband	457	0.8
Wife 15–19 years older than husband	120	0.2
Wife 20 or more years older than husband	88	0.2

Source: Bureau of the Census, America's Families and Living Arrangements: March 2000, *detailed tables for Current Population Report P20-537, Internet site <www.census.gov/population/www/socdemo/hh-fam/p20-537_00.html>; calculations by New Strategist*

Race of Husbands and Wives, 2000

(number and percent distribution of married-couple family groups by race of husband and wife, 2000; numbers in thousands)

	number	percent distribution
Total married couples	**56,497**	**100.0%**
Both white	48,917	86.6
Both black	3,989	7.1
Both American Indian	209	0.4
Both Asian	1,914	3.4
Husband white, wife black	95	0.2
Husband white, wife American Indian	203	0.4
Husband white, wife Asian	452	0.8
Husband black, wife white	268	0.5
Husband black, wife American Indian	12	0.0
Husband black, wife Asian	25	0.0
Husband American Indian, wife white	193	0.3
Husband American Indian, wife black	13	0.0
Husband American Indian, wife Asian	2	0.0
Husband Asian, wife white	203	0.4
Husband Asian, wife American Indian	2	0.0

Note: These figures include Hispanics, who may be of any race.
Source: Bureau of the Census, America's Families and Living Arrangements: March 2000, *detailed tables for Current Population Report P20-537, Internet site <www.census.gov/population/www/socdemo/hh-fam/p20-537_00.html>; calculations by New Strategist*

Race and Hispanic Origin of Husbands and Wives, 2000

(number and percent distribution of married-couple family groups by race and Hispanic origin of husband and wife, 2000; numbers in thousands)

	number	percent distribution
Total married couples	**56,497**	**100.0%**
Both non-Hispanic white	42,845	75.8
Both non-Hispanic black	3,809	6.7
Both Hispanic	4,739	8.4
Both non-Hispanic other race	2,059	3.6
Husband non-Hispanic white, wife non-Hispanic black	80	0.1
Husband non-Hispanic white, wife Hispanic	824	1.5
Husband non-Hispanic white, wife non-Hispanic other	600	1.1
Husband non-Hispanic black, wife non-Hispanic white	227	0.4
Husband non-Hispanic black, wife Hispanic	72	0.1
Husband non-Hispanic black, wife non-Hispanic other	35	0.1
Husband Hispanic, wife non-Hispanic white	723	1.3
Husband Hispanic, wife non-Hispanic black	41	0.1
Husband Hispanic, wife non-Hispanic other	47	0.1
Husband non-Hispanic other, wife non-Hispanic white	348	0.6
Husband non-Hispanic other, wife non-Hispanic black	11	0.0
Husband non-Hispanic other, wife Hispanic	35	0.1

Source: Bureau of the Census, America's Families and Living Arrangements: March 2000, *detailed tables for Current Population Report P20-537, Internet site <www.census.gov/population/www/socdemo/hh-fam/p20-537_00.html>; calculations by New Strategist*

Educational Difference between Husbands and Wives, 2000

(number and percent distribution of husbands and wives by educational attainment, and number and percent of married-couple family groups by educational difference between husband and wife, 2000; numbers in thousands)

	number	percent distribution
Total husbands	**56,497**	**100.0%**
Not a high school graduate	8,314	14.7
High school graduate	17,506	31.0
Some college	14,002	24.8
Bachelor's degree or higher	16,674	29.5
Total wives	**56,497**	**100.0**
Not a high school graduate	7,160	12.7
High school graduate	19,950	35.3
Some college	14,968	26.5
Bachelor's degree or higher	14,419	25.5
Total married couples	**56,497**	**100.0**
Husband more educated than wife	13,843	24.5
Husband and wife same education	30,590	54.1
Wife more educated than husband	12,064	21.4

Source: Bureau of the Census, America's Families and Living Arrangements: March 2000, *detailed tables for Current Population Report P20-537, Internet site <www.census.gov/population/www/socdemo/hh-fam/p20-537_00.html>; calculations by New Strategist*

Nearly 4 Million Men Are Unmarried Partners to Women

Men aged 25 to 29 are most likely to be unmarried partners.

In 2000, more than 3.8 million men were partners in opposite-sex unmarried-partner households. In other words, they were living as married but had not tied the knot. While the proportion of households headed by married couples has been shrinking over the past few decades, if unmarried partners were counted in the total, the decline in married couples would be smaller than the official numbers suggest.

The 53 percent majority of male partners are under age 35. Only 21 percent are aged 45 or older. Being an unmarried partner is most common among men aged 25 to 29, at 8 percent. The proportion stands at 7 percent among men aged 30 to 34, then falls with increasing age.

■ Although the number of cohabiting couples has grown over the years, it is still tiny in comparison to married couples.

Many twentysomething men are unmarried partners

(percent of men who are partners in opposite-sex unmarried-partner households, by age, 2000)

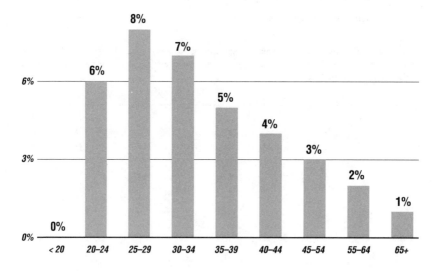

Men in Unmarried-Partner Households by Age, 2000

(total number of men, number and percent distribution of men who are partners in opposite sex unmarried-partner households, and unmarried-partner share of total men, by age, 2000; numbers in thousands)

| | total | unmarried partners | | |
		number	percent distribution	share of total
Total men	**103,114**	**3,822**	**100.0%**	**3.7%**
Under age 20	10,295	50	1.3	0.5
Aged 20 to 24	9,208	547	14.3	5.9
Aged 25 to 29	8,942	734	19.2	8.2
Aged 30 to 34	9,621	679	17.8	7.1
Aged 35 to 39	11,032	518	13.6	4.7
Aged 40 to 44	11,103	482	12.6	4.3
Aged 45 to 54	17,889	459	12.0	2.6
Aged 55 to 64	11,137	232	6.1	2.1
Aged 65 or older	13,886	120	3.1	0.9

Source: Bureau of the Census, America's Families and Living Arrangements: March 2000, *detailed tables for Current Population Report P20-537, Internet site <www.census.gov/population/www/socdemo/hh-fam/p20-537_00.html>; calculations by New Strategist*

8

Population

Fiftysomethings grew fastest during the 1990s.

The number of men aged 50 to 54 climbed 57 percent between 1990 and 2000 as boomers filled the age group.

Women outnumber men by a growing margin with age.

Men account for only 41 percent of Americans aged 65 or older. Among people aged 85 or older, men are an even smaller 29 percent share.

Fewer than 70 percent of the nation's males are non-Hispanic white.

Hispanics outnumber blacks among the nation's males. The 2000 census counted 18 million Hispanic males and 17 million black males.

The number of males grew fastest in Nevada.

The number of males grew in all 50 states, but males declined by 5 percent in the District of Columbia.

Sixteen percent of males moved between 1999 and 2000.

Men in their twenties are most likely to move. Among movers, older men are most likely to move out of state.

Males account for half the nation's foreign-born.

They are a 45 percent minority of legal immigrants, but they accounted for most immigrants from Cuba in 2000.

Forty- and Fiftysomethings Grew the Fastest

The number of 50-to-54-year-olds males grew more than 50 percent during the 1990s.

The number of American males increased 14 percent between 1990 and 2000, climbing from 121 million to 138 million. Some age groups grew much faster than average, while others saw declines.

The aging of the baby-boom generation was behind the rapid growth in the number of men in their late forties and early fifties during the 1990s. The oldest boomers, born in 1946, turned 54 in 2000. During the next ten years, the oldest boomers will enter their sixties, making the sixtysomething age group grow faster than any other.

The number of men declined in several age groups during the 1990s. As generation X, which is much smaller than the baby-boom generation, entered its late twenties and early thirties, the number of men aged 25 to 34 fell. And as the small generation born during the Depression aged, the number of men aged 65 to 69 dropped by 2 percent.

■ When boomers were teens and young adults, youth issues commanded attention. Now that boomers are approaching old age, retirement planning is taking center stage.

The 25-to-29 age group experienced the biggest decline

(percent change in number of males in selected age groups, 1990–2000)

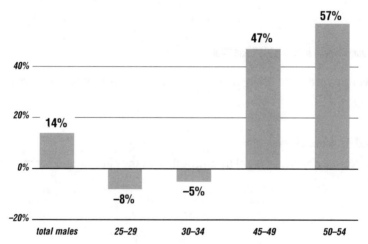

Males by Age, 1990 and 2000 Censuses

(number of males, 1990 and 2000, percent change in number, 1990–2000; numbers in thousands)

	1990	2000	percent change 1990–2000
Total males	**121,284**	**138,054**	**13.8%**
Under age 5	9,603	9,811	2.2
Aged 5 to 9	9,236	10,523	13.9
Aged 10 to 14	8,742	10,520	20.3
Aged 15 to 19	9,178	10,391	13.2
Aged 20 to 24	9,749	9,688	–0.6
Aged 25 to 29	10,708	9,799	–8.5
Aged 30 to 34	10,866	10,322	–5.0
Aged 35 to 39	9,837	11,319	15.1
Aged 40 to 44	8,679	11,129	28.2
Aged 45 to 49	6,741	9,890	46.7
Aged 50 to 54	5,494	8,608	56.7
Aged 55 to 59	5,009	6,509	29.9
Aged 60 to 64	4,947	5,137	3.8
Aged 65 to 69	4,508	4,400	–2.4
Aged 70 to 74	3,400	3,903	14.8
Aged 75 to 79	2,389	3,044	27.4
Aged 80 to 84	1,356	1,835	35.3
Aged 85 or older	842	1,227	45.7
Aged 18 to 24	13,744	13,874	0.9
Aged 18 or older	88,520	100,994	14.1
Aged 65 or older	12,495	14,410	15.3

Source: U.S. Census Bureau, Census 2000 Summary File 1; and <www.census.gov/population/estimates/ nation/intfile2-1.txt>; calculations by New Strategist

Males Are a Minority

Only among children and young adults are males more numerous.

Among the nation's 281 million inhabitants in 2000, 138 million were male—49 percent of the total. Females outnumber males by more than 5 million although more boys are born than girls. Because the death rate is higher for males than females at every age, females eventually begin to outnumber males. This shift occurs in the 35-to-39 age group.

With age, women increasingly outnumber men. Men account for only 41 percent of people aged 65 or older. Among the oldest Americans, men account for fewer than one-third of the total—just 29 percent of people aged 85 or older are men.

■ Because men are a minority of older Americans, women are the primary consumers of health care and the great majority of nursing home residents.

Females outnumber males by more than 5 million

(total population by sex, 2000; numbers in millions)

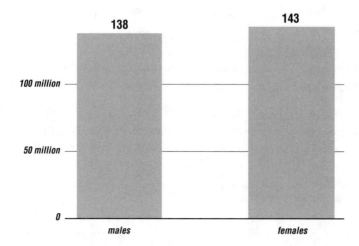

Male Share of Total Population by Age, 2000 Census

(number of total people, number of males, and male share of total, by age, 2000)

	total	males number	share of total
Total people	**281,421,906**	**138,053,563**	**49.1%**
Under age 5	19,175,798	9,810,733	51.2
Aged 5 to 9	20,549,505	10,523,277	51.2
Aged 10 to 14	20,528,072	10,520,197	51.2
Aged 15 to 19	20,219,890	10,391,004	51.4
Aged 20 to 24	18,964,001	9,687,814	51.1
Aged 25 to 29	19,381,336	9,798,760	50.6
Aged 30 to 34	20,510,388	10,321,769	50.3
Aged 35 to 39	22,706,664	11,318,696	49.8
Aged 40 to 44	22,441,863	11,129,102	49.6
Aged 45 to 49	20,092,404	9,889,506	49.2
Aged 50 to 54	17,585,548	8,607,724	48.9
Aged 55 to 59	13,469,237	6,508,729	48.3
Aged 60 to 64	10,805,447	5,136,627	47.5
Aged 65 to 69	9,533,545	4,400,362	46.2
Aged 70 to 74	8,857,441	3,902,912	44.1
Aged 75 to 79	7,415,813	3,044,456	41.1
Aged 80 to 84	4,945,367	1,834,897	37.1
Aged 85 or older	4,239,587	1,226,998	28.9
Aged 18 to 24	27,143,454	13,873,829	51.1
Aged 18 or older	209,128,094	100,994,367	48.3
Aged 65 or older	34,991,753	14,409,625	41.2

Source: U.S. Census Bureau, Census 2000 Summary File 1; calculations by New Strategist

Hispanics Outnumber Blacks among American Males

Fewer than 70 percent of males are non-Hispanic white.

The 2000 census counted 95 million non-Hispanic white males, 69 percent of the total male population. Hispanics outnumber blacks among males by more than 800,000. Hispanics accounted for 13.2 percent and blacks for 12.5 percent of the male population in 2000.

Among children, Hispanics and blacks make up even larger shares of the population. Only 59 percent of boys under age 5 are non-Hispanic white, while 19 percent are Hispanic and 16 percent are black. In contrast, among men aged 65 or older, 84 percent are non-Hispanic white, only 5 percent are Hispanic, and 8 percent are black.

There are fewer males than females in most racial and ethnic groups. Among Hispanics, however, the opposite is true because of the youthfulness of the Hispanic population. With age, women increasingly outnumber men. The male share of people aged 65 or older ranges from a low of 38 percent among blacks to a high of 44 percent among Native Hawaiians.

■ As the nation's youth grow older, the racial and ethnic diversity of both the male and the female populations will increase.

About one in four males is Hispanic or black

(percent distribution of males by race and Hispanic origin, 2000)

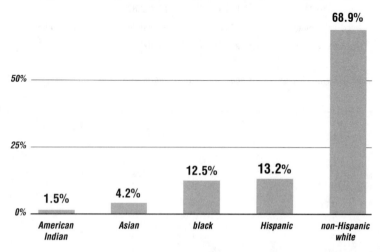

Males by Race and Hispanic Origin, 2000 Census

(number and percent distribution of males by race and Hispanic origin, 2000)

	number	percent distribution
Total males	**138,053,563**	**100.0%**
American Indian	2,033,242	1.5
Asian	5,779,038	4.2
Black	17,315,333	12.5
Hispanic	18,161,795	13.2
Native Hawaiian	439,681	0.3
White	106,521,196	77.2
Non-Hispanic	95,157,731	68.9
Other race	9,635,774	7.0

Note: Numbers will not add to total because each racial category includes those who identified themselves as the race alone and those who identified themselves as the race in combination with one or more other races, and because Hispanics may be of any race. Non-Hispanic whites are those who identified themselves as white alone and non-Hispanic. For more information about the other race population, see glossary.
Source: U.S. Census Bureau, Census 2000 Summary File 1; calculations by New Strategist

Males by Age, Race, and Hispanic Origin, 2000 Census

(total number of males and percent distribution by age, race, and Hispanic origin, 2000)

	total		American Indian	Asian	black	Hispanic	Native Hawaiian	white		other race
	number	percent						total	non-Hispanic	
Total males	**138,053,563**	**100.0%**	**1.5%**	**4.2%**	**12.5%**	**13.2%**	**0.3%**	**77.2%**	**68.9%**	**7.0%**
Under age 5	9,810,733	100.0	1.9	4.7	16.4	19.4	0.5	71.4	58.6	10.5
Aged 5 to 9	10,523,277	100.0	1.9	4.4	16.8	17.6	0.4	71.4	60.1	9.5
Aged 10 to 14	10,520,197	100.0	1.9	4.3	16.1	15.4	0.4	72.8	63.0	8.2
Aged 15 to 19	10,391,004	100.0	1.9	4.5	15.0	16.3	0.4	72.6	62.9	8.9
Aged 20 to 24	9,687,814	100.0	1.7	5.0	13.9	19.4	0.4	71.2	60.5	11.0
Aged 25 to 29	9,798,760	100.0	1.5	5.6	12.9	18.6	0.4	71.9	61.6	10.5
Aged 30 to 34	10,321,769	100.0	1.4	5.0	12.5	16.2	0.4	74.4	65.1	8.9
Aged 35 to 39	11,318,696	100.0	1.4	4.3	12.1	13.0	0.3	77.1	69.2	6.9
Aged 40 to 44	11,129,102	100.0	1.4	4.0	11.7	10.6	0.3	79.0	72.4	5.6
Aged 45 to 49	9,889,506	100.0	1.3	3.9	11.0	9.0	0.2	80.7	74.9	4.7
Aged 50 to 54	8,607,724	100.0	1.3	3.7	9.9	7.7	0.2	82.8	77.5	3.8
Aged 55 to 59	6,508,729	100.0	1.2	3.4	9.3	7.0	0.2	84.3	79.2	3.1
Aged 60 to 64	5,136,627	100.0	1.1	3.4	9.3	6.8	0.2	84.6	79.4	2.8
Aged 65 to 69	4,400,362	100.0	0.9	2.9	8.7	6.1	0.2	86.3	81.3	2.3
Aged 70 to 74	3,902,912	100.0	0.8	2.6	7.6	5.3	0.1	88.1	83.7	1.8
Aged 75 to 79	3,044,456	100.0	0.7	2.4	6.9	4.4	0.1	89.3	85.5	1.6
Aged 80 to 84	1,834,897	100.0	0.6	2.1	6.4	3.7	0.1	90.3	87.0	1.3
Aged 85 or older	1,226,998	100.0	0.6	2.2	7.1	4.0	0.1	89.5	86.0	1.5

(continued)

(continued from previous page)

	total		American Indian	Asian	black	Hispanic	Native Hawaiian	white		other race
	number	percent						total	non-Hispanic	
Aged 18 to 24	13,873,829	100.0%	1.7%	4.9%	14.1%	18.7%	0.4%	71.4%	61.0%	10.6%
Aged 18 or older	100,994,367	100.0	1.3	4.1	11.2	11.7	0.3	79.0	71.8	6.2
Aged 65 or older	14,409,625	100.0	0.8	2.5	7.6	5.0	0.1	88.2	84.0	1.8

Note: Percentages will not add to 100 because each racial category includes those who identified themselves as the race alone and those who identified themselves as the race in combination with one or more other races, and because Hispanics may be of any race. Non-Hispanic whites are those who identified themselves as white alone and non-Hispanic. For more information about the other race population, see glossary.
Source: U.S. Census Bureau, Census 2000 Summary File 1; calculations by New Strategist

Male Share of American Indian Population by Age, 2000 Census

(total number of American Indians, number of American Indian males, and male share of total, by age, 2000)

	total	number	share of total
		males	
Total American Indians	**4,119,301**	**2,033,242**	**49.4%**
Under age 5	358,816	182,829	51.0
Aged 5 to 9	389,906	197,044	50.5
Aged 10 to 14	400,989	203,414	50.7
Aged 15 to 19	381,024	194,223	51.0
Aged 20 to 24	315,568	161,565	51.2
Aged 25 to 29	292,807	148,841	50.8
Aged 30 to 34	294,716	147,876	50.2
Aged 35 to 39	326,794	160,339	49.1
Aged 40 to 44	317,193	152,855	48.2
Aged 45 to 49	273,977	131,555	48.0
Aged 50 to 54	227,045	109,094	48.0
Aged 55 to 59	162,057	77,624	47.9
Aged 60 to 64	118,746	56,759	47.8
Aged 65 to 69	88,510	40,822	46.1
Aged 70 to 74	68,110	30,019	44.1
Aged 75 to 79	49,271	20,080	40.8
Aged 80 to 84	29,374	10,642	36.2
Aged 85 or older	24,398	7,661	31.4
Aged 18 to 24	462,801	236,924	51.2
Aged 18 or older	2,735,799	1,331,091	48.7
Aged 65 or older	259,663	109,224	42.1

Note: American Indians include those who identified themselves as American Indian alone and those who identified themselves as American Indian in combination with one or more other races; American Indians include Alaska Natives.
Source: U.S. Census Bureau, Census 2000 Summary File 1; calculations by New Strategist

Male Share of Asian Population by Age, 2000 Census

(total number of Asians, number of Asian males, and male share of total, by age, 2000)

	total	males number	males share of total
Total Asian	**11,898,828**	**5,779,038**	**48.6%**
Under age 5	919,078	463,968	50.5
Aged 5 to 9	897,412	459,741	51.2
Aged 10 to 14	873,617	448,573	51.3
Aged 15 to 19	916,676	466,383	50.9
Aged 20 to 24	961,389	479,613	49.9
Aged 25 to 29	1,116,520	548,855	49.2
Aged 30 to 34	1,062,354	517,995	48.8
Aged 35 to 39	1,014,467	491,818	48.5
Aged 40 to 44	938,398	445,291	47.5
Aged 45 to 49	820,538	381,487	46.5
Aged 50 to 54	678,180	314,262	46.3
Aged 55 to 59	468,743	220,490	47.0
Aged 60 to 64	369,731	173,174	46.8
Aged 65 to 69	295,106	129,185	43.8
Aged 70 to 74	236,587	99,979	42.3
Aged 75 to 79	167,596	72,229	43.1
Aged 80 to 84	94,760	39,079	41.2
Aged 85 or older	67,676	26,916	39.8
Aged 18 to 24	1,346,262	674,375	50.1
Aged 18 or older	8,676,918	4,135,135	47.7
Aged 65 or older	861,725	367,388	42.6

Note: Asians include those who identified themselves as Asian alone and those who identified themselves as Asian in combination with one or more other races.
Source: U.S. Census Bureau, Census 2000 Summary File 1; calculations by New Strategist

Male Share of Black Population by Age, 2000 Census

(total number of blacks, number of black males, and male share of total, by age, 2000)

		males	
	total	*number*	*share of total*
Total blacks	**36,419,434**	**17,315,333**	**47.5%**
Under age 5	3,166,859	1,607,056	50.7
Aged 5 to 9	3,490,717	1,770,636	50.7
Aged 10 to 14	3,332,324	1,689,401	50.7
Aged 15 to 19	3,093,824	1,562,487	50.5
Aged 20 to 24	2,759,272	1,342,046	48.6
Aged 25 to 29	2,658,466	1,262,912	47.5
Aged 30 to 34	2,715,440	1,285,177	47.3
Aged 35 to 39	2,917,159	1,370,837	47.0
Aged 40 to 44	2,781,722	1,305,119	46.9
Aged 45 to 49	2,339,345	1,086,162	46.4
Aged 50 to 54	1,855,083	853,543	46.0
Aged 55 to 59	1,340,069	603,483	45.0
Aged 60 to 64	1,088,474	480,152	44.1
Aged 65 to 69	900,785	382,575	42.5
Aged 70 to 74	746,514	297,934	39.9
Aged 75 to 79	560,952	210,980	37.6
Aged 80 to 84	353,135	118,261	33.5
Aged 85 or older	319,294	86,572	27.1
Aged 18 to 24	3,997,739	1,958,702	49.0
Aged 18 or older	24,574,177	11,302,409	46.0
Aged 65 or older	2,880,680	1,096,322	38.1

Note: Black numbers include those who identified themselves as black alone and those who identified themselves as black in combination with one or more other races.
Source: U.S. Census Bureau, Census 2000 Summary File 1; calculations by New Strategist

Male Share of Hispanic Population by Age, 2000 Census

(total number of Hispanics, number of Hispanic males, and male share of total, by age, 2000)

		males	
	total	*number*	*share of total*
Total Hispanics	**35,305,818**	**18,161,795**	**51.4%**
Under age 5	3,717,974	1,900,431	51.1
Aged 5 to 9	3,623,680	1,851,885	51.1
Aged 10 to 14	3,163,412	1,617,185	51.1
Aged 15 to 19	3,171,646	1,688,556	53.2
Aged 20 to 24	3,409,427	1,875,139	55.0
Aged 25 to 29	3,385,334	1,826,146	53.9
Aged 30 to 34	3,124,901	1,668,064	53.4
Aged 35 to 39	2,825,158	1,474,462	52.2
Aged 40 to 44	2,304,152	1,178,548	51.1
Aged 45 to 49	1,775,168	886,695	49.9
Aged 50 to 54	1,360,935	664,236	48.8
Aged 55 to 59	960,033	456,165	47.5
Aged 60 to 64	750,407	347,409	46.3
Aged 65 to 69	599,353	268,184	44.7
Aged 70 to 74	477,266	205,691	43.1
Aged 75 to 79	326,726	135,463	41.5
Aged 80 to 84	179,538	67,919	37.8
Aged 85 or older	150,708	49,617	32.9
Aged 18 to 24	4,743,880	2,598,352	54.8
Aged 18 or older	22,963,559	11,826,951	51.5
Aged 65 or older	1,733,591	726,874	41.9

Source: U.S. Census Bureau, Census 2000 Summary File 1; calculations by New Strategist

Male Share of Native Hawaiian Population by Age, 2000 Census

(total number of Native Hawaiians, number of Native Hawaiian males, and male share of total, by age, 2000)

	total	males number	males share of total
Total Native Hawaiians	**874,414**	**439,681**	**50.3%**
Under age 5	88,495	45,389	51.3
Aged 5 to 9	90,039	45,782	50.8
Aged 10 to 14	85,129	43,715	51.4
Aged 15 to 19	86,341	44,303	51.3
Aged 20 to 24	81,872	42,171	51.5
Aged 25 to 29	71,967	36,948	51.3
Aged 30 to 34	67,769	34,082	50.3
Aged 35 to 39	67,419	33,631	49.9
Aged 40 to 44	58,697	29,332	50.0
Aged 45 to 49	47,899	23,599	49.3
Aged 50 to 54	37,994	18,849	49.6
Aged 55 to 59	27,111	13,278	49.0
Aged 60 to 64	19,880	9,495	47.8
Aged 65 to 69	15,429	7,299	47.3
Aged 70 to 74	11,572	5,052	43.7
Aged 75 to 79	7,927	3,319	41.9
Aged 80 to 84	4,793	1,896	39.6
Aged 85 or older	4,081	1,541	37.8
Aged 18 to 24	118,405	60,790	51.3
Aged 18 or older	560,943	279,111	49.8
Aged 65 or older	43,802	19,107	43.6

Note: Native Hawaiians include those who identified themselves as Native Hawaiian alone and those who identified themselves as Native Hawaiian in combination with one or more other races; Native Hawaiians include other Pacific Islanders.
Source: U.S. Census Bureau, Census 2000 Summary File 1; calculations by New Strategist

Male Share of White Population by Age, 2000 Census

(total number of whites, number of white males, and male share of total, by age, 2000)

	total	males number	males share of total
Total whites	**216,930,975**	**106,521,196**	**49.1%**
Under age 5	13,656,252	7,002,928	51.3
Aged 5 to 9	14,632,897	7,509,387	51.3
Aged 10 to 14	14,899,672	7,654,064	51.4
Aged 15 to 19	14,666,888	7,542,069	51.4
Aged 20 to 24	13,497,559	6,897,429	51.1
Aged 25 to 29	13,901,171	7,050,004	50.7
Aged 30 to 34	15,194,805	7,683,565	50.6
Aged 35 to 39	17,395,108	8,730,298	50.2
Aged 40 to 44	17,588,919	8,795,219	50.0
Aged 45 to 49	16,070,375	7,985,576	49.7
Aged 50 to 54	14,423,239	7,126,081	49.4
Aged 55 to 59	11,256,685	5,488,177	48.8
Aged 60 to 64	9,059,558	4,347,007	48.0
Aged 65 to 69	8,130,453	3,795,563	46.7
Aged 70 to 74	7,722,044	3,440,027	44.5
Aged 75 to 79	6,585,517	2,719,299	41.3
Aged 80 to 84	4,442,647	1,656,659	37.3
Aged 85 or older	3,807,186	1,097,844	28.8
Aged 18 to 24	19,389,359	9,912,019	51.1
Aged 18 or older	164,967,066	79,827,338	48.4
Aged 65 or older	30,687,847	12,709,392	41.4

Note: Whites include those who identified themselves as white alone and those who identified themselves as white in combination with one or more other races.
Source: U.S. Census Bureau, Census 2000 Summary File 1; calculations by New Strategist

Male Share of Non-Hispanic White Population by Age, 2000 Census

(total number of non-Hispanic whites, number of non-Hispanic white males, and male share of total, by age, 2000)

	total	males number	males share of total
Total non-Hispanic whites	**194,552,774**	**95,157,731**	**48.9%**
Under age 5	11,194,346	5,747,742	51.3
Aged 5 to 9	12,303,903	6,321,695	51.4
Aged 10 to 14	12,882,540	6,623,228	51.4
Aged 15 to 19	12,759,934	6,530,937	51.2
Aged 20 to 24	11,594,742	5,865,075	50.6
Aged 25 to 29	11,990,863	6,038,628	50.4
Aged 30 to 34	13,365,410	6,723,177	50.3
Aged 35 to 39	15,665,973	7,835,996	50.0
Aged 40 to 44	16,135,362	8,058,013	49.9
Aged 45 to 49	14,908,211	7,410,884	49.7
Aged 50 to 54	13,478,949	6,669,501	49.5
Aged 55 to 59	10,545,669	5,151,858	48.9
Aged 60 to 64	8,482,012	4,079,327	48.1
Aged 65 to 69	7,650,827	3,578,792	46.8
Aged 70 to 74	7,327,622	3,267,502	44.6
Aged 75 to 79	6,307,373	2,603,467	41.3
Aged 80 to 84	4,284,906	1,597,046	37.3
Aged 85 or older	3,674,132	1,054,863	28.7
Aged 18 to 24	16,708,378	8,460,829	50.6
Aged 18 or older	150,525,687	72,529,883	48.2
Aged 65 or older	29,244,860	12,101,670	41.4

Note: Non-Hispanic whites include only those who identified themselves as white alone and non-Hispanic.
Source: U.S. Census Bureau, Census 2000 Summary File 1; calculations by New Strategist

Male Share of the Other Race Population by Age, 2000 Census

(total number of people of other race, number of other race males, and male share of total, by age, 2000)

	total	males number	males share of total
Total people of other race	**18,521,486**	**9,635,774**	**52.0%**
Under age 5	2,016,773	1,032,510	51.2
Aged 5 to 9	1,948,423	997,252	51.2
Aged 10 to 14	1,699,140	866,995	51.0
Aged 15 to 19	1,748,498	922,430	52.8
Aged 20 to 24	1,941,639	1,066,863	54.9
Aged 25 to 29	1,887,344	1,028,593	54.5
Aged 30 to 34	1,691,079	915,139	54.1
Aged 35 to 39	1,487,065	785,647	52.8
Aged 40 to 44	1,205,498	626,174	51.9
Aged 45 to 49	901,493	460,413	51.1
Aged 50 to 54	651,338	325,617	50.0
Aged 55 to 59	416,516	203,150	48.8
Aged 60 to 64	301,449	142,365	47.2
Aged 65 to 69	222,380	99,313	44.7
Aged 70 to 74	169,146	72,061	42.6
Aged 75 to 79	116,047	47,912	41.3
Aged 80 to 84	64,082	24,678	38.5
Aged 85 or older	53,576	18,662	34.8
Aged 18 to 24	2,688,472	1,467,536	54.6
Aged 18 or older	11,855,485	6,217,260	52.4
Aged 65 or older	625,231	262,626	42.0

Note: People of other race include those who identified themselves as other race alone and those who identified themselves as other race in combination with one or more other races; for more about the other race population, see glossary.
Source: U.S. Census Bureau, Census 2000 Summary File 1; calculations by New Strategist

Male Population Grew Fastest in the West

Every state gained males, the number growing the fastest in Nevada.

The number of males grew 14 percent between 1990 and 2000, but in the West it rose 20 percent. Not far behind was the 18 percent gain in the South, which is home to the largest share of the population.

The number of males grew in all 50 states during the 1990s, the biggest gain (66 percent) occurring in Nevada. The number of males fell by 5 percent in the District of Columbia. State populations are split nearly fifty-fifty between males and females, but males have a slight edge in some states. Alaska has the largest share of males (52 percent) followed by Nevada (51 percent). The District of Columbia has the smallest percentage of males (47 percent), followed by Rhode Island (48 percent).

■ States with youthful populations, such as Utah, tend to have more males than females. States with older populations, such as Pennsylvania, tend to have more females than males.

The South is home to the largest share of males

(percent distribution of males by region, 2000)

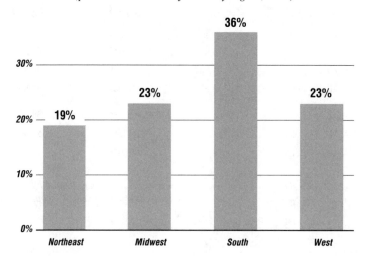

Males by Region, 1990 and 2000 Censuses

(number and percent distribution of males by region, 1990 and 2000; percent change in number, 1990–2000)

| | 1990 | | 2000 | | |
	number	percent distribution	number	percent distribution	percent change 1990–2000
Total males	**121,239,418**	**100.0%**	**138,053,563**	**100.0%**	**13.9%**
Northeast	24,435,623	20.2	25,897,327	18.8	6.0
Midwest	28,971,653	23.9	31,555,438	22.9	8.9
South	41,491,327	34.2	49,057,320	35.5	18.2
West	26,340,815	21.7	31,543,478	22.8	19.8

Source: Bureau of the Census, Gender: 2000, Census 2000 Brief, C2KBR/01-9, 2001

Males by State, 1990 and 2000 Censuses

(number of males by state, 1990 and 2000; percent change, 1990–2000)

	1990	2000	percent change 1990–2000
Total males	**121,239,418**	**138,053,563**	**13.9%**
Alabama	1,936,162	2,146,504	10.9
Alaska	289,867	324,112	11.8
Arizona	1,810,691	2,561,057	41.4
Arkansas	1,133,076	1,304,693	15.1
California	14,897,627	16,874,892	13.3
Colorado	1,631,295	2,165,983	32.8
Connecticut	1,592,873	1,649,319	3.5
Delaware	322,968	380,541	17.8
District of Columbia	282,970	269,366	-4.8
Florida	6,261,719	7,797,715	24.5
Georgia	3,144,503	4,027,113	28.1
Hawaii	563,891	608,671	7.9
Idaho	500,956	648,660	29.5
Illinois	5,552,233	6,080,336	9.5
Indiana	2,688,281	2,982,474	10.9
Iowa	1,344,802	1,435,515	6.7
Kansas	1,214,645	1,328,474	9.4
Kentucky	1,785,235	1,975,368	10.7
Louisiana	2,031,386	2,162,903	6.5
Maine	597,850	620,309	3.8
Maryland	2,318,671	2,557,794	10.3
Massachusetts	2,888,745	3,058,816	5.9
Michigan	4,512,781	4,873,095	8.0
Minnesota	2,145,183	2,435,631	13.5
Mississippi	1,230,617	1,373,554	11.6
Missouri	2,464,315	2,720,177	10.4
Montana	395,769	449,480	13.6
Nebraska	769,439	843,351	9.6
Nevada	611,880	1,018,051	66.4
New Hampshire	543,544	607,687	11.8
New Jersey	3,735,685	4,082,813	9.3
New Mexico	745,253	894,317	20.0

(continued)

(continued from previous page)

	1990	2000	percent change 1990–2000
New York	8,625,673	9,146,748	6.0%
North Carolina	3,214,290	3,942,695	22.7
North Dakota	318,201	320,524	0.7
Ohio	5,226,340	5,512,262	5.5
Oklahoma	1,530,819	1,695,895	10.8
Oregon	1,397,073	1,696,550	21.4
Pennsylvania	5,694,265	5,929,663	4.1
Rhode Island	481,496	503,635	4.6
South Carolina	1,688,510	1,948,929	15.4
South Dakota	342,498	374,558	9.4
Tennessee	2,348,928	2,770,275	17.9
Texas	8,365,963	10,352,910	23.8
Utah	855,759	1,119,031	30.8
Vermont	275,492	298,337	8.3
Virginia	3,033,974	3,471,895	14.4
Washington	2,413,747	2,934,300	21.6
West Virginia	861,536	879,170	2.0
Wisconsin	2,392,935	2,649,041	10.7
Wyoming	227,007	248,374	9.4

Source: Bureau of the Census, Gender: 2000, Census 2000 Brief, C2KBR/01-9, 2001

Male Share of Total Population by State, 2000 Census

(total number of people, number of males, and male share of total, by state, 2000)

	total	males number	males share of total
Total population	**281,421,906**	**138,053,563**	**49.1%**
Alabama	4,447,100	2,146,504	48.3
Alaska	626,932	324,112	51.7
Arizona	5,130,632	2,561,057	49.9
Arkansas	2,673,400	1,304,693	48.8
California	33,871,648	16,874,892	49.8
Colorado	4,301,261	2,165,983	50.4
Connecticut	3,405,565	1,649,319	48.4
Delaware	783,600	380,541	48.6
District of Columbia	572,059	269,366	47.1
Florida	15,982,378	7,797,715	48.8
Georgia	8,186,453	4,027,113	49.2
Hawaii	1,211,537	608,671	50.2
Idaho	1,293,953	648,660	50.1
Illinois	12,419,293	6,080,336	49.0
Indiana	6,080,485	2,982,474	49.0
Iowa	2,926,324	1,435,515	49.1
Kansas	2,688,418	1,328,474	49.4
Kentucky	4,041,769	1,975,368	48.9
Louisiana	4,468,976	2,162,903	48.4
Maine	1,274,923	620,309	48.7
Maryland	5,296,486	2,557,794	48.3
Massachusetts	6,349,097	3,058,816	48.2
Michigan	9,938,444	4,873,095	49.0
Minnesota	4,919,479	2,435,631	49.5
Mississippi	2,844,658	1,373,554	48.3
Missouri	5,595,211	2,720,177	48.6
Montana	902,195	449,480	49.8
Nebraska	1,711,263	843,351	49.3
Nevada	1,998,257	1,018,051	50.9
New Hampshire	1,235,786	607,687	49.2
New Jersey	8,414,350	4,082,813	48.5
New Mexico	1,819,046	894,317	49.2

(continued)

(continued from previous page)

	total	males number	males share of total
New York	18,976,457	9,146,748	48.2%
North Carolina	8,049,313	3,942,695	49.0
North Dakota	642,200	320,524	49.9
Ohio	11,353,140	5,512,262	48.6
Oklahoma	3,450,654	1,695,895	49.1
Oregon	3,421,399	1,696,550	49.6
Pennsylvania	12,281,054	5,929,663	48.3
Rhode Island	1,048,319	503,635	48.0
South Carolina	4,012,012	1,948,929	48.6
South Dakota	754,844	374,558	49.6
Tennessee	5,689,283	2,770,275	48.7
Texas	20,851,820	10,352,910	49.6
Utah	2,233,169	1,119,031	50.1
Vermont	608,827	298,337	49.0
Virginia	7,078,515	3,471,895	49.0
Washington	5,894,121	2,934,300	49.8
West Virginia	1,808,344	879,170	48.6
Wisconsin	5,363,675	2,649,041	49.4
Wyoming	493,782	248,374	50.3

Source: Bureau of the Census, Gender: 2000, Census 2000 Brief, C2KBR/01-9, 2001; calculations by New Strategist

Sixteen Percent of Males Move Each Year

Most move within the same county.

The mobility rate is highest among men aged 20 to 29, about one-third of whom moved between March 1999 and March 2000. There are many reasons why the mobility rate is highest for people in their twenties. Some young men are moving out of their parents' home into their own apartment. Some are going to college, while others are leaving college or the military for jobs elsewhere. The mobility rate falls with age as people buy homes and establish roots in a community. The mobility rate is lowest among men aged 65 or older, fewer than 5 percent of whom move each year.

Most moves are local. The 56 percent majority of male movers stayed within the same county. Only 9 percent moved to a different state. Among movers, men aged 40 or older are more likely than younger men to move to a different state. Many of these moves are job related. Retirement accounts for a large share of moves among older men. Among movers, men aged 62 or older are most likely to move to a different region, many leaving the North for the South in retirement.

■ Americans are less likely to move today than in the 1950s and 1960s, in part because of the increase in two-income couples. When both husband and wife have a job, moving is more difficult.

Few moves are out-of-state

(percent distribution of male movers by type of move, 1999–2000)

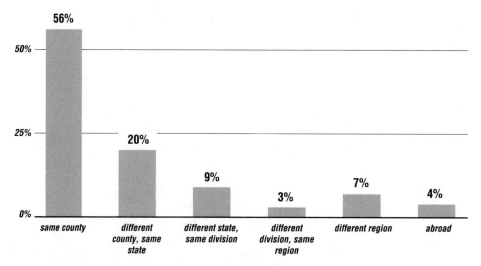

Geographical Mobility of Males by Age, 1999–2000

(total number of males aged 1 or older, and number and percent who moved between March 1999 and March 2000; by age; numbers in thousands)

	total	movers	
		number	percent
Total males	**131,969**	**21,573**	**16.3%**
Aged 1 to 5	8,043	1,929	24.0
Aged 5 to 9	10,439	1,868	17.9
Aged 10 to 14	10,372	1,442	13.9
Aged 15 to 17	6,212	771	12.4
Aged 18 to 19	4,082	793	19.4
Aged 20 to 24	9,208	2,997	32.5
Aged 25 to 29	8,942	3,072	34.4
Aged 30 to 34	9,621	2,235	23.2
Aged 35 to 39	11,032	1,912	17.3
Aged 40 to 44	11,103	1,538	13.9
Aged 45 to 49	9,654	969	10.0
Aged 50 to 54	8,235	658	8.0
Aged 55 to 59	6,105	504	8.3
Aged 60 to 61	2,105	146	6.9
Aged 62 to 64	2,927	171	5.8
Aged 65 to 69	4,376	188	4.3
Aged 70 to 74	3,673	160	4.4
Aged 75 to 79	2,989	102	3.4
Aged 80 to 84	1,807	77	4.3
Aged 85 or older	1,041	44	4.2

Source: Bureau of the Census, Current Population Survey, Internet site <www.census.gov/population/socdemo/migration/p20-538/tab02.xls>; calculations by New Strategist

Geographical Mobility of Males by Age and Type of Move, 1999–2000

(number of males aged 1 or older who moved between March 1999 and March 2000, and percent distribution by type of move, by age; numbers in thousands)

	total		same county	different county, same state	different state, same division	different division, same region	different region	abroad
	number	percent						
Male movers	**21,573**	**100.0 %**	**55.9%**	**20.5%**	**9.4%**	**2.9%**	**7.0%**	**4.4%**
Under age 5	1,929	100.0	60.1	19.9	6.6	3.1	6.7	3.7
Aged 5 to 9	1,868	100.0	60.8	16.5	9.6	2.3	7.3	3.5
Aged 10 to 14	1,442	100.0	59.3	16.0	10.3	1.8	7.6	5.1
Aged 15 to 17	771	100.0	54.0	20.9	8.6	3.2	8.0	5.3
Aged 18 to 19	793	100.0	53.5	20.8	14.5	2.1	5.3	3.8
Aged 20 to 24	2,997	100.0	56.9	20.5	7.5	3.1	6.0	6.0
Aged 25 to 29	3,072	100.0	55.3	22.1	8.1	3.3	7.3	3.9
Aged 30 to 34	2,235	100.0	56.1	21.0	7.8	3.7	6.6	4.9
Aged 35 to 39	1,912	100.0	55.4	21.0	9.8	1.5	7.4	4.8
Aged 40 to 44	1,538	100.0	54.7	20.2	12.7	2.4	6.2	3.8
Aged 45 to 49	969	100.0	52.2	25.0	11.8	2.5	5.4	3.2
Aged 50 to 54	658	100.0	51.8	21.9	11.7	3.6	6.7	4.3
Aged 55 to 59	504	100.0	52.2	19.0	13.3	4.4	7.7	3.4
Aged 60 to 61	146	100.0	47.9	26.0	15.8	4.1	4.8	1.4
Aged 62 to 64	171	100.0	36.3	30.4	13.5	5.3	12.9	1.8
Aged 65 to 69	188	100.0	53.2	15.4	10.1	7.4	11.2	2.7
Aged 70 to 74	160	100.0	47.5	15.6	10.0	6.3	12.5	8.1
Aged 75 to 79	102	100.0	43.1	27.5	4.9	6.9	15.7	2.0
Aged 80 to 84	77	100.0	40.3	31.2	14.3	1.3	13.0	–
Aged 85 or older	44	100.0	47.7	31.8	–	4.5	11.4	4.5

Note: (–) means sample is too small to make a reliable estimate.
Source: Bureau of the Census, Current Population Survey, Internet site <www.census.gov/population/socdemo/ migration/p20-538/tab01 .xls>; calculations by New Strategist

Half the Foreign-Born Are Male

Forty percent came to the U.S. since 1990.

The nation's foreign-born numbered more than 28 million in 2000, and males accounted for exactly half the population. More than 7 million foreign-born males are from Latin America, accounting for the 52 percent majority. Asia accounts for another 24 percent and Europe for just 15 percent.

The foreign-born share of males varies by age. It is well below average among those under age 20 and peaks at 17 percent among men aged 25 to 34. Forty percent of foreign born males live in the West, where they account for more than 18 percent of the population. Although foreign-born men are less likely than the average man to be high school graduates (68 versus 84 percent), they are slightly more likely to be college graduates. Foreign born men are more likely to be in the labor force than the average man, 80 versus 74 percent. Their earnings are below average, however, and they are more likely to be poor. Foreign-born males account for 16 percent of all males in poverty.

■ Because the foreign born are more likely to settle in some regions than others, their cultural influence varies greatly across the nation.

The foreign-born account for a large share of the West's population

(foreign-born share of male population, by region, 2000)

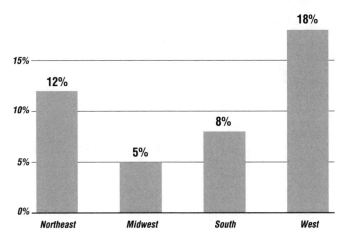

Foreign-Born Males by Place of Birth and Year of Entry, 2000

(total number of foreign-born, and number and percent male; number and percent distribution of foreign-born males by place of birth and year of entry to the U.S., 2000; numbers in thousands)

	number	*percent*
Total foreign-born	**28,379**	**100.0%**
Foreign-born males	14,179	50.0
Foreign-born males	**14,179**	**100.0**
World region of birth		
Asia	3,466	24.4
Europe	2,118	14.9
Latin America	7,373	52.0
Other area	1,244	8.8
Year of entry		
1990 or later	5,692	40.1
1980–1989	4,186	29.5
1970–1979	2,243	15.8
Before 1970	2,079	14.7

Source: Bureau of the Census, detailed tables for The Foreign Born Population in the United States: March 2000, *Current Population Report P20-534; Internet site <www.census.gov/population/www/socdemo/foreign/p20-534.html>; calculations by New Strategist*

Foreign-Born Males by Selected Characteristics, 2000

(number and percent distribution of total males, number and percent distribution of foreign-born males, and foreign-born share of total, by selected characteristics, 2000; numbers in thousands)

	total		foreign-born		
	number	percent distribution	number	percent distribution	share of total
Total males	133,933	100.0%	14,200	100.0%	10.6%
Age					
Under age 5	10,007	7.5	137	1.0	1.4
Aged 5 to 9	10,439	7.8	344	2.4	3.3
Aged 10 to 14	10,372	7.7	577	4.1	5.6
Aged 15 to 19	10,295	7.7	824	5.8	8.0
Aged 20 to 24	9,208	6.9	1,352	9.5	14.7
Aged 25 to 29	8,942	6.7	1,488	10.5	16.6
Aged 30 to 34	9,621	7.2	1,668	11.7	17.3
Aged 35 to 44	22,135	16.5	3,177	22.4	14.4
Aged 45 to 54	17,890	13.4	2,093	14.7	11.7
Aged 55 to 64	11,137	8.3	1,193	8.4	10.7
Aged 65 or older	13,886	10.4	1,347	9.5	9.7
Region of residence					
Northeast	24,959	18.6	3,063	21.6	12.3
Midwest	31,279	23.4	1,608	11.3	5.1
South	46,880	35.0	3,843	27.1	8.2
West	30,815	23.0	5,686	40.0	18.5
Education, aged 25 or older					
High school grad. or more	70,395	84.2	7,408	67.6	10.5
Bachelor's degree or more	23,251	27.8	3,135	28.6	13.5
Labor force, aged 16 or older					
Number and percent in labor force	74,517	74.2	10,334	79.6	13.9
Median earnings of full-time workers	$36,572	–	$27,239	–	–
Number and percent in poverty	13,813	10.3	2,157	15.2	15.6

Note: (–) means not applicable.
Source: Bureau of the Census, detailed tables for The Foreign Born Population in the United States: March 2000, *Current Population Report P20-534; Internet site <www.census.gov/population/www/socdemo/foreign/p20-534.html>; calculations by New Strategist*

Males Are a Minority of Immigrants

They are the majority of immigrants from Cuba, however.

In 2000, more than 849,000 legal immigrants were admitted to the United States—only 45 percent of them male. While boys outnumber girls among immigrants aged 5 to 19, females outnumber males in all other age groups.

The male share of immigrants varies by country of birth. Among the 45,652 immigrants from China in 2000, only 40 percent were male. In contrast, 53 percent of the 20,831 immigrants from Cuba were male. Males also accounted for the majority of immigrants from Bosnia-Herzegovina, Pakistan, and the United Kingdom.

■ Many immigrants to the U.S. are the relatives of America's foreign-born population, including wives, mothers, and sisters.

More than 378,000 males immigrated to the U.S. in 2000

(number of total and male immigrants, 2000)

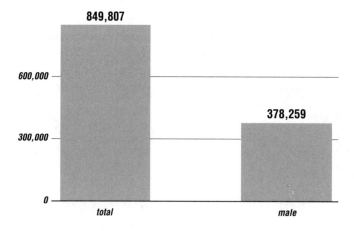

Male Immigrants by Age, 2000

(total number of immigrants admitted for legal permanent residence, number of male immigrants, and male share of total, by age, fiscal year 2000)

| | | male | |
| | | number | share of total |
	total		
Total immigrants	**849,807**	**378,259**	**44.5%**
Under age 5	39,215	17,443	44.5
Aged 5 to 9	45,945	23,309	50.7
Aged 10 to 14	66,734	34,323	51.4
Aged 15 to 19	85,947	43,539	50.7
Aged 20 to 24	70,696	29,885	42.3
Aged 25 to 29	112,793	46,509	41.2
Aged 30 to 34	115,575	50,987	44.1
Aged 35 to 39	85,703	37,515	43.8
Aged 40 to 44	60,443	25,654	42.4
Aged 45 to 49	44,217	18,573	42.0
Aged 50 to 54	33,513	14,082	42.0
Aged 55 to 59	25,315	10,013	39.6
Aged 60 to 64	23,407	9,450	40.4
Aged 65 to 69	17,620	7,385	41.9
Aged 70 to 74	11,161	4,718	42.3
Aged 75 to 79	5,933	2,512	42.3
Aged 80 or older	3,470	1,379	39.7

Note: Numbers will not add to total because immigrants of unknown age and sex are not shown.
Source: U.S. Immigration and Naturalization Service, 2000 Statistical Yearbook of the Immigration and Naturalization Service, Internet site <www.ins.usdoj.gov/graphics/aboutins/statistics/IMM00yrbk/ IMM2000list.htm>; calculations by New Strategist

Male Immigrants by Country of Birth, 2000

(total number of immigrants admitted for legal permanent residence, number of male immigrants, and male share of total, by country of birth, fiscal year 2000)

	total	males number	males share of total
Total immigrants	**849,807**	**378,259**	**44.5%**
Bosnia-Herzegovina	11,828	6,133	51.9
Canada	16,210	7,485	46.2
China, People's Republic	45,652	18,312	40.1
Colombia	14,498	5,611	38.7
Cuba	20,831	10,993	52.8
Dominican Republic	17,536	8,121	46.3
Ecuador	7,685	3,553	46.2
El Salvador	22,578	10,359	45.9
Germany	7,638	3,255	42.6
Guatemala	9,970	4,787	48.0
Haiti	22,364	9,740	43.6
India	42,046	20,710	49.3
Iran	8,519	3,909	45.9
Jamaica	16,000	7,353	46.0
Korea	15,830	6,961	44.0
Mexico	173,919	70,441	40.5
Nicaragua	24,029	10,883	45.3
Nigeria	7,853	3,910	49.8
Pakistan	14,535	7,377	50.8
Peru	9,613	4,117	42.8
Philippines	42,474	16,493	38.8
Poland	10,114	4,576	45.2
Russia	17,110	7,147	41.8
Taiwan	9,040	3,890	43.0
Ukraine	15,810	7,214	45.6
United Kingdom	13,385	7,438	55.6
Vietnam	26,747	10,637	39.8
Other	205,993	96,854	47.0

Source: U.S. Immigration and Naturalization Service, 2000 Statistical Yearbook of the Immigration and Naturalization Service, Internet site <www.ins.usdoj.gov/graphics/aboutins/statistics/IMM00yrbk/IMM2000list.htm>; calculations by New Strategist

9

Spending

Married couples with children spend the most.

They spent an average of $53,586 in 2000, or 41 percent more than average. Those with school-aged children spend 57 percent more than average on shoes.

Married couples without children at home spend more on some items.

Many are empty-nesters and big spenders on public transportation, which includes cruises and air fares. They also spend more than average on alcoholic beverages, health care, reading material, cash contributions, and gifts.

Men who live alone spend less than average.

They spent an average of $29,267 in 1999–2000, just 66 percent as much as the $37,622 spent by the average household during that time period.

Men who live alone spend more than average on some items.

They spend 43 percent more than the average household on alcoholic beverages, 13 percent more than average on men's clothes, and three times the average on gifts of jewelry and watches.

Married Couples Spend More than Average

Those with children at home spend the most.

Because the majority of men are married, examining the spending patterns of married couples reveals much of what men do with their money. Married couples spent $48,619 in 2000, a substantial 28 percent more than the $38,045 spent by the average household. But married couples with children spent a larger $53,586, or 41 percent more than the average household.

The Bureau of Labor Statistics collects spending data from households rather than individuals. The data in this chapter, showing the spending of married couples and men who live alone, include more than 80 percent of male householders. The average spending table shows how much married couples spent in 2000. The indexed spending table compares the spending of each type of married-couple household to the spending of the average household. An index of 100 means the household type spends an average amount on the item. An index above 100 means the household type spends more than average on the item, while an index below 100 signifies below-average spending.

Married couples with children at home spend more than average on most items because their households are larger than average. They spend 44 percent more than average on food at home and 35 percent more on food away from home. They are big spenders on

Empty-nesters spend less than couples with children

(average annual spending of consumer units by type, 2000)

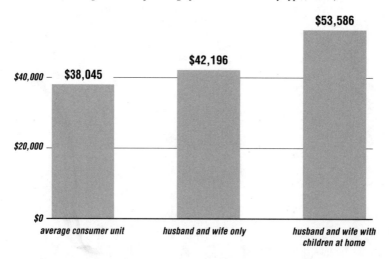

household personal services (mostly day care), with an index of 230. They spend well above average on children's clothes, vehicles, entertainment, and education. They spend close to the average on alcoholic beverages, with an index of 106.

Married couples without children at home (many of them empty-nesters) spend only 11 percent more than the average household. But they spend 24 percent more than average on alcoholic beverages. They spend 36 percent more on public transportation, which includes cruises and air fares. They spend well above average on cash contributions, health care, household furnishings, and gifts for people living in other households.

■ The spending of parents is largely devoted to children. As boomers become empty-nesters, spending will shift to more personal wants and needs.

Spending of Married Couples, 2000

(number, selected characteristics, and average annual spending of total consumer units (CU) and consumer units headed by married couples, by spending category and presence of children at home, 2000)

	average consumer unit	married couples total	husband and wife only	couples with children of any age at home total	oldest child under 6	oldest child 6 to 17	oldest child 18 or older	other husband/wife consumer units
Number of consumer units (in thousands)	109,367	56,287	22,805	28,777	5,291	15,396	8,090	4,705
Income before taxes	$44,649	$60,588	$53,232	$66,913	$62,928	$69,472	$64,725	$56,796
Age of reference person	48	48	57	42	32	40	51	48
Average number of persons in CU	2.5	3.2	2.0	3.9	3.5	4.1	3.8	4.9
Average number of earners in CU	1.4	1.7	1.2	2.0	1.7	1.9	2.6	2.4
Average number of vehicles owned by CU	1.9	2.6	2.4	2.7	2.2	2.6	3.2	2.8
Percent homeowners	66%	81%	85%	79%	68%	79%	87%	78%
With mortgage	39	53	41	63	62	66	59	54
Without mortgage	27	28	44	16	6	13	28	24
Percent renters	34	19	15	21	32	21	13	22
Percent black	12	8	5	9	7	10	9	16
Average annual expenditures	$38,045	$48,619	$42,196	$53,586	$50,756	$54,170	$54,550	$49,646
FOOD	$5,158	$6,575	$5,575	$7,251	$5,817	$7,508	$7,858	$7,506
Food at home	3,021	3,892	3,155	4,357	3,659	4,458	4,724	4,815
Cereals and bakery products	453	590	456	680	542	702	749	723
Cereals and cereal products	156	203	149	240	186	256	251	255
Bakery products	297	387	307	440	356	445	497	468

(continued)

(continued from previous page)

	average consumer unit	married couples total	husband and wife only	couples with children of any age at home total	oldest child under 6	oldest child 6 to 17	oldest child 18 or older	other husband/wife consumer units
Meats, poultry, fish, and eggs	$795	$1,018	$846	$1,113	$819	$1,155	$1,271	$1,333
Beef	238	307	251	335	245	345	391	432
Pork	167	213	189	226	151	236	268	249
Other meats	101	129	100	148	108	153	170	166
Poultry	145	183	143	207	171	210	230	241
Fish and seafood	110	144	126	153	109	168	156	185
Eggs	34	43	37	44	33	44	56	59
Dairy products	325	420	335	481	415	497	505	474
Fresh milk and cream	131	169	121	201	176	209	206	213
Other dairy products	193	252	214	280	239	288	299	261
Fruits and vegetables	521	665	578	710	619	717	771	839
Fresh fruits	163	206	180	216	188	215	241	276
Fresh vegetables	159	204	183	211	184	213	229	271
Processed fruits	115	147	123	164	152	169	163	164
Processed vegetables	84	108	91	119	94	120	138	126
Other food at home	927	1,199	940	1,373	1,265	1,388	1,428	1,446
Sugar and other sweets	117	156	123	172	127	176	202	227
Fats and oils	83	106	94	113	74	118	135	127
Miscellaneous foods	437	566	413	677	733	678	628	650
Nonalcoholic beverages	250	316	252	356	286	357	413	397
Food prepared by cu on trips	40	55	58	54	45	59	50	46
Food away from home	**2,137**	**2,683**	**2,420**	**2,894**	**2,158**	**3,050**	**3,134**	**2,692**

(continued)

(continued from previous page)

		married couples						
				couples with children of any age at home				other husband/wife
	average consumer unit	total	husband and wife only	total	oldest child under 6	oldest child 6 to 17	oldest child 18 or older	consumer units
ALCOHOLIC BEVERAGES	**$372**	**$420**	**$461**	**$396**	**$375**	**$365**	**$477**	**$362**
HOUSING	**12,319**	**15,204**	**12,832**	**17,132**	**18,702**	**17,433**	**15,537**	**14,891**
Shelter	**7,114**	**8,536**	**7,153**	**9,693**	**10,398**	**10,035**	**8,581**	**8,155**
Owned dwellings*	4,602	6,505	5,234	7,587	7,864	7,937	6,743	6,050
Mortgage interest and charges	2,639	3,922	2,692	4,940	5,485	5,280	3,938	3,653
Property taxes	1,139	1,534	1,460	1,618	1,504	1,604	1,719	1,372
Maintenance, repair, insurance, other expenses	825	1,050	1,082	1,029	874	1,053	1,086	1,024
Rented dwellings	2,034	1,355	1,121	1,502	2,162	1,543	993	1,590
Other lodging	478	675	798	604	372	556	845	516
Utilities, fuels, and public services	**2,489**	**3,006**	**2,689**	**3,180**	**2,804**	**3,193**	**3,401**	**3,485**
Natural gas	307	368	318	396	360	397	418	435
Electricity	911	1,116	1,022	1,161	956	1,170	1,277	1,300
Fuel oil and other fuels	97	120	129	120	114	118	130	80
Telephone	877	1,016	871	1,097	1,045	1,096	1,133	1,224
Water and other public services	296	386	348	405	329	412	443	447
Household services	**684**	**911**	**533**	**1,221**	**2,380**	**1,183**	**534**	**850**
Personal services	326	444	54	750	1,990	661	107	462
Other household services	358	467	478	471	390	523	427	388
Housekeeping supplies	**482**	**647**	**573**	**703**	**618**	**724**	**730**	**669**
Laundry and cleaning supplies	131	173	134	203	150	226	200	188
Other household products	226	317	286	338	302	345	353	349
Postage and stationery	126	156	154	162	166	153	177	132

(continued)

(continued from previous page)

| | average consumer unit | married couples | | | | | | other husband/wife consumer units |
| | | total | husband and wife only | couples with children of any age at home | | | | |
				total	oldest child under 6	oldest child 6 to 17	oldest child 18 or older	
Household furnishings and equipment	**$1,549**	**$2,103**	**$1,884**	**$2,336**	**$2,502**	**$2,297**	**$2,291**	**$1,732**
Household textiles	106	144	129	162	179	157	163	107
Furniture	391	521	437	608	722	635	484	397
Floor coverings	44	65	61	71	46	60	108	47
Major appliances	189	258	218	290	265	274	342	256
Small appliances, misc. housewares	87	117	110	122	125	120	124	114
Miscellaneous household equipment	731	999	929	1,082	1,165	1,052	1,071	809
APPAREL AND SERVICES	**1,856**	**2,312**	**1,725**	**2,749**	**2,590**	**2,838**	**2,698**	**2,552**
Men and boys	**440**	**565**	**424**	**683**	**538**	**717**	**727**	**531**
Men, aged 16 or older	344	434	400	467	390	421	620	404
Boys, aged 2 to 15	96	131	25	216	148	296	107	126
Women and girls	**725**	**906**	**691**	**1,052**	**777**	**1,094**	**1,190**	**1,094**
Women, aged 16 or older	607	736	657	778	623	695	1,079	887
Girls, aged 2 to 15	118	170	34	274	154	400	111	206
Children under age 2	**82**	**118**	**38**	**173**	**498**	**102**	**63**	**188**
Footwear	**343**	**406**	**298**	**480**	**449**	**537**	**387**	**495**
Other apparel products and services	266	316	274	361	328	388	331	245
TRANSPORTATION	**7,417**	**9,910**	**8,309**	**11,088**	**10,745**	**10,644**	**12,158**	**10,470**
Vehicle purchases	**3,418**	**4,709**	**3,824**	**5,365**	**5,594**	**5,102**	**5,716**	**4,989**
Cars and trucks, new	1,605	2,277	2,113	2,478	2,640	2,379	2,559	1,844
Cars and trucks, used	1,770	2,379	1,685	2,817	2,816	2,658	3,119	3,070
Other vehicles	43	53	26	70	137	65	38	76

(continued)

| | average consumer unit | married couples | | | | | | other husband/wife consumer units |
| | | total | husband and wife only | couples with children of any age at home | | | | |
				total	oldest child under 6	oldest child 6 to 17	oldest child 18 or older	
Gasoline and motor oil	$1,291	$1,697	$1,411	$1,879	$1,594	$1,866	$2,092	$1,966
Other vehicle expenses	2,281	2,984	2,493	3,352	3,150	3,192	3,793	3,112
Vehicle finance charges	328	457	350	534	551	517	556	500
Maintenance and repairs	624	776	673	851	712	827	988	827
Vehicle insurance	778	994	837	1,097	957	982	1,408	1,126
Vehicle rentals, leases, licenses, other charges	551	757	633	871	929	866	841	660
Public transportation	427	520	581	491	407	485	558	403
HEALTH CARE	2,066	2,640	3,044	2,306	1,897	2,251	2,681	2,727
Health insurance	983	1,288	1,479	1,131	1,025	1,078	1,303	1,318
Medical services	568	717	738	698	548	731	732	733
Drugs	416	504	671	361	241	327	509	572
Medical supplies	99	132	157	116	84	115	138	104
ENTERTAINMENT	1,863	2,454	1,968	2,864	2,191	3,250	2,586	2,304
Fees and admissions	515	714	595	850	486	1,049	708	456
Television, radios, sound equipment	622	735	570	854	717	917	825	812
Pets, toys, and playground equipment	334	444	388	498	481	547	423	384
Other entertainment products and services	393	561	414	662	506	736	629	651
PERSONAL CARE PRODUCTS AND SERVICES	564	700	611	769	649	774	845	723
READING	146	182	197	176	174	174	181	141
EDUCATION	632	811	447	1,126	420	1,032	1,769	651

(continued)

(continued from previous page)

| | average consumer unit | total | husband and wife only | married couples with children of any age at home | | | | other husband/wife consumer units |
				total	oldest child under 6	oldest child 6 to 17	oldest child 18 or older	
TOBACCO PRODUCTS AND SMOKING SUPPLIES	$319	$343	$286	$358	$275	$336	$455	$533
MISCELLANEOUS	776	908	878	893	687	960	909	1,140
CASH CONTRIBUTIONS	1,192	1,512	1,915	1,220	848	1,270	1,370	1,339
PERSONAL INSURANCE, PENSIONS	3,365	4,648	3,949	5,257	5,388	5,334	5,027	4,308
Life and other personal insurance	399	608	613	601	482	590	702	629
Pensions and Social Security	2,966	4,039	3,335	4,656	4,906	4,744	4,325	3,679
PERSONAL TAXES	3,117	4,308	4,358	4,457	4,164	4,734	4,120	3,189
Federal income taxes	2,409	3,361	3,396	3,467	3,260	3,646	3,261	2,565
State and local income taxes	562	752	726	816	756	906	678	496
Other taxes	146	195	236	175	147	182	181	128
GIFTS**	1,083	1,355	1,477	1,266	918	1,147	1,728	1,312
Food	70	109	101	116	58	87	213	105
Alcoholic beverages	14	19	14	24	45	14	27	10
Housing	291	379	417	358	345	324	436	323
Housekeeping supplies	39	50	50	52	49	45	69	43
Household textiles	13	19	14	24	10	15	53	11
Appliances and misc. housewares	28	35	44	27	35	23	28	44
Major appliances	8	10	11	6	2	7	5	34
Small appliances and misc. housewares	21	25	33	21	34	16	23	10
Miscellaneous household equipment	70	85	87	83	70	66	122	87
Other housing	140	190	221	172	181	174	164	138

(continued)

(continued from previous page)

	average consumer unit $244	married couples						other husband/wife consumer units $295
		total $280	husband and wife only $301	couples with children of any age at home				
				total $261	oldest child under 6 $270	oldest child 6 to 17 $221	oldest child 18 or older $334	
Apparel and services								
Males, aged 2 or older	68	74	87	68	59	45	124	47
Females, aged 2 or older	85	100	122	82	65	79	100	107
Children under age 2	41	57	38	65	105	51	60	106
Other apparel products and services	51	48	54	46	41	46	50	34
Jewelry and watches	20	14	17	13	16	8	19	6
All other apparel products and services	30	35	38	33	25	38	31	28
Transportation	70	72	101	57	15	61	75	32
Health care	38	28	29	14	3	14	21	116
Entertainment	94	112	123	96	100	92	102	155
Toys, games, hobbies, and tricycles	30	36	47	27	34	24	29	37
Other entertainment	64	76	76	69	67	68	73	119
Personal care products and services	19	23	15	29	26	31	28	24
Reading	2	2	3	2	2	1	2	1
Education	151	237	271	229	19	234	355	122
All other gifts	89	94	102	81	35	67	136	131

* This figure does not include the amount paid for mortgage principle, which is considered an asset.
** Expenditures on gifts include only gifts purchased for non-household members. Gift spending is also included in the preceding product and service categories.
Note: The Bureau of Labor Statistics uses consumer unit rather than household as the sampling unit in the Consumer Expenditure survey. For the definition of consumer unit, see glossary.
Source: Bureau of Labor Statistics, 2000 Consumer Expenditure Survey, Internet site <ftp://ftp.bls.gov/pub/special.requests/ce/standard/2000/cucomp.txt>

Indexed Spending of Married Couples, 2000

(indexed spending of consumer units (CU) headed by married couples by category of spending and presence of children at home, 2000)

	average consumer unit	married couples		couples with children of any age at home				other husband/wife consumer units
		total	husband and wife only	total	oldest child under 6	oldest child 6 to 17	oldest child 18 or older	
Average annual expenditures	100	128	111	141	133	142	143	130
FOOD	**100**	**127**	**108**	**141**	**113**	**146**	**152**	**146**
Food at home	**100**	**129**	**104**	**144**	**121**	**148**	**156**	**159**
Cereals and bakery products	100	130	101	150	120	155	165	160
Cereals and cereal products	100	130	96	154	119	164	161	163
Bakery products	100	130	103	148	120	150	167	158
Meats, poultry, fish, and eggs	100	128	106	140	103	145	160	168
Beef	100	129	105	141	103	145	164	182
Pork	100	128	113	135	90	141	160	149
Other meats	100	128	99	147	107	151	168	164
Poultry	100	126	99	143	118	145	159	166
Fish and seafood	100	131	115	139	99	153	142	168
Eggs	100	126	109	129	97	129	165	174
Dairy products	100	129	103	148	128	153	155	146
Fresh milk and cream	100	129	92	153	134	160	157	163
Other dairy products	100	131	111	145	124	149	155	135
Fruits and vegetables	100	128	111	136	119	138	148	161
Fresh fruits	100	126	110	133	115	132	148	169
Fresh vegetables	100	128	115	133	116	134	144	170

(continued)

(continued from previous page)

| | average consumer unit | married couples | | | | | | other husband/wife consumer units |
| | | total | husband and wife only | couples with children of any age at home | | | | |
				total	oldest child under 6	oldest child 6 to 17	oldest child 18 or older	
Processed fruits	100	128	107	143	132	147	142	143
Processed vegetables	100	129	108	142	112	143	164	150
Other food at home	100	129	101	148	136	150	154	156
Sugar and other sweets	100	133	105	147	109	150	173	194
Fats and oils	100	128	113	136	89	142	163	153
Miscellaneous foods	100	130	95	155	168	155	144	149
Nonalcoholic beverages	100	126	101	142	114	143	165	159
Food prepared by CU on trips	100	138	145	135	113	148	125	115
Food away from home	**100**	**126**	**113**	**135**	**101**	**143**	**147**	**126**
ALCOHOLIC BEVERAGES	**100**	**113**	**124**	**106**	**101**	**98**	**128**	**97**
HOUSING	**100**	**123**	**104**	**139**	**152**	**142**	**126**	**121**
Shelter	**100**	**120**	**101**	**136**	**146**	**141**	**121**	**115**
Owned dwellings	100	141	114	165	171	172	147	131
Mortgage interest and charges	100	149	102	187	208	200	149	138
Property taxes	100	135	128	142	132	141	151	120
Maintenance, repair, insurance, other expenses	100	127	131	125	106	128	132	124
Rented dwellings	100	67	55	74	106	76	49	78
Other lodging	100	141	167	126	78	116	177	108
Utilities, fuels, and public services	**100**	**121**	**108**	**128**	**113**	**128**	**137**	**140**
Natural gas	100	120	104	129	117	129	136	142
Electricity	100	123	112	127	105	128	140	143
Fuel oil and other fuels	100	124	133	124	118	122	134	82

(continued)

(continued from previous page)

| | average consumer unit | married couples | | couples with children of any age at home | | | | other husband/wife consumer units |
		total	husband and wife only	total	oldest child under 6	oldest child 6 to 17	oldest child 18 or older	
Telephone	100	116	99	125	119	125	129	140
Water and other public services	100	130	118	137	111	139	150	151
Household services	**100**	**133**	**78**	**179**	**348**	**173**	**78**	**124**
Personal services	100	136	17	230	610	203	33	142
Other household services	100	130	134	132	109	146	119	108
Housekeeping supplies	**100**	**134**	**119**	**146**	**128**	**150**	**151**	**139**
Laundry and cleaning supplies	100	132	102	155	115	173	153	144
Other household products	100	140	127	150	134	153	156	154
Postage and stationery	100	124	122	129	132	121	140	105
Household furnishings and equipment	**100**	**136**	**122**	**151**	**162**	**148**	**148**	**112**
Household textiles	100	136	122	153	169	148	154	101
Furniture	100	133	112	155	185	162	124	102
Floor coverings	100	148	139	161	105	136	245	107
Major appliances	100	137	115	153	140	145	181	135
Small appliances, misc. housewares	100	134	126	140	144	138	143	131
Miscellaneous household equipment	100	137	127	148	159	144	147	111
APPAREL AND SERVICES	**100**	**125**	**93**	**148**	**140**	**153**	**145**	**138**
Men and boys	**100**	**128**	**96**	**155**	**122**	**163**	**165**	**121**
Men, aged 16 or older	100	126	116	136	113	122	180	117
Boys, aged 2 to 15	100	136	26	225	154	308	111	131
Women and girls	**100**	**125**	**95**	**145**	**107**	**151**	**164**	**151**
Women, aged 16 or older	100	121	108	128	103	114	178	146
Girls, aged 2 to 15	100	144	29	232	131	339	94	175
Children under age 2	**100**	**144**	**46**	**211**	**607**	**124**	**77**	**229**

(continued)

(continued from previous page)

| | average consumer unit | total | husband and wife only | married couples | | | | other husband/wife consumer units |
| | | | | couples with children of any age at home | | | | |
				total	oldest child under 6	oldest child 6 to 17	oldest child 18 or older	
Footwear	**100**	**118**	**87**	**140**	**131**	**157**	**113**	**144**
Other apparel products and services	**100**	**119**	**103**	**136**	**123**	**146**	**124**	**92**
TRANSPORTATION	**100**	**134**	**112**	**149**	**145**	**144**	**164**	**141**
Vehicle purchases	**100**	**138**	**112**	**157**	**164**	**149**	**167**	**146**
Cars and trucks, new	100	142	132	154	164	148	159	115
Cars and trucks, used	100	134	95	159	159	150	176	173
Other vehicles	100	123	60	163	319	151	88	177
Gasoline and motor oil	**100**	**131**	**109**	**146**	**123**	**145**	**162**	**152**
Other vehicle expenses	**100**	**131**	**109**	**147**	**138**	**140**	**166**	**136**
Vehicle finance charges	100	139	107	163	168	158	170	152
Maintenance and repairs	100	124	108	136	114	133	158	133
Vehicle insurance	100	128	108	141	123	126	181	145
Vehicle rentals, leases, licenses, other charges	100	137	115	158	169	157	153	120
Public transportation	**100**	**122**	**136**	**115**	**95**	**114**	**131**	**94**
HEALTH CARE	**100**	**128**	**147**	**112**	**92**	**109**	**130**	**132**
Health insurance	100	131	150	115	104	110	133	134
Medical services	100	126	130	123	96	129	129	129
Drugs	100	121	161	87	58	79	122	138
Medical supplies	100	133	159	117	85	116	139	105
ENTERTAINMENT	**100**	**132**	**106**	**154**	**118**	**174**	**139**	**124**
Fees and admissions	100	139	116	165	94	204	137	89
Television, radios, sound equipment	100	118	92	137	115	147	133	131

(continued)

(continued from previous page)

| | average consumer unit | married couples | | | | | | other husband/wife consumer units |
| | | total | husband and wife only | couples with children of any age at home | | | | |
				total	oldest child under 6	oldest child 6 to 17	oldest child 18 or older	
Pets, toys, and playground equipment	100	133	116	149	144	164	127	115
Other entertainment products and services	100	143	105	168	129	187	160	166
PERSONAL CARE PRODUCTS AND SERVICES	**100**	**124**	**108**	**136**	**115**	**137**	**150**	**128**
READING	**100**	**125**	**135**	**121**	**119**	**119**	**124**	**97**
EDUCATION	**100**	**128**	**71**	**178**	**66**	**163**	**280**	**103**
TOBACCO PRODUCTS AND SMOKING SUPPLIES	**100**	**108**	**90**	**112**	**86**	**105**	**143**	**167**
MISCELLANEOUS	**100**	**117**	**113**	**115**	**89**	**124**	**117**	**147**
CASH CONTRIBUTIONS	**100**	**127**	**161**	**102**	**71**	**107**	**115**	**112**
PERSONAL INSURANCE AND PENSIONS	**100**	**138**	**117**	**156**	**160**	**159**	**149**	**128**
Life and other personal insurance	100	152	154	151	121	148	176	158
Pensions and Social Security	100	136	112	157	165	160	146	124
PERSONAL TAXES	**100**	**138**	**140**	**143**	**134**	**152**	**132**	**102**
Federal income taxes	100	140	141	144	135	151	135	106
State and local income taxes	100	134	129	145	135	161	121	88
Other taxes	100	134	162	120	101	125	124	88
GIFTS	**100**	**125**	**136**	**117**	**85**	**106**	**160**	**121**
Food	**100**	**156**	**144**	**166**	**83**	**124**	**304**	**150**
Alcoholic beverages	**100**	**136**	**100**	**171**	**321**	**100**	**193**	**71**
Housing	**100**	**130**	**143**	**123**	**119**	**111**	**150**	**111**
Housekeeping supplies	100	128	128	133	126	115	177	110
Household textiles	100	146	108	185	77	115	408	85

(continued)

(continued from previous page)

	average consumer unit	total	husband and wife only	married couples couples with children of any age at home				other husband/wife consumer units
				total	oldest child under 6	oldest child 6 to 17	oldest child 18 or older	
Appliances and misc. housewares	100	125	157	96	125	82	100	157
Major appliances	100	125	138	75	25	88	63	425
Small appliances and misc. housewares	100	119	157	100	162	76	110	48
Miscellaneous household equipment	100	121	124	119	100	94	174	124
Other housing	100	136	158	123	129	124	117	99
Apparel and services	**100**	**115**	**123**	**107**	**111**	**91**	**137**	**121**
Males, aged 2 or older	100	109	128	100	87	66	182	69
Females, aged 2 or older	100	118	144	96	76	93	118	126
Children under age 2	100	139	93	159	256	124	146	259
Other apparel products and services	100	94	106	90	80	90	98	67
Jewelry and watches	100	70	85	65	80	40	95	30
All other apparel products and services	100	117	127	110	83	127	103	93
Transportation	**100**	**103**	**144**	**81**	**21**	**87**	**107**	**46**
Health care	**100**	**74**	**76**	**37**	**8**	**37**	**55**	**305**
Entertainment	**100**	**119**	**131**	**102**	**106**	**98**	**109**	**165**
Toys, games, hobbies, and tricycles	100	120	157	90	113	80	97	123
Other entertainment	100	119	119	108	105	106	114	186
Personal care products and services	**100**	**121**	**79**	**153**	**137**	**163**	**147**	**126**
Reading	**100**	**100**	**150**	**100**	**100**	**50**	**100**	**50**
Education	**100**	**157**	**179**	**152**	**13**	**155**	**235**	**81**
All other gifts	**100**	**106**	**115**	**91**	**39**	**75**	**153**	**147**

Note: The index compares the spending of each type of consumer unit with the spending of the average consumer unit. 100 is the average. An index of 132 means the spending of the consumer unit type is 32 percent above average, while an index of 75 means the spending of the consumer unit type is 25 percent below average. The Bureau of Labor Statistics uses consumer unit rather than household as the sampling unit in the Consumer Expenditure Survey. For the definition of consumer unit, see glossary.
Source: Calculations by New Strategist based on the Bureau of Labor Statistics' 2000 Consumer Expenditure Survey, Internet site <ftp://ftp.bls.gov/pub/special.requests/ce/standard/2000/cucomp.txt>>

Men Who Live Alone Spend Less than Average

They spend more than the average household on alcoholic beverages, however.

Men who live alone spent an annual average of $29,267 in 1999–2000, only 66 percent of the $37,622 spent by the average household during the time period.

The Bureau of Labor Statistics collects spending data from households rather than individuals. The data in this chapter, showing the spending of married couples and men who live alone, include more than 80 percent of male householders. The average spending table shows how much men who live alone spent annually in 1999–2000, by age group. The indexed spending table compares the spending of men who live alone to the spending of the average consumer unit. An index of 100 means men in the age group spend an average amount on an item. An index above 100 means men in the age group spend more than average on an item, while an index below 100 signifies below-average spending.

Among men who live alone, those under age 25 spend much more than the average household on education, with an index of 252. They spent $650 on alcoholic beverages in 1999-2000, more than any other household type.

Men aged 25 to 64 who live alone have higher incomes and spend more than younger men. Men aged 25 to 34 who live alone spend 12 percent more than the average household on food away from home despite their smaller household size. They spend 66 percent more

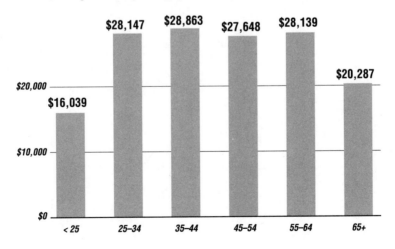

Among men living alone, those aged 25 to 64 spend the most

(average annual spending of men living alone by age, 1999–2000)

than average on men's clothes, more than almost any other household type. They spend eight times the average on gifts of jewelry and watches.

Men aged 65 or older who live alone spend less than their middle-aged counterparts, an average of $20,287 in 1999–2000. They spend more than the average household on health care and cash contributions.

■ As single-person households become a larger share of all households, their spending will become increasingly important to the economy.

Spending of Men Who Live Alone by Age, 1999–2000

(number, selected characteristics, and average annual spending of total and single-person consumer units (CU) headed by men, by spending category and age, 1999–2000)

	average consumer unit	total	< 25	25–34	35–44	45–54	55–64	65 +
					men living alone			
Number of consumer units (in 000s)	108,916	13,667	2,199	2,725	2,485	2,220	1,470	2,569
Income before taxes	$44,299	$29,267	$11,561	$36,007	$35,005	$39,313	$33,318	$21,439
Percent homeowners	65%	43%	7%	29%	46%	49%	60%	71%
With mortgage	38	21	3	23	33	29	30	9
Without mortgage	27	23	5	6	13	21	30	61
Renters	35	57	93	71	54	51	40	29
Black	12	11	10	9	13	15	11	10
Average annual expenditures	$37,622	$24,760	$16,039	$28,147	$28,863	$27,648	$28,139	$20,287
FOOD	**$5,094**	**$3,110**	**$2,190**	**$3,716**	**$3,615**	**$3,269**	**$3,439**	**$2,447**
Food at home	2,968	1,386	820	1,325	1,510	1,552	1,700	1,433
Cereals and bakery products	451	202	116	189	207	237	241	224
Cereals and cereal products	158	67	37	68	71	73	73	80
Bakery products	293	135	79	121	136	164	168	144
Meats, poultry, fish, and eggs	772	346	183	308	412	415	448	326
Beef	229	97	57	81	115	116	135	87
Pork	162	70	28	58	85	83	90	76
Other meats	99	50	27	43	55	57	68	52
Poultry	141	61	34	56	78	75	69	51
Fish and seafood	108	52	27	55	60	67	63	43
Eggs	33	17	10	14	19	18	22	18

(continued)

(continued from previous page)

	average consumer unit	men living alone						
		total	<25	25–34	35–44	45–54	55–64	65+
Dairy products	$323	$147	$86	$135	$157	$164	$180	164
Fresh milk and cream	127	57	32	44	57	68	62	75
Other dairy products	197	91	54	91	100	95	118	89
Fruits and vegetables	510	238	117	214	243	257	295	296
Fresh fruits	158	74	32	66	70	71	107	99
Fresh vegetables	154	69	38	62	70	85	84	78
Processed fruits	114	56	30	51	59	55	61	74
Processed vegetables	85	39	17	35	44	46	43	44
Other food at home	912	452	317	479	491	479	536	423
Sugar and other sweets	114	47	35	46	50	50	50	51
Fats and oils	83	36	22	34	40	37	40	40
Miscellaneous foods	428	212	135	222	222	241	245	210
Nonalcoholic beverages	246	133	105	145	149	133	167	108
Food prepared by CU on trips	40	25	20	32	31	18	35	15
Food away from home	**2,126**	**1,724**	**1,370**	**2,391**	**2,105**	**1,717**	**1,739**	**1,013**
ALCOHOLIC BEVERAGES	**345**	**493**	**650**	**577**	**628**	**361**	**495**	**281**
HOUSING	**12,188**	**8,210**	**4,416**	**9,310**	**9,544**	**9,573**	**9,335**	**7,148**
Shelter	**7,065**	**5,401**	**3,172**	**6,407**	**6,546**	**6,375**	**5,744**	**4,095**
Owned dwellings*	4,564	2,281	292	1,993	3,206	2,873	3,477	2,198
Mortgage interest and charges	2,593	1,152	130	1,350	2,002	1,617	1,625	321
Property taxes	1,131	647	133	367	688	794	1,087	964
Maintenance, repair, insurance, other expenses	839	482	28	276	516	462	765	913
Rented dwellings	2,030	2,738	2,453	4,119	3,020	2,793	1,920	1,663

(continued)

(continued from previous page)

	average consumer unit	men living alone						
		total	< 25	25-34	35-44	45-54	55-64	65 +
Other lodging	$471	$382	$427	$295	$319	$709	$346	$234
Utilities, fuels, and public services	**2,433**	**1,491**	**682**	**1,560**	**1,684**	**1,632**	**1,684**	**1,693**
Natural gas	289	174	48	152	176	199	229	251
Electricity	905	536	227	532	606	582	642	637
Fuel oil and other fuels	86	51	7	29	43	48	53	121
Telephone	863	585	356	736	711	642	563	464
Water and other public services	291	145	44	111	148	160	197	219
Household services	**675**	**283**	**51**	**207**	**211**	**339**	**408**	**510**
Personal services	324	68	–	–	–	–	–	–
Other household services	351	215	46	166	189	264	402	285
Housekeeping supplies	**490**	**178**	**67**	**154**	**192**	**198**	**207**	**233**
Laundry and cleaning supplies	126	47	20	46	58	58	50	46
Other household products	238	87	27	66	88	88	104	137
Postage and stationery	126	44	20	42	46	52	54	49
Household furnishings and equipment	**1,524**	**857**	**444**	**982**	**911**	**1,028**	**1,292**	**618**
Household textiles	110	41	10	40	73	65	43	17
Furniture	378	212	102	342	223	230	244	122
Floor coverings	44	10	–	16	–	–	–	–
Major appliances	186	92	24	82	104	101	132	112
Small appliances, misc. housewares	94	58	17	31	35	72	49	129
Miscellaneous household equipment	711	445	289	472	466	558	816	219
APPAREL AND SERVICES	**1,816**	**836**	**769**	**1,246**	**1,003**	**833**	**725**	**408**
Men and boys	**438**	**396**	**395**	**582**	**512**	**381**	**295**	**185**
Men, aged 16 or older	343	387	391	568	497	371	284	180
Boys, aged 2 to 15	94	10	3	14	15	10	11	5

(continued)

	average consumer unit	men living alone						
		total	<25	25-34	35-44	45-54	55-64	65+
Women and girls	$695	$46	$31	$57	$58	$71	$59	$10
Women, aged 16 or older	582	35	23	28	46	64	53	5
Girls, aged 2 to 15	113	11	8	29	13	6	6	4
Children under age 2	80	9	19	15	6	8	7	3
Footwear	323	152	170	221	132	197	121	74
Other apparel products and services	281	233	154	372	294	177	242	137
TRANSPORTATION	7,215	4,571	3,679	4,946	5,755	4,411	5,455	3,428
Vehicle purchases	3,362	2,000	1,934	1,753	2,706	1,647	2,534	1,635
Cars and trucks, new	1,616	962	684	887	1,405	769	1,115	930
Cars and trucks, used	1,706	972	1,242	738	1,213	783	1,371	688
Other vehicles	40	67	–	–	–	–	–	–
Gasoline and motor oil	1,173	796	629	916	969	851	807	592
Other vehicle expenses	2,268	1,482	881	1,871	1,710	1,703	1,773	1,009
Vehicle finance charges	324	150	102	217	182	158	187	63
Maintenance and repairs	644	475	338	491	583	521	589	366
Vehicle insurance	767	489	259	557	571	568	535	439
Vehicle rentals, leases, licenses, other charges	532	368	182	606	375	455	463	141
Public transportation	412	292	234	406	370	210	342	193
HEALTH CARE	2,012	1,121	323	640	818	1,196	1,466	2,336
Health insurance	953	488	108	319	405	441	584	1,056
Medical services	563	374	147	192	252	475	568	681
Drugs	393	211	49	90	135	232	264	496
Medical supplies	104	48	20	38	25	48	49	103

(continued)

(continued from previous page)

	average consumer unit	total	men living alone					
			< 25	25-34	35-44	45-54	55-64	65 +
ENTERTAINMENT	$1,902	$1,244	$1,003	$1,610	$1,488	$1,129	$1,293	$905
Fees and admissions	509	341	308	481	390	285	341	221
Television, radios, sound equipment	615	522	467	642	579	530	551	369
Pets, toys, and playground equipment	339	159	73	163	231	179	197	117
Other entertainment products and services	439	222	155	324	289	135	203	199
PERSONAL CARE PRODUCTS AND SERVICES	552	226	147	258	290	254	210	178
READING	153	108	62	108	105	140	127	109
EDUCATION	633	502	1,597	616	154	313	253	87
TOBACCO PRODUCTS AND SMOKING SUPPLIES	309	271	159	226	375	402	321	172
MISCELLANEOUS	821	636	162	757	886	639	776	592
CASH CONTRIBUTIONS	1,187	1,151	178	1,211	1,161	1,425	1,435	1,510
PERSONAL INSURANCE AND PENSIONS	3,393	2,282	704	2,928	3,041	3,704	2,809	684
Life and other personal insurance	397	166	34	109	156	236	255	236
Pensions and Social Security	2,997	2,117	670	2,819	2,885	3,468	2,554	448
PERSONAL TAXES	3,208	2,858	679	3,597	3,080	4,284	4,934	1,422
Federal income taxes	2,461	2,256	527	2,888	2,392	3,373	3,996	1,069
State and local income taxes	589	497	148	668	608	784	731	149
Other taxes	158	104	4	41	79	126	207	203
GIFTS**	1,090	883	565	934	949	994	902	928
Food	76	30	29	26	16	81	29	7
Alcohol	15	11	11	15	19	6	14	4

(continued)

(continued from previous page)

	average consumer unit	men living alone						
		total	< 25	25–34	35–44	45–54	55–64	65 +
Housing	$291	$174	$129	$166	$147	$215	$196	$199
Housekeeping supplies	40	13	6	13	17	16	14	9
Apparel and services	231	182	142	299	205	156	189	92
Males, aged 2 or older	61	28	16	22	44	31	36	19
Females, aged 2 or older	78	45	31	57	58	71	47	9
Children under age 2	40	9	19	15	6	8	7	3
Other apparel products and services	51	100	76	206	97	47	100	61
Jewelry and watches	23	79	39	189	70	29	68	56
Transportation	67	59	102	47	43	89	48	32
Entertainment	101	93	26	99	159	68	76	104
Toys, games, hobbies, and tricycles	31	22	5	30	32	18	28	22
Other entertainment products and services	70	70	21	69	127	50	47	83
Personal care products and services	19	11	–	9	35	7	–	–
Education	159	110	82	103	73	225	150	58
All other gifts	90	131	38	156	213	109	119	133

* This figure does not include the amount paid for mortgage principle, which is considered an asset.
** Expenditures on gifts include only gifts purchased for non-household members. Gift spending is also included in the preceding product and service categories. Gift categories will not add to total gift spending because not all categories are shown.
Note: The Bureau of Labor Statistics uses consumer unit rather than household as the sampling unit in the Consumer Expenditure survey. For the definition of consumer unit, see glossary. (–) means sample is too small to make a reliable estimate.
Source: Bureau of Labor Statistics, 2000 Consumer Expenditure Survey, Internet site <ftp://ftp.bls.gov/pub/special.requests/ce/CrossTabs/y9900/SEXbyAGE/malesage.TXT>

Indexed Spending of Men Who Live Alone by Age, 1999–2000

(indexed spending of single-person consumer units (CU) headed by men, by spending category and age, 1999–2000)

	average consumer unit	men living alone						
		total	<25	25–34	35–44	45–54	55–64	65+
Average annual expenditures	100	66	43	75	77	73	75	54
FOOD	**100**	**61**	**43**	**73**	**71**	**64**	**68**	**48**
Food at home	**100**	**47**	**28**	**45**	**51**	**52**	**57**	**48**
Cereals and bakery products	100	45	26	42	46	53	53	50
Cereals and cereal products	100	42	23	43	45	46	46	51
Bakery products	100	46	27	41	46	56	57	49
Meats, poultry, fish, and eggs	100	45	24	40	53	54	58	42
Beef	100	42	25	35	50	51	59	38
Pork	100	43	17	36	52	51	56	47
Other meats	100	51	27	43	56	58	69	53
Poultry	100	43	24	40	55	53	49	36
Fish and seafood	100	48	25	51	56	62	58	40
Eggs	100	52	30	42	58	55	67	55
Dairy products	100	46	27	42	49	51	56	51
Fresh milk and cream	100	45	25	35	45	54	49	59
Other dairy products	100	46	27	46	51	48	60	45
Fruits and vegetables	100	47	23	42	48	50	58	58
Fresh fruits	100	47	20	42	44	45	68	63
Fresh vegetables	100	45	25	40	45	55	55	51
Processed fruits	100	49	26	45	52	48	54	65
Processed vegetables	100	46	20	41	52	54	51	52

(continued)

(continued from previous page)

	average consumer unit	men living alone						
		total	<25	25–34	35–44	45–54	55–64	65+
Other food at home	100	50	35	53	54	53	59	46
Sugar and other sweets	100	41	31	40	44	44	44	45
Fats and oils	100	43	27	41	48	45	48	48
Miscellaneous foods	100	50	32	52	52	56	57	49
Nonalcoholic beverages	100	54	43	59	61	54	68	44
Food prepared by CU on trips	100	63	50	80	78	45	88	38
Food away from home	**100**	**81**	**64**	**112**	**99**	**81**	**82**	**48**
ALCOHOLIC BEVERAGES	**100**	**143**	**188**	**167**	**182**	**105**	**143**	**81**
HOUSING	**100**	**67**	**36**	**76**	**78**	**79**	**77**	**59**
Shelter	**100**	**76**	**45**	**91**	**93**	**90**	**81**	**58**
Owned dwellings	100	50	6	44	70	63	76	48
Mortgage interest and charges	100	44	5	52	77	62	63	12
Property taxes	100	57	12	32	61	70	96	85
Maintenance, repair, insurance, other expenses	100	57	3	33	62	55	91	109
Rented dwellings	100	135	121	203	149	138	95	82
Other lodging	100	81	91	63	68	151	73	50
Utilities, fuels, and public services	**100**	**61**	**28**	**64**	**69**	**67**	**69**	**70**
Natural gas	100	60	17	53	61	69	79	87
Electricity	100	59	25	59	67	64	71	70
Fuel oil and other fuels	100	59	8	34	50	56	62	141
Telephone	100	68	41	85	82	74	65	54
Water and other public services	100	50	15	38	51	55	68	75

(continued)

(continued from previous page)

	average consumer unit	men living alone						
		total	< 25	25–34	35–44	45–54	55–64	65 +
Household services	100	42	8	31	31	50	60	76
Personal services	100	21	–	–	–	–	–	–
Other household services	100	61	13	47	54	75	115	81
Housekeeping supplies	100	36	14	31	39	40	42	48
Laundry and cleaning supplies	100	37	16	37	46	46	40	37
Other household products	100	37	11	28	37	37	44	58
Postage and stationery	100	35	16	33	37	41	43	39
Household furnishings and equipment	100	56	29	64	60	67	85	41
Household textiles	100	37	9	36	66	59	39	15
Furniture	100	56	27	90	59	61	65	32
Floor coverings	100	23	–	36	–	–	–	–
Major appliances	100	49	13	44	56	54	71	60
Small appliances, misc. housewares	100	62	18	33	37	77	52	137
Miscellaneous household equipment	100	63	41	66	66	78	115	31
APPAREL AND SERVICES	100	46	42	69	55	46	40	22
Men and boys	100	90	90	133	117	87	67	42
Men, aged 16 or older	100	113	114	166	145	108	83	52
Boys, aged 2 to 15	100	11	3	15	16	11	12	5
Women and girls	100	7	4	8	8	10	8	1
Women, aged 16 or older	100	6	4	5	8	11	9	1
Girls, aged 2 to 15	100	10	7	26	12	5	5	4
Children under age 2	100	11	24	19	8	10	9	4
Footwear	100	47	53	68	41	61	37	23
Other apparel products and services	100	83	55	132	105	63	86	49

(continued)

	average consumer unit	men living alone						
		total	<25	25–34	35–44	45–54	55–64	65 +
TRANSPORTATION	**100**	**63**	**51**	**69**	**80**	**61**	**76**	**48**
Vehicle purchases	**100**	**59**	**58**	**52**	**80**	**49**	**75**	**49**
Cars and trucks, new	100	60	42	55	87	48	69	58
Cars and trucks, used	100	57	73	43	71	46	80	40
Other vehicles	100	168	–	–	–	–	–	–
Gasoline and motor oil	**100**	**68**	**54**	**78**	**83**	**73**	**69**	**50**
Other vehicle expenses	**100**	**65**	**39**	**82**	**75**	**75**	**78**	**44**
Vehicle finance charges	100	46	31	67	56	49	58	19
Maintenance and repairs	100	74	52	76	91	81	91	57
Vehicle insurance	100	64	34	73	74	74	70	57
Vehicle rentals, leases, licenses, other charges	100	69	34	114	70	86	87	27
Public transportation	**100**	**71**	**57**	**99**	**90**	**51**	**83**	**47**
HEALTH CARE	**100**	**56**	**16**	**32**	**41**	**59**	**73**	**116**
Health insurance	100	51	11	33	42	46	61	111
Medical services	100	66	26	34	45	84	101	121
Drugs	100	54	12	23	34	59	67	126
Medical supplies	100	46	19	37	24	46	47	99
ENTERTAINMENT	**100**	**65**	**53**	**85**	**78**	**59**	**68**	**48**
Fees and admissions	100	67	61	94	77	56	67	43
Television, radios, sound equipment	100	85	76	104	94	86	90	60
Pets, toys, and playground equipment	100	47	22	48	68	53	58	35
Other entertainment products and services	100	51	35	74	66	31	46	45

(continued)

(continued from previous page)

	average consumer unit	men living alone						
		total	< 25	25–34	35–44	45–54	55–64	65 +
PERSONAL CARE PRODUCTS AND SERVICES	**100**	**41**	**27**	**47**	**53**	**46**	**38**	**32**
READING	**100**	**71**	**41**	**71**	**69**	**92**	**83**	**71**
EDUCATION	**100**	**79**	**252**	**97**	**24**	**49**	**40**	**14**
TOBACCO PRODUCTS AND SMOKING SUPPLIES	**100**	**88**	**51**	**73**	**121**	**130**	**104**	**56**
MISCELLANEOUS	**100**	**77**	**20**	**92**	**108**	**78**	**95**	**72**
CASH CONTRIBUTIONS	**100**	**97**	**15**	**102**	**98**	**120**	**121**	**127**
PERSONAL INSURANCE AND PENSIONS	**100**	**67**	**21**	**86**	**90**	**109**	**83**	**20**
Life and other personal insurance	100	42	9	27	39	59	64	59
Pensions and Social Security	100	71	22	94	96	116	85	15
PERSONAL TAXES	**100**	**89**	**21**	**112**	**96**	**134**	**154**	**44**
Federal income taxes	100	92	21	117	97	137	162	43
State and local income taxes	100	84	25	113	103	133	124	25
Other taxes	100	66	3	26	50	80	131	128
GIFTS	**100**	**81**	**52**	**86**	**87**	**91**	**83**	**85**
Food	**100**	**39**	**38**	**34**	**21**	**107**	**38**	**9**
Alcohol	**100**	**73**	**73**	**100**	**127**	**40**	**93**	**27**
Housing	**100**	**60**	**44**	**57**	**51**	**74**	**67**	**68**
Housekeeping supplies	100	33	15	33	43	40	35	23
Apparel and services	**100**	**79**	**61**	**129**	**89**	**68**	**82**	**40**
Males, aged 2 or older	100	46	26	36	72	51	59	31
Females, aged 2 or older	100	58	40	73	74	91	82	60

(continued)

(continued from previous page)

	average consumer unit	men living alone						
		total	<25	25–34	35–44	45–54	55–64	65+
Children under age 2	100	23	48	38	15	20	18	8
Other apparel products and services	100	196	149	404	190	92	196	120
Jewelry and watches	100	343	170	822	304	126	296	243
Transportation	**100**	**88**	**152**	**70**	**64**	**133**	**72**	**48**
Entertainment	**100**	**92**	**26**	**98**	**157**	**67**	**75**	**103**
Toys, games, hobbies, and tricycles	100	71	16	97	103	58	90	71
Other entertainment products and services	100	100	30	99	181	71	67	119
Personal care products and services	**100**	**58**	**–**	**47**	**184**	**37**	**–**	**–**
Education	**100**	**69**	**52**	**65**	**46**	**142**	**94**	**36**
All other gifts	**100**	**146**	**42**	**173**	**237**	**121**	**132**	**148**

Note: The index compares the spending of men living alone by age with the spending of the average consumer unit. 100 is the average. An index of 132 means the spending of men in the age group is 32 percent above the average for all consumer units, while an index of 75 means the spending of men in the age group is 25 percent below the average for all consumer units. The Bureau of Labor Statistics uses consumer unit rather than household as the sampling unit in the Consumer Expenditure Survey. For the definition of consumer unit, see glossary. (–) means sample is too small to make a reliable estimate.

Source: Calculations by New Strategist based on the Bureau of Labor Statistics' 2000 Consumer Expenditure Survey, Internet site <ftp://ftp.bls.gov/pub/special.requests/ce/CrossTabs/y9900/SEXbyAGE/malesage.TXT>

10

Wealth

Household net worth peaks in the older age groups.

Householders aged 65 to 74 had the highest net worth, a median of $146,500 in 1998.

The average household had just $22,400 in financial assets in 1998.

Financial assets account for 41 percent of all household assets, up from 30 percent in 1989.

The home is the single most valuable asset owned by most Americans.

The median value of their primary residence stood at $100,000 in 1998.

Most households have debts.

The average household with debt owed $33,300 in 1998, a surprisingly modest figure considering that it includes mortgages.

More than 80 percent of married couples are homeowners.

The majority of male-headed families are homeowners as well.

Nearly half of working men have pension coverage.

Those most likely to be covered by pensions are middle-aged professionals working for large corporations.

Net Worth Rises with Age

Householders aged 65 to 74 have the largest net worth.

The median net worth (assets minus debts) of American households stood at $71,600 in 1998 (the latest available data), according to the Federal Reserve Board's 1998 Survey of Consumer Finances. Thanks to the booming economy of the 1990s, median net worth grew 20 percent between 1989 and 1998, after adjusting for inflation.

The government collects data on the net worth, assets, and debts of households rather than individuals. Examining these measures by age of householder and household income reveals much about the wealth of the nation's men and women.

Net worth naturally rises with income, although it does not amount to much until annual household income tops $100,000. Net worth also rises with age, peaking in the 65-to-74 age group as people accumulate assets and pay off debts. The net worth of householders aged 65 or older grew rapidly in the 1990s because a more affluent generation entered the older age groups and because of housing value and stock market gains. The net worth of householders aged 65 to 74 grew 51 percent between 1989 and 1998, after adjusting for inflation. The net worth of householders aged 75 or older grew 36 percent during those years. In contrast, householders under age 55 saw their net worth decline.

■ The net worth of householders under age 55 has fallen because of lower homeownership rates in the younger age groups and growing mortgage debt among homeowners.

The youngest householders have little wealth

(median net worth of households by age of householder, 1998)

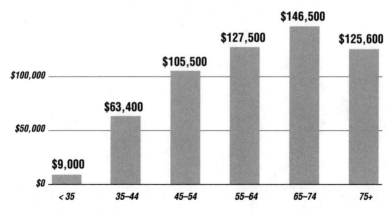

Net Worth of Households, 1989 and 1998

(median net worth of households by household income and age of householder, 1989 and 1998, and percent change, 1989–98; in 1998 dollars; numbers in thousands)

	1998	1989	percent change 1989–98
Total households	**$71,600**	**$59,700**	**19.9%**
Household income			
Under $10,000	3,600	1,900	89.5
$10,000 to $24,999	24,800	22,800	8.8
$25,000 to $49,999	60,300	58,100	3.8
$50,000 to $99,999	152,000	131,400	15.7
$100,000 or more	510,800	542,100	−5.8
Age of householder			
Under age 35	9,000	9,900	−9.1
Aged 35 to 44	63,400	71,800	−11.7
Aged 45 to 54	105,500	125,700	−16.1
Aged 55 to 64	127,500	124,600	2.3
Aged 65 to 74	146,500	97,100	50.9
Aged 75 or older	125,600	92,200	36.2

Source: Federal Reserve Board, Recent Changes in U.S. Family Finances: Results from the 1998 Survey of Consumer Finances, *Federal Reserve Bulletin, January 2000; calculations by New Strategist*

Financial Assets Are Growing

The median value of the financial assets owned by the average household stood at $22,400 in 1998.

The financial assets of households grew sharply in the 1990s as Americans poured money into the booming stock market. Financial assets accounted for 41 percent of all household assets in 1998, up from 30 percent in 1989. During those years, the percentage of households owning stock either directly or indirectly (through mutual funds and retirement accounts) grew from 32 to 49 percent.

The most commonly held financial asset is a transaction account, such as a checking account, owned by more than 90 percent of households. Retirement accounts are owned by 49 percent, and life insurance by 30 percent. The median value of retirement accounts was just $24,000 in 1998, peaking at $93,000 among households with incomes of $100,000 or more and, by age, at $46,800 among householders aged 55 to 64.

■ Because of the recent stock market decline, the financial assets of Americans are probably worth less today than in 1998, but the proportion of households owning financial assets is not likely to have changed much.

Nearly half of households own retirement accounts

(percent of households owning selected financial assets, 1998)

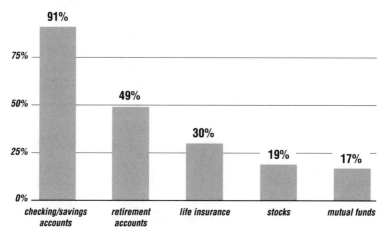

Financial Assets of Households, 1998

(percentage of households owning financial assets and median value of assets for owners, by household income, age of householder, and type of asset, 1998)

	any financial asset	transaction accounts	CDs	savings bonds	bonds	stocks	mutual funds	retirement accounts	life insurance	other managed	other financial
Percent owning, total households	92.9%	90.5%	15.3%	19.3%	3.0%	19.2%	16.5%	48.8%	29.6%	5.9%	9.4%
Household income											
Under $10,000	70.6	61.9	7.7	3.5	–	3.8	1.9	6.4	15.7	–	8.0
$10,000 to $24,999	89.9	86.5	16.8	10.2	1.3	7.2	7.6	25.4	20.9	4.9	8.2
$25,000 to $49,999	97.3	95.8	15.9	20.4	2.4	17.7	14.0	54.2	28.1	3.9	10.2
$50,000 to $99,999	99.8	99.3	16.4	30.6	3.3	27.7	25.8	73.5	39.8	8.0	9.1
$100,000 or more	100.0	100.0	16.8	32.3	12.2	56.6	44.8	88.6	50.1	15.8	12.7
Age of householder											
Under age 35	88.6	84.6	6.2	17.2	1.0	13.1	12.2	39.8	18.0	1.9	10.1
Aged 35 to 44	93.3	90.5	9.4	24.9	1.5	18.9	16.0	59.5	29.0	3.9	11.8
Aged 45 to 54	94.9	93.5	11.8	21.8	2.8	22.6	23.0	59.2	32.9	6.5	9.1
Aged 55 to 64	95.6	93.9	18.6	18.1	3.5	25.0	15.2	58.3	35.8	6.5	8.4
Aged 65 to 74	95.6	94.1	29.9	16.1	7.2	21.0	18.0	46.1	39.1	11.8	7.3
Aged 75 or older	92.1	89.7	35.9	12.0	5.9	18.0	15.1	16.7	32.6	11.6	6.4

(continued)

(continued from previous page)

	any financial asset	transaction accounts	CDs	savings bonds	bonds	stocks	mutual funds	retirement accounts	life insurance	other managed	other financial
Median value, total households	**$22,400**	**$3,100**	**$15,000**	**$1,000**	**$44,800**	**$17,500**	**$25,000**	**$24,000**	**$7,300**	**$31,500**	**$3,000**
Household income											
Under $10,000	$1,100	$500	$7,000	$1,800	–	$14,000	$6,000	$7,500	$3,000	–	$500
$10,000 to $24,999	4,800	1,300	20,000	1,000	$8,400	10,000	26,000	8,000	5,000	$30,000	1,100
$25,000 to $49,999	17,600	2,500	14,500	600	25,000	8,000	11,000	13,000	5,000	15,000	2,000
$50,000 to $99,999	57,200	6,000	13,300	1,000	19,000	15,000	25,000	31,000	9,500	32,000	5,000
$100,000 or more	244,300	19,000	22,000	1,500	108,000	55,000	65,000	93,000	18,000	100,000	25,000
Age of householder											
Under age 35	4,500	1,500	2,500	500	3,000	500	7,000	7,000	2,700	19,400	1,000
Aged 35 to 44	22,900	2,800	8,000	700	55,300	12,000	14,000	21,000	8,500	25,000	2,500
Aged 45 to 54	37,800	4,500	11,500	1,000	31,700	24,000	30,000	34,000	10,000	39,300	6,000
Aged 55 to 64	45,600	4,100	17,000	1,500	100,000	21,000	58,000	46,800	9,500	65,000	10,000
Aged 65 to 74	45,800	5,600	20,000	2,000	52,000	50,000	60,000	38,000	8,500	41,300	6,000
Aged 75 or older	36,600	6,100	30,000	5,000	18,800	50,000	59,000	30,000	5,000	30,000	8,200

Note: (–) means sample is too small to make a reliable estimate.
Source: Federal Reserve Board, Recent Changes in U.S. Family Finances: Results from the 1998 Survey of Consumer Finances, Federal Reserve Bulletin, January 2000

For Most Americans, the Home Is Their Most Valuable Asset

The median value of the primary residence stood at $100,000 in 1998.

Although a larger percentage of households own a vehicle (83 percent) than own a home (66 percent), the median value of vehicles was just $10,800 in 1998. For homeowners, the value of their house is greater than the value of any other single asset they own. Few households own other types of nonfinancial assets such as other residential property, nonresidential property, or businesses.

The median value of vehicles owned by households rises from just $4,000 for households with incomes below $10,000 to a peak of $26,800 for households with incomes of $100,000 or more. From ages 35 to 74, the median value of owned vehicles exceeds $10,000, with a peak of $13,500 among householders aged 55 to 64.

Not surprisingly, the value of owned homes also rises with income, to a peak of $240,000 among households with incomes of $100,000 or more. By age, housing values peak in the 45-to-54 age group at $120,000. Many of these households have hefty mortgages, however, lowering their net worth.

■ Because most older Americans have paid off their mortgages, their net worth is far higher than that of younger householders.

Home values rise with income

(median value of primary residence by household income, 1998)

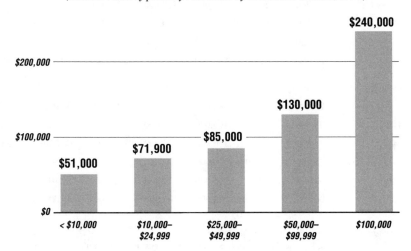

Nonfinancial Assets of Households, 1998

(percentage of households owning nonfinancial assets, and median value of assets for owners, by household income, age of householder, and type of asset, 1998; numbers in thousands)

	any nonfinancial asset	vehicles	primary residence	other residential property	equity in nonresi- dential property	business	other non- financial
Percent owning, total households	**89.9%**	**82.8%**	**66.2%**	**12.8%**	**8.6%**	**11.5%**	**8.5%**
Household income							
Under $10,000	62.7	51.3	34.5	–	–	3.8	2.6
$10,000 to $24,999	85.9	78.0	51.7	5.8	5.0	5.0	5.6
$25,000 to $49,999	95.6	89.6	68.2	11.4	7.6	10.3	9.4
$50,000 to $99,999	98.0	93.6	85.0	19.0	12.0	15.0	10.2
$100,000 or more	98.9	88.7	93.3	37.3	22.6	34.7	17.1
Age of householder							
Under age 35	83.3	78.3	38.9	3.5	2.7	7.2	7.3
Aged 35 to 44	92.0	85.8	67.1	12.2	7.5	14.7	8.8
Aged 45 to 54	92.9	87.5	74.4	16.2	12.2	16.2	9.2
Aged 55 to 64	93.8	88.7	80.3	20.4	10.4	14.3	8.5
Aged 65 to 74	92.0	83.4	81.5	18.4	15.3	10.1	10.3
Aged 75 or older	87.2	69.8	77.0	13.6	8.1	2.7	7.0
Median value, total households	**$97,800**	**$10,800**	**$100,000**	**$65,000**	**$38,000**	**$60,000**	**$10,000**
Household income							
Under $10,000	$16,300	$4,000	$51,000	–	–	$37,500	$5,000
$10,000 to $24,999	43,700	5,700	71,900	$70,000	$25,000	31,100	5,000
$25,000 to $49,999	83,500	10,200	85,000	50,000	28,000	37,500	6,000
$50,000 to $99,999	156,300	16,600	130,000	60,000	30,000	56,000	12,000
$100,000 or more	380,000	26,800	240,000	132,000	114,100	230,000	36,000
Age of householder							
Under age 35	22,700	8,900	84,000	42,500	25,000	34,000	5,000
Aged 35 to 44	103,500	11,400	101,000	45,000	20,000	62,500	8,000
Aged 45 to 54	126,800	12,800	120,000	74,000	45,000	100,000	14,000
Aged 55 to 64	126,900	13,500	110,000	70,000	54,000	62,500	28,000
Aged 65 to 74	109,900	10,800	95,000	75,000	45,000	61,100	10,000
Aged 75 or older	96,100	7,000	85,000	103,000	54,000	40,000	10,000

Note: (–) means sample is too small to make a reliable estimate.
Source: Federal Reserve Board, Recent Changes in U.S. Family Finances: Results from the 1998 Survey of Consumer Finances, *Federal Reserve Bulletin, January 2000*

Most Households Have Debts

Only among householders aged 75 or older is the majority debt free.

The average household with debt owed $33,300 in 1998. This figure is surprisingly modest, considering that it includes mortgage debt. Overall, 43 percent of households owed on a mortgage. Those with mortgages owed a median of $62,000. Forty-four percent of households owed a median of $8,700 on installment loans (such as car loans). The same percentage carried a median unpaid balance of $1,700 on their credit cards.

The percentage of households with debt rises with income. Households with incomes of $100,000 or more owe a median of $135,400, but much of that is mortgage debt. The richest households owe a median of $3,200 on their credit cards, and they owe a median of $15,400 on installment loans.

The percentage of households in debt declines with age after peaking in the 35-to-54 age group. The expenses of buying a home and raising children explain why 87 to 88 percent of 35-to-54-year-olds are in debt. Among householders aged 75 or older, only 25 percent are in debt.

■ As the large baby-boom generation pays off its mortgages and other debts, the net worth of Americans will rise.

The amount of money owed by households declines with age

(median amount of debt for households with debt, by age of householder, 1998)

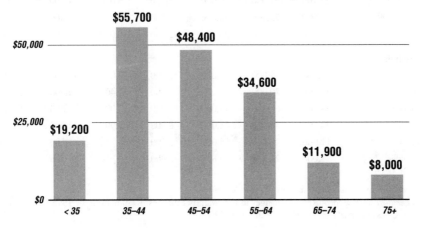

Households with Debt, 1998

(percentage of households with debt, and median value of debt for debtors, by household income, age of householder, and type of debt, 1998; numbers in thousands)

	any debt	home secured	other residential property	installment loans	other lines of credit	credit card balances	other debt
Percent with debt, total households	**74.1%**	**43.1%**	**5.1%**	**43.7%**	**2.3%**	**44.1%**	**8.8%**
Household income							
Under $10,000	41.7	8.3	–	25.7	–	20.6	3.6
$10,000 to $24,999	63.7	21.3	1.8	34.4	1.2	37.9	7.0
$25,000 to $49,999	79.6	43.7	4.1	50.0	2.9	49.9	7.7
$50,000 to $99,999	89.4	71.0	7.7	55.0	3.3	56.7	12.2
$100,000 or more	87.8	73.4	16.4	43.2	2.6	40.4	14.8
Age of householder							
Under age 35	81.2	33.2	2.0	60.0	2.4	50.7	9.6
Aged 35 to 44	87.6	58.7	6.7	63.3	3.6	51.3	11.4
Aged 45 to 54	87.0	58.8	6.7	51.2	3.6	52.5	11.1
Aged 55 to 64	76.4	49.4	7.8	37.9	1.6	45.7	8.3
Aged 65 to 74	51.4	26.0	5.1	20.2	–	29.2	4.1
Aged 75 or older	24.6	11.5	1.8	4.2	–	11.2	2.0
Median amount owed, total households	**$33,300**	**$62,000**	**$40,000**	**$8,700**	**$2,500**	**$1,700**	**$3,000**
Household income							
Under $10,000	$4,100	$16,000	–	$4,000	–	$1,100	$600
$10,000 to $24,999	8,000	34,200	$34,000	6,000	$1,100	1,000	1,300
$25,000 to $49,999	27,100	47,000	20,000	8,000	3,000	1,900	2,200
$50,000 to $99,999	75,000	75,000	42,000	11,300	2,800	2,400	3,800
$100,000 or more	135,400	123,800	60,000	15,400	5,000	3,200	10,000
Age of householder							
Under age 35	19,200	71,000	55,000	9,100	1,000	1,500	1,700
Aged 35 to 44	55,700	70,000	40,000	7,700	1,400	2,000	3,000
Aged 45 to 54	48,400	68,800	40,000	10,000	3,000	1,800	5,000
Aged 55 to 64	34,600	49,400	41,000	8,300	4,900	2,000	5,000
Aged 65 to 74	11,900	29,000	56,000	6,500	–	1,100	4,500
Aged 75 or older	8,000	21,200	29,800	8,900	–	700	1,700

Note: (–) means sample is too small to make a reliable estimate.
Source: Federal Reserve Board, Recent Changes in U.S. Family Finances: Results from the 1998 Survey of Consumer Finances, *Federal Reserve Bulletin, January 2000*

Homeownership Is Likely for Older Men

Married men are most likely to own a home.

Married couples are more likely to own a home than any other household type. While 67 percent of all households owned a home in 2000, the figure was a much higher 82 percent among married couples. Homeownership is more affordable for married couples than other household types because most couples are dual earners.

The 57 percent majority of male-headed families own a home, but among men who live alone only 47 percent are homeowners. The homeownership rate is an even lower 38 percent among men living with nonrelatives.

Regardless of household type, most older male householders are homeowners. Even among men heading nonfamily households, the majority of those aged 45 or older are homeowners. Among married men, 92 percent of those aged 65 or older are homeowners.

■ As the large baby-boom generation ages, the nation's homeownership rate will rise.

Most male family heads are homeowners

(homeownership rate by household type, 2000)

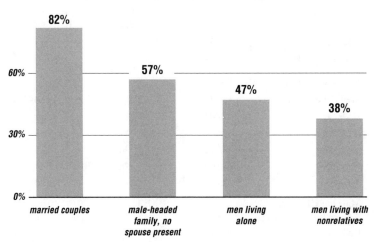

Male Homeowners by Household Type and Age of Householder, 2000

(total number of households, number of households owning a home, and homeowner share of total, by household type and age of householder, 2000; numbers in thousands)

		homeowners	
	total	number	share of total
Total households	**105,719**	**71,249**	**67.4%**
Under age 35	24,922	10,161	40.8
Aged 35 to 44	24,211	16,429	67.9
Aged 45 to 54	20,998	16,058	76.5
Aged 55 to 64	13,817	11,100	80.3
Aged 65 or older	21,771	17,501	80.4
FAMILY HOUSEHOLDS			
Married couples	**55,294**	**45,535**	**82.4**
Under age 35	10,799	6,584	61.0
Aged 35 to 44	14,260	11,668	81.8
Aged 45 to 54	12,605	11,169	88.6
Aged 55 to 64	8,269	7,485	90.5
Aged 65 or older	9,361	8,629	92.2
Male householder, no spouse present	**4,224**	**2,427**	**57.5**
Under age 35	1,546	617	39.9
Aged 35 to 44	1,122	673	60.0
Aged 45 to 54	773	527	68.2
Aged 55 to 64	359	259	72.1
Aged 65 or older	424	351	82.8
NONFAMILY HOUSEHOLDS			
Men living alone	**11,573**	**5,480**	**47.4**
Under age 35	3,007	782	26.0
Aged 35 to 44	2,584	1,157	44.8
Aged 45 to 54	2,212	1,126	50.9
Aged 55 to 64	1,360	776	57.1
Aged 65 or older	2,410	1,639	68.0
Male householder, living with nonrelatives	**3,625**	**1,377**	**38.0**
Under age 35	2,016	473	23.5
Aged 35 to 44	727	340	46.8
Aged 45 to 54	454	264	58.1
Aged 55 to 64	231	160	69.3
Aged 65 or older	197	140	71.1

Source: Bureau of the Census, Housing Vacancy Survey, Internet site <www.census.gov/hhes/www/housing/hvs/historic/histt15.html>; calculations by New Strategist

Nearly Half of Men Have Pension Coverage

Few of those working for small employers are covered, however.

Among employed men in 2000, 57 percent worked for an employer who offered a pension plan. Forty-six percent were covered by a plan. Pension coverage varies greatly by worker and employer characteristics.

Among men who work full-time, year-round, 56 percent are included in their employer's pension plan. But few men working part-time are covered. At least half of employed men aged 25 to 64 are covered by an employer's pension plan. Among men under age 25, however, only 15 percent are covered by a plan. Similarly, most men who earn $25,000 or more have pension coverage compared with only 30 percent of men earning between $15,000 and $25,000.

Only 19 percent of men who work for small employers—with fewer than 25 employees—are covered by a pension plan. Among those working for the largest employers, 65 percent are covered.

By occupation, white-collar workers are most likely to have pension coverage. From 61 to 64 percent of men in managerial, professional specialty, and technical occupations are covered. Among men in the armed forces, 65 percent are in a pension plan. Among men in precision production, craft, and repair occupations, however—which employ the largest share of men—only 45 percent are covered by a pension plan.

■ Men who devote their careers to big corporations are likely to be better off in retirement than those who worked for small companies.

Pension coverage is above 70 percent for high earners

(percent of employed men covered by employer-offered pension plans, by earnings, 2000)

Pension Coverage of Men, 2000

(total number of employed men aged 15 or older, number and percent with an employer-offered pension plan, and number and percent included in pension plan by selected characteristics, 2000; numbers in thousands)

| | | with employer-offered pension plan at work | | | |
| | | | | included in plan | |
	total	*number*	*percent*	*number*	*percent*
Total employed men	**79,180**	**45,200**	**57.1%**	**36,591**	**46.2%**
Age					
Under age 65	75,918	43,921	57.9	35,716	47.0
Aged 15 to 24	12,962	4,980	38.4	1,929	14.9
Aged 25 to 44	37,985	22,795	60.0	19,009	50.0
Aged 45 to 64	24,972	16,147	64.7	14,778	59.2
Aged 65 or older	3,261	1,278	39.2	875	26.8
Worked					
Full-time	68,985	41,804	60.6	35,492	51.4
50 weeks or more	58,765	37,251	63.4	32,790	55.8
27 to 49 weeks	6,106	3,008	49.3	2,043	33.5
26 weeks or less	4,114	1,545	37.6	659	16.0
Part-time	10,194	3,396	33.3	1,099	10.8
50 weeks or more	4,546	1,654	36.4	711	15.6
27 to 49 weeks	1,981	737	37.2	191	9.6
26 weeks or less	3,667	1,005	27.4	197	5.4
Size of employer					
Under 25 employees	23,924	5,693	23.8	4,622	19.3
25 to 99 employees	10,650	5,633	52.9	4,361	40.9
100 to 499 employees	10,692	7,280	68.1	5,897	55.1
500 to 999 employees	3,817	2,809	73.6	2,242	58.7
1,000 or more employees	30,096	23,784	79.0	19,469	64.7

(continued)

(continued from previous page)

Occupation	total	with employer-offered pension plan at work		included in plan	
		number	percent	number	percent
Executive, administrative, and managerial	11,413	7,698	67.5%	6,912	60.6%
Professional specialty	10,289	7,555	73.4	6,558	63.7
Technical, related support	2,224	1,669	75.0	1,388	62.4
Sales workers	8,815	4,628	52.5	3,518	39.9
Administrative support, including clerical	4,430	2,938	66.3	2,189	49.4
Precision production, craft, and repair	14,493	7,500	51.7	6,473	44.7
Machine operators, assemblers, inspectors	4,875	2,961	60.7	2,423	49.7
Transportation, material moving occupations	5,485	3,018	55.0	2,365	43.1
Handlers, equip. cleaners, helpers, and laborers	5,205	2,357	45.3	1,287	24.7
Service workers	8,142	3,799	46.7	2,679	32.9
Private household	50	2	4.0	2	4.0
Service workers except private household	8,092	3,797	46.9	2,677	33.1
Farming, forestry, fishing	3,180	606	19.1	389	12.2
Armed forces	630	471	74.8	409	64.8
Earnings					
Under $15,000	18,171	5,564	30.6	1,903	10.5
$15,000 to $24,999	13,268	5,896	44.4	4,022	30.3
$25,000 to $49,999	26,267	17,315	65.9	15,121	57.6
$50,000 to $74,999	12,122	9,310	76.8	8,815	72.7
$75,000 to $99,999	4,549	3,568	78.4	3,370	74.1
$100,000 or more	4,723	3,536	74.9	3,357	71.1

Source: Bureau of the Census, Current Population Survey, Internet site <http://ferret.bls.census.gov/macro/ 032001/noncash/nc8_002 .htm>; calculations by New Strategist

For More Information

The federal government is a rich source of data on almost every aspect of American life. Below are the Internet addresses of federal and other agencies that collect the demographic data analyzed in this book. Also shown are phone numbers of the agencies and of the subject specialists at the Census Bureau and the Bureau of Labor Statistics, organized alphabetically by name of agency or specialty topic. A list of State Data Centers and Small Business Development Centers is also included to help you track down demographic and economic information for your state or local area. E-mail addresses are shown when available.

Internet addresses

- Bureau of the Census; http://www.census.gov
- Bureau of Labor Statistics; http://www.bls.gov
- Current Population Survey; http://www.bls .census.gov/cps
- Higher Education Research Institute; http://www. gseis.ucla.edu/heri/heri.html
- Immigration and Naturalization Service; http:// www.ins.usdoj.gov/graphics/aboutins/statistics/ index.htm
- National Center for Education Statistics; http:// nces.ed.gov
- National Center for Health Statistics; http:// www.cdc.gov/nchs
- National Opinion Research Center; http:// www.norc.uchicago.edu
- National Telecommunications and Information Administration; http://www.ntia.doc.gov
- Federal Reserve Board, Survey of Consumer Finances; http://www.federalreserve.gov/pubs/ OSS/oss2/scfindex.html
- USDA Agricultural Research Service, Food Surveys Research Group; http://www.barc.usda.gov/ bhnrc/foodsurvey/home.htm

Subject specialists

Absences from work, Staff 202-691-6378
Aging population, Staff 301-457-2422
American Community Survey/C2SS Results, Larry McGinn 301-457-8050
Ancestry, Staff 301-457-2403
Apportionment, Edwin Byerly 301-457-2381
Apportionment and redistricting, Cathy McCully 301-457-4039
Business expenditures, Sheldon Ziman 301-457-3315

Business investment, Charles Funk 301-457-3324
Census 2000
- Aging population, Staff 301-457-2378
- American Community Survey, Larry McGinn 301-457-8050
- American Factfinder, Staff 301-763-INFO (4636)
- Annexations/boundary changes, Joe Marinucci 301-457-1099
- Apportionment, Edwin Byerly 301-457-2381
- Briefs, Staff 301-457-2437
- Census 2010, Paulette Lichtman-Panzer 301-457-4027
- Census history, Dave Pemberton 301-457-1167
- Citizenship, Staff 301-457-2403
- Commuting and place of work, Clara Reschovsky/Celia Boertlein 301-457-2454
- Confidentiality and privacy, Jerry Gates 301-457-2515
- Count question resolution, Staff 866-546-0527
- Count review, Paul Campbell 301-457-2390
- Data dissemination, Staff 301-763-INFO(4636)
- Disability, Sharon Stern 301-457-3213
- Education, Staff 301-457-2464
- Employment/unemployment, Staff 301-457-3242
- Foreign born, Staff 301-457-2403
- Geographic entities, Staff 301-457-1099
- Grandparents as caregivers, Staff 301-457-2465
- Group quarters population, Denise Smith 301-457-2378
- Hispanic origin, ethnicity, ancestry, Staff 301-457-2403
- Homeless, Edison Gore/Fay Nash 301-457-3998
- Housing, Staff 301-457-3237
- Immigration/emigration, Dianne Schmidley 301-457-2403
- Income, Staff 301-457-3242
- Island areas, Idabelle Hovland 301-457-8443
- Labor force status/work experience, Staff 301-457-3220
- Language spoken in home, Staff 301-457-2464
- Living arrangements, Staff 301-457-2465
- Marital status, Staff 301-457-2465
- Metropolitan areas, concepts and standards, Michael Ratcliffe 301-457-2419
- Microdata files, Amanda Shields 301-457-1326
- Migration, Jason Schachter/Carol Faber

202-691-6373

Employment and unemployment trends, Staff 202-691-6378

Employment projections, Staff 202-691-5745

Enterprise statistics, Trey Cole 301-457-3321

Equal employment opportunity data, Staff 301-457-3242

Fertility, Barbara Downs 301-457-2449

Finance, insurance and real estate, Economic Census, Faye Jacobs 301-457-2824

Flexitime and shift work, Staff 202-691-6378

Foreign-Born
• Current Population Survey, Staff 301-457-2403
• Decennial census, Kevin Deardorff 301-457-2403

Geographic concepts
• American Indian areas, Vince Osier 301-457-1099
• Annexations and boundary changes, Dorothy Stroz 301-457-1099
• Census blocks, Valerie Pfeiffer 301-457-1099
• Census county divisions, Pat Ream 301-457-1099
• Census designated places, Pat Ream 301-457-1099
• Census geographic concepts, Staff 301-457-1099
• Census tracts, Dan Flynn 301-457-1099
• Centers of population, Staff 301-457-1128
• Congressional districts, boundaries, Donna Zorn 301-457-1099
• Island areas, Jim Davis 301-457-1099
• Metropolitan areas, Rodger Johnson 301-457-2419
• Postal geography, Dan Sweeney 301-457-1106
• School districts, Dave Aultman 301-457-1106
• Traffic analysis zones, Carrie Saunders 301-457-1099
• Urban/rural concepts, Ryan Short 301-457-1099
• Urbanized areas, Ryan Short 301-457-1099
• Voting districts, John Byle 301-457-1099
• Zip code tabulation areas, Andy Flora 301-457-1100
• Zip codes, demographic data, Staff 301-763-INFO(4636)
• Zip codes, economic data, Andy Hait 301-457-8125
• Zip codes, geography, Andy Flora 301-457-1100

Governments
• Census of governments, Stephen Poyta 301-457-1486
• Criminal justice, Charlene Sebold 301-457-1591
• Education and library statistics, Johnny Monaco 301-457-2584
• Education, elementary-secondary, Larry MacDonald 301-457-1563

• Employment, Ellen Thompson 301-457-1531
• Federal expenditure data, Gerard Keffer 301-457-1522
• Finance, Stephen Owens 301-457-1485
• Government information, Staff 301-457-1580
• Governmental organization, Robert McArthur 301-457-1582
• Public retirement systems, Sandra Reading 301-457-1517

Group quarters population, Denise Smith 301-457-2378

Health insurance statistics, Staff 301-457-3242

Health surveys, Adrienne Oneto 301-457-3879

Higher Education Research Institute, 310-825-1925

Hispanic statistics, Staff 301-457-2403

Home-based work, Staff 202-691-6378

Homeless, Fay Nash 301-457-3998

Households and families, Staff 301-457-2465

Household wealth, Staff 301-457-3242

Housing
• American Housing Survey, Jane Kneessi/Barbara Williams 301-457-3235
• Census, Staff 301-457-3237
• Homeownership, vacancy data, Linda Cavanaugh/Robert Callis 301-457-3199
• Housing affordability, Howard Savage 301-457-3199
• Market absorption, Alan Friedman/Mary Schwartz 301-457-3199
• New York City Housing and Vacancy Survey, Alan Friedman/Robert Callis 301-457-3199
• Residential finance, Howard Savage 301-457-3199

Illegal immigration, Staff 301-457-2403

Immigration, general information, Staff 301-457-2422

Income statistics, Staff 301-457-3242

Industry and commodity classification, James Kristoff 301-457-4631

International Statistics
• Africa, Asia, Latin Am., North Am., and Oceania, Patricia Rowe 301-457-1358
• Aging population, Victoria Velkoff 301-457-1371
• China, People's Republic, Loraine West 301-457-1363
• Europe, former Soviet Union, Marc Rubin 301-457-1362
• Health, Karen Stanecki 301-457-1406
• International data base, Pat Dickerson/Peter Johnson 301-457-1403

- Technical assistance and training, Diana Lopez-Meisel 301-457-1444
- Women in development, Victoria Velkoff 301-457-1371

Job tenure, Staff 202-691-6378

Journey to work, Phil Salopek/Celia Boertlein 301-457-2454

Labor force concepts, Staff 202-691-6378

Language, Staff 301-457-2464

Longitudinal data/gross flows, Staff 202-691-6345

Longitudinal surveys, Ron Dopkowski 301-457-3801

Manufacturing and Mining
- Concentration, Patrick Duck 301-457-4699
- Exports from manufacturing establishments, John Gates 301-457-4589
- Financial statistics (Quarterly Financial Report), Ronald Horton 301-457-3343
- Foreign direct investment, Ron Taylor 301-457-1313
- Fuels, electric energy consumed and prod. index, Pat Horning 301-457-4680
- General information and data request, Nishea Quash 301-457-4673
- Industries
  - Electrical and trans. equip., instruments, misc., Milbren Thomas 301-457-4821
  - Food, textiles, and apparel, Robert Reinard 301-457-4810
  - Furniture, printing, Robert Reinard 301-457-4810
  - Metals and industrial machinery, Kenneth Hansen 301-457-4757
  - Wood, paper, chem., pet. prod., rubber, plastics, Nat Shelton 301-457-6614
- Mining, Pat Horning 301-457-4680
- Monthly shipments, inventories, and orders, Lee Wentela 301-457-4832
- Technology, research and development, and capacity use, Ron Taylor 301-457-4683

Marital and family characteristics of workers, Staff 202-691-6378

Metropolitan areas, Staff 301-457-2422

Metropolitan standards, Rodger Johnson 301-457-2419

Migration, Jason Schachter/Carol Faber 301-457-2454

Mineral industries, Pat Horning 301-457-4680

Minimum wage data, Steven Haugen 202-691-6378

Minority/women-owned businesses, Valerie Strang 301-457-3316

Minority workers, Staff 202-691-6378

Multiple jobholders, Staff 202-691-6373

National Center for Education Statistics, Staff 202-502-7300

National Center for Health Statistics, Staff 301-458-4636,

National Opinion Research Center, Staff 773-256-6000; norcinfo@norcmail.uchicago.edu

National Telecommunications and Information Administration, Staff 202-482-7002

North Am. Industry Class. System (NAICS), Wanda Dougherty 301-457-2772

Occupational and industrial statistics, Staff 301-457-3242

Occupational data, Staff 202-691-6378

Occupational employment statistics, Staff 202-691-6569; oesinfo@bls.gov

Older workers, Staff 202-691-6378

Outlying areas, population, Michael Levin 301-457-1444

Part-time workers, Staff 202-691-6378

Place of birth, Bonnie Berkner/Carol Faber 301-457-2454

Population estimates and projections, Staff 301-457-2422

Population information, Staff 301-457-2422

Poverty statistics, Staff 301-457-3242

Prisoner surveys, Marilyn Monahan 301-457-3925

Puerto Rico, Idabelle Hovland 301-457-8443

Quarterly Financial Report, Ronald Horton 301-457-3343

Race, concepts and interpretation, Staff 301-457-2402

Race statistics, Staff 301-457-2422

Retail Trade
- Advance monthly, Scott Scheleur 301-457-2713; svsd@census.gov
- Annual retail, Scott Scheleur 301-457-2713; svsd@census.gov
- Economic census, Fay Dorsett 301-457-2687; rcb@census.gov
- Monthly sales and inventory, Nancy Piesto 301-457-2706; retail.trade@census.gov
- Quarterly Financial Report, Ronald Horton 301-457-3343; cad@census.gov

School enrollment, Staff 301-457-2464

Seasonal adjustment methodology, Robert McIntire 202-691-6345

Services
- Current Reports, Ruth Bramblett 301-457-2766

- Economic census, Jack Moody 301-457-2689
- General information, Staff 1-800-541-8345

Small-area income and poverty estimates, David Waddington 301-457-3195

Special censuses, Josephine Ruffin 301-457-3577

Special surveys, Ron Dopkowski 301-457-3801

Special tabulations, Marie Pees 301-457-2447

State population estimates, Staff 301-457-2422

Statistics of U.S. businesses, Trey Cole 301-457-3321

Survey of Income and Program Participation (SIPP), Staff 301-457-3242

Transportation
- Commodity Flow Survey, John Fowler 301-457-2108; svsd@census.gov
- Economic census, James Barron 301-457-2811; ucb@census.gov
- Vehicle inventory and use, Kim Moore 301-457-2797; vius@census.gov
- Warehousing and trucking, Ruth Bramblett 301-457-2766; svsd@census.gov

Undercount, demographic analysis, Gregg Robinson 301-457-2103

Union membership, Staff 202-691-6378

Urban/rural population, Michael Ratcliff/Rodger Johnson 301-457-2419

USDA Agricultural Research Service, Food Surveys Research Group, Staff 301-504-0170

Veterans in labor force, Staff 202-691-6378

Veterans' status, Staff 301-457-3242

Voters, characteristics, Staff 301-457-2445

Voting age population, Jennifer Day 301-457-2464

Weekly earnings, Staff 202-691-6378

Wholesale Trade
- Annual wholesale, Scott Scheleur 301-457-2713; svsd@census.gov
- Current sales and inventories, Scott Scheleur 301-457-2713; svsd@census.gov
- Economic census, Donna Hambric 301-457-2725; wcb@census.gov
- Quarterly Financial Report, Ronald Horton 301-457-3343; csd@census.gov

Women, Staff 301-457-2378

Women in the labor force, Staff 202-691-6378

Work experience, Staff 202-691-6378

Working poor, Staff 202-691-6378

Youth, students, and dropouts in labor force, Staff 202-691-6378

Census Regional Offices

Information specialists in the Census Bureau's 12 regional offices answer thousands of questions each year. If you have questions about the Census Bureau's products and services, you can contact the regional office serving your state. The states served by each regional office are listed in parentheses.

- Atlanta (AL, FL, GA) 404-730-3833; www.census.gov/atlanta
- Boston, MA (CT, MA, ME, NH, NY, RI, VT) 617-424-0510; www.census.gov/boston
- Charlotte (KY, NC, SC, TN, VA) 704-344-6144; www.census.gov/charlotte
- Chicago (IL, IN, WI) 708-562-1350; www.census.gov/chicago
- Dallas (LA, MS, TX) 214-253-4481; www.census.gov/dallas
- Denver (AZ, CO, MT, NE, ND, NM, NV, SD, UT, WY) 303-969-7750; www.census.gov/denver
- Detroit (MI, OH, WV) 313-259-1875; www.census.gov/detroit
- Kansas City (AR, IA, KS, MN, MO, OK) 913-551-6711; www.census.gov/kansascity
- Los Angeles (southern CA, HI) 818-904-6339; www.census.gov/losangeles
- New York (NY, NJ—selected counties) 212-264-4730; www.census.gov/newyork
- Philadelphia (DE, DC, MD, NJ—selected counties, PA) 215-656-7578; www.census.gov/philadelphia
- Seattle (northern CA, AK, ID, OR, WA) 206-553-5835; www.census.gov/seattle
- Puerto Rico and the U.S. Virgin Islands are serviced by the Boston regional office. All other outlying areas are serviced by the Los Angeles regional office.

State Data Centers and Business and Industry Data Centers

For demographic and economic information about states and local areas, contact your State Data Center (SDC) or Business and Industry Data Center (BIDC). Every state has a State Data

Center. Below are listed the leading centers for each state—usually a state government agency, university, or library that heads a network of affiliate centers. Asterisks (*) identify states that also have BIDCs. In some states, one agency serves as the lead for both the SDC and the BIDC. The BIDC is listed separately if a separate agency serves as the lead.

- Alabama, Annette Watters, University of Alabama 205-348-6191; awatters@cba.ua.edu
- Alaska, Kathryn Lizik, Department of Labor 907-465-2437; kathryn_lizik@labor.state.ak.us
- American Samoa, Vaitoelav Filiga, Department of Commerce 684-633-5155; vfiliga@doc.asg.as
- Arizona,* Betty Jeffries, Department of Economic Security 602-542-5984; popstats@de.state.az.us
- Arkansas, Sarah Breshears, Univ. of Arkansas/ Little Rock 501-569-8530; sgbreshears@ualr.edu
- California, Julie Hoang, Department of Finance 916-323-4086; fijhoang@dof.ca.gov
- Colorado, Rebecca Picaso, Dept. of Local Affairs 303-866-2156; rebecca.picaso@state.co.us
- Connecticut, Bill Kraynak, Office of Policy and Management 860-418-6230; william.kraynak@po.state.ct.us
- Delaware,* O'Shell Howell, Economic Development Office 302-739-4271; oshowell@state.de.us
- District of Columbia, Herb Bixhorn, Mayor's Office of Planning 202-442-7603; herb.bixhorn@dc.gov
- Florida,* Pam Schenker, Dept. of Labor and Employment Security 850-488-1048; pamela.schenker@awi.state.fl.us
- Georgia, Robert Giacomini, Office of Planning and Budget 404-463-1115; robert.giacomini@sdrc.gadata.org
- Guam, Isabel Lujan, Department of Commerce 671-475-0321; idlujan@mail.gov.gu
- Hawaii, Jan Nakamoto, Dept. of Business, Econ. Dev., and Tourism 808-586-2493; jnakamot@dbedt.hawaii.gov
- Idaho, Alan Porter, Department of Commerce 208-334-2470; aporter@idoc.state.id.us
- Illinois, Suzanne Ebetsch, Bureau of the Budget 217-782-1381; sebetsch@commerce.state.il.us
- Indiana,* Roberta Brooker, State Library 317-232-3733; rbooker@statelib.lib.in.us

- Indiana BIDC, Carol Rogers, Business Research Center 317-274-2205; rogersc@iupui.edu
- Iowa, Beth Henning, State Library 515-281-4350; beth.henning@lib.state.ia.us
- Kansas, Marc Galbraith, State Library 785-296-3296; ksstl3lb@ink.org
- Kentucky,* Ron Crouch, University of Louisville 502-852-7990; rtcrou01gwise@louisville.edu
- Louisiana, Karen Paterson, Office of Planning and Budget 225-219-4025; webmaster@doa.state.la.us
- Maine,* Eric Vonmagnus, State Planning Office 207-287-2989; eric.vonmagnus@state.me.us
- Maryland,* Jane Traynham, Office of Planning 410-767-4450; jtraynham@mdp.state.md.us
- Massachusetts,* John Gaviglio, Institute for Social and Econ. Research 413-545-3460; miser@miser.umass.edu
- Michigan, Carolyn Lauer, Dept. of Management and Budget 517-373-7910; Lauerc@state.mi.us
- Minnesota,* David Birkholz, State Demographer's Office 651-296-2557; david.birkholz@mnplan.state.mn.us
- Minnesota BIDC, Barbara Ronningen, State Demographer's Office 651-296-2557; barbara.ronningen@mnplan.state.mn.us
- Mississippi,* Rachel McNeely, University of Mississippi 662-915-7288; rmcneely@olemiss.edu
- Mississippi BIDC, Deloise Tate, Dept. of Econ. and Comm. Dev. 601-359-3593; dtate@mississippi.org
- Missouri,* Debra Pitts, State Library 573-526-7648; pittsd@sosmail.state.mo.us
- Missouri BIDC, Fred Goss, Small Business Development Center 573-341-4559; fredgoss@umr.edu
- Montana,* Pam Harris, Department of Commerce 406-444-4302; paharris@state.mt.us
- Nebraska, Jerome Deichert, University of Nebraska at Omaha 402-554-2134; jerome_deichert@unomaha.edu
- Nevada, Ramona Reno, State Library and Archives 775-684-3326; rlreno@clan.lib.nv.us
- New Hampshire, Thomas Duffy, Office of State Planning 603-271-2155; t_duffy@osp.state.nh.us
- New Jersey,* David Joye, Department of Labor 609-984-2595; djoye@dol.state.nj.us
- New Mexico,* Kevin Kargacin, University of New Mexico 505-277-6626; kargacin@unm.edu
- New Mexico BIDC, Beth Davis, Economic Development Dept. 505-827-0264; edavis@yucca.edd.state.nm.us

- New York,* Staff, Department of Economic Development 518-292-5300; rscardamalia@empire.state.ny.us
- North Carolina,* Staff, State Library 919-733-3270; francine@ospl.state.nc.us
- North Dakota, Richard Rathge, State University 701-231-8621; Richard.rathge@ndsu.nodak.edu
- Northern Mariana Islands, Diego A. Sasamoto, Dept. of Commerce 670-664-3034; csd@itecnmi.com
- Ohio,* Barry Bennett, Department of Development 614-466-2115; bbennett@odod.state.oh.us
- Oklahoma,* Jeff Wallace, Dept. of Commerce 405-815-5184; jeff_wallace@odoc.state.ok.us
- Oregon, George Hough, Portland State University. 503-725-5159; houghg@mail.pdx.edu
- Pennsylvania,* Sue Copella, Pennsylvania State Univ./Harrisburg 717-948-6336; sdc3@psu.edu
- Puerto Rico, Lillian Torres Aguirre, Planning Bd. 787-728-4430; torres_l@jp.prstar.net
- Rhode Island, Mark Brown, Department of Administration 401-222-6183; mbrown@planning.state.ri.us
- South Carolina, Mike MacFarlane, Budget and Control Board 803-734-3780; mmacfarl@drss.state.sc.us
- South Dakota, Nancy Nelson, Univ. of South Dakota 605-677-5287; nnelson@usd.edu
- Tennessee, Betty Vickers, University of Tennessee 423-974-6080; bvickers@utk.edu
- Texas,* Steve Murdock, Texas A&M University 409-845-5115/5332; smurdock@rsocsun.tamu.edu
- Texas BIDC, Michael West, Dept. of Econ. Dev. 512-936-0292; mwest@ded.state.tx.us
- Utah,* Lisa Hillman, Office of Planning and Budget 801-537-9013; lhillman@gov.state.ut.us
- Vermont, Sharon Whitaker, University of Vermont 802-656-3021; sharon.whitaker@uvm.edu
- Virgin Islands, Frank Mills, University of the Virgin Islands 340-693-1027; fmills@uvi.edu
- Virginia,* Don Lillywhite, Virginia Employment Comm. 804-786-7496; dlillywhite@vec.state.va.us
- Washington,* Yi Zhao, Office of Financial Management 360-902-0599; yi.zhao@ofm.wa.gov
- West Virginia,* Delphine Coffey, Office of Comm. and Ind. Dev. 304-558-4010; dcoffey@wvdo.org
- West Virginia BIDC, Randy Childs, Center for Economic Research 304-293-6524; childs@be.wvu.edu
- Wisconsin,* Robert Naylor, Depart of Admin. 608-266-1927; bob.naylor@doa.state.wi.us
- Wisconsin BIDC, Dan Veroff, Univ. of Wisc. 608-265-9545; dlveroff@facstaff.wisc.edu
- Wyoming, Wenlin Liu, Dept. of Admin. and Information 307-766-2925; wliu@state.wy.us

Glossary

adjusted for inflation Income or a change in income that has been adjusted for the rise in the cost of living, or the consumer price index (CPI-U-XI).

age Classification by age is based on the age of the person at his/her last birthday.

American Indians and Alaska Natives American Indians and Alaska Natives (Eskimos and Aleuts) are people who reported their race as American Indian and/or entered the name of an American Indian tribe on the 2000 census form. In 2000 census data, the term "American Indian" includes those who identified themselves as American Indian and no other race (called "American Indian alone") and those who identified themselves as American Indian and some other race (called "American Indian in combination"). The combination of the two groups is termed "American Indian, alone or in combination."

Asian The term "Asian" is defined differently depending on whether census or survey data are shown. In 2000 census data, Asians do not include Pacific Islanders. The term "Asian" includes those who identified themselves as Asian and no other race (called "Asian alone") and those who identified themselves as Asian and some other race (called "Asian in combination"). The combination of the two groups is termed "Asian, alone or in combination." Asian estimates in survey data differ from 2000 census counts in part because the multiracial option was not yet included in surveys and other data collection efforts in 2000. Also, in surveys and other data collections, Asian figures include Pacific Islanders.

baby boom Americans born between 1946 and 1964. Baby boomers were aged 36 to 54 in 2000.

baby bust Americans born between 1965 and 1976, also known as Generation X. In 2000, baby busters were aged 24 to 35.

black The black racial category includes those who identified themselves as "black or African American." The term "black" is defined differently depending on whether census or survey data are shown. In 2000 census data, the term "black" includes those who identified themselves as black and no other race (called "black alone") and those who identified themselves as black and some other race (called "black in combination"). The combination of the two groups is termed "black, alone or in combination." Because the multiracial option was not yet included in surveys and other

data collection efforts in 2000, black estimates from survey data will be different from 2000 census counts.

central cities The largest city in a metropolitan area is called the central city. The balance of the metropolitan area outside the central city is regarded as the "suburbs."

Consolidated Metropolitan Statistical Area (CMSA) A geographic entity defined by the federal Office of Management and Budget for use by federal statistical agencies. An area becomes a CMSA if it qualifies as a metropolitan statistical area, has a population of 1,000,000 or more, if component parts are recognized as Primary Metropolitan Statistical Areas, and if local opinion favors the designation.

Consumer Expenditure Survey The Consumer Expenditure Survey (CEX) is an ongoing survey of the day-to-day spending of American households administered by the Bureau of Labor Statistics. Results are used to update prices for the Consumer Price Index. The CEX includes an interview survey and a diary survey. The average spending figures shown in this book are the integrated data from both the diary and interview components of the survey. Two separate, nationally representative samples are used for the interview and diary surveys. For the interview survey, about 7,500 consumer units are interviewed on a rotating panel basis each quarter for five consecutive quarters. For the diary survey, 7,500 consumer units keep weekly diaries of spending for two consecutive weeks.

consumer unit For convenience, the terms consumer unit and household are used interchangeably in the spending tables of this book, although consumer units are somewhat different from the Census Bureau's households. Consumer units are all related members of a household, or financially independent members of a household. A household may include more than one consumer unit.

Current Population Survey A nationally representative survey of the civilian noninstitutional population aged 15 or older. It is taken monthly by the Census Bureau, collecting information from 50,000 households on employment and unemployment. In March of each year, the survey includes a demographic supplement which is the source of most national data on the characteristics of Americans, such as their educational attainment, living arrangements, and incomes. The survey has been conducted for more than 50 years.

disability People were considered to have a disability if they met any of the following criteria: 1) used a wheelchair, cane, crutches, or walker; 2) had difficulty performing one or more functional activities (seeing, hearing, speaking, lifting, carrying, using stairs, walking, or grasping small objects); 3) had difficulty with one or more activities of daily living (the ADLs include getting around inside the home, getting in or out of a bed or chair, bathing, dressing, eating, and toileting); 4) had difficulty with one or more instrumental activities of daily living (the IADLs include going outside the home, keeping track of money and bills, preparing meals, doing light housework, taking prescription medicines in the right amount at the right time, and using the telephone); 5) had one or more conditions (learning disability, mental retardation, Alzheimer's disease, or some other type of mental or emotional condition); 6) had any other mental or emotional condition that seriously interfered with everyday activities (frequently depressed or anxious, trouble getting along with others, trouble concentrating, trouble coping with day-to-day stress); 7) had a condition that limited the ability to work around the house; 8) if age 16 to 67, had a condition that made it difficult to work at a job or business; 9) received federal benefits based on an inability to work. Individuals were considered to have a severe disability if they met criteria 1, 6, or 9; or had Alzheimer's disease, mental retardation, or another developmental disability; or were unable to perform or needed help to perform one or more of the activities in criteria 2, 3, 4, 7, or 8.

dual-earner couple A married couple in which both husband and wife are in the labor force.

earnings A type of income, earnings is the amount of money a person receives from his or her job. See also Income.

economic census Collective name for the censuses of construction, manufactures, minerals, minority- and women-owned businesses, retail trade, service industries, transportation, and wholesale trade. The economic censuses are conducted by the Census Bureau every five years, in years ending in 2 and 7.

employed All civilians who did any work as a paid employee or farmer/self-employed worker, or who worked 15 hours or more as an unpaid farm worker or in a family-owned business, during the reference period. All those who have jobs but who are temporarily absent from their jobs due to illness, bad weather, vacation, labor management dispute, or personal reasons are considered employed.

expenditure The transaction cost including excise and sales taxes of goods and services acquired during the survey period. The full cost of each purchase is recorded even though full payment may not have been made at the date of purchase. Average expenditure figures may be artificially low for infrequently purchased items such as cars because figures are calculated using all consumer units within a demographic segment rather than just purchasers. Expenditure estimates include money spent on gifts.

family A group of two or more people (one of whom is the householder) related by birth, marriage, or adoption and living in the same household.

family household A household maintained by a householder who lives with one or more people related to him or her by blood, marriage, or adoption.

female/male householder A woman or man who maintains a household without a spouse present. May head family or nonfamily households.

firm In the business tables, a firm is a business consisting of one or more domestic establishments specified by the reporting firm as under its ownership or control at the end of 1997. If a company owned or controlled other companies, all establishments of the subsidiaries are included as part of the owning or controlling company.

foreign-born population People who are not U.S. citizens at birth.

full-time employment Full-time is 35 or more hours of work per week during a majority of the weeks worked during the preceding calendar year.

full-time, year-round Indicates 50 or more weeks of full-time employment during the previous calendar year.

General Social Survey The General Social Survey (GSS) is a biennial survey of the attitudes of Americans taken by the University of Chicago's National Opinion Research Center (NORC). NORC conducts the GSS through face-to-face interviews with an independently drawn, representative sample of 1,500 to 3,000 noninstitutionalized English-speaking people aged 18 or older who live in the United States.

generation X Americans born between 1965 and 1976, also known as the baby-bust generation. Generation Xers were aged 24 to 35 in 2000.

geographic regions The four major regions and nine census divisions of the United States are the state groupings as shown below:

Northeast:
—New England: Connecticut, Maine, Massachusetts, New Hampshire, Rhode Island, and Vermont

—Middle Atlantic: New Jersey, New York, and Pennsylvania

Midwest:
—East North Central: Illinois, Indiana, Michigan, Ohio, and Wisconsin
—West North Central: Iowa, Kansas, Minnesota, Missouri, Nebraska, North Dakota, and South Dakota

South:
—South Atlantic: Delaware, District of Columbia, Florida, Georgia, Maryland, North Carolina, South Carolina, Virginia, and West Virginia
—East South Central: Alabama, Kentucky, Mississippi, and Tennessee
—West South Central: Arkansas, Louisiana, Oklahoma, and Texas

West:
—Mountain: Arizona, Colorado, Idaho, Montana, Nevada, New Mexico, Utah, and Wyoming
—Pacific: Alaska, California, Hawaii, Oregon, and Washington

Hispanic Hispanic origin is self-reported in a question separate from race. Because Hispanic is an ethnic origin rather than a race, Hispanics may be of any race. While most Hispanics are white, there are black, Asian, American Indian, and even Native Hawaiian Hispanics. On the 2000 census, many Hispanics identified their race as "other" rather than white, black, and so on. In fact, 90 percent of people identifying their race as "other" also identified themselves as Hispanic. The 2000 census count of Hispanics differs from estimates in the Current Population Survey and other data collections in part due to methodological differences. Numbers from the 2000 census are more accurate than survey data.

household All the people who occupy a housing unit. A household includes the related family members and all the unrelated people, if any, such as lodgers, foster children, wards, or employees who share the housing unit. A person living alone is counted as a household. A group of unrelated people who share a housing unit as roommates or unmarried partners also counts as a household. Households do not include group quarters such as college dormitories, prisons, or nursing homes.

household, race/ethnicity of Households are categorized according to the race or ethnicity of the householder only.

householder The householder is the person (or one of the persons) in whose name the housing unit is owned or rented or, if there is no such person, any adult member. With married couples, the householder may be either the husband or wife. The householder is the reference person for the household.

householder, age of The age of the householder is used to categorize households into age groups such as those used in this book. Married couples, for example, are classified according to the age of either the husband or wife, depending on which one identified him or herself as the householder.

housing unit A housing unit is a house, an apartment, a group of rooms, or a single room occupied or intended for occupancy as separate living quarters. Separate living quarters are those in which the occupants do not live and eat with any other persons in the structure and that have direct access from the outside of the building or through a common hall that is used or intended for use by the occupants of another unit or by the general public. The occupants may be a single family, one person living alone, two or more families living together, or any other group of related or unrelated persons who share living arrangements.

immigrants Aliens admitted for legal permanent residence in the United States.

income Money received in the preceding calendar year by each person aged 15 or older from each of the following sources: (1) earnings from longest job (or self-employment); (2) earnings from jobs other than longest job; (3) unemployment compensation; (4) workers' compensation; (5) Social Security; (6) Supplemental Security income; (7) public assistance; (8) veterans' payments; (9) survivor benefits; (10) disability benefits; (11) retirement pensions; (12) interest; (13) dividends; (14) rents and royalties or estates and trusts; (15) educational assistance; (16) alimony; (17) child support; (18) financial assistance from outside the household, and other periodic income. Income is reported in several ways in this book. Household income is the combined income of all household members. Income of persons is all income accruing to a person from all sources. Earnings is the amount of money a person receives from his or her job.

industry The kind of business conducted by a worker's employing organization. For those who work at two or more jobs, the data refer to the job at which the person worked the greatest number of hours.

job tenure The length of time a worker has been employed continuously by the same employer.

labor force The labor force tables in this book show the civilian labor force only. The labor force includes both the employed and the unemployed (people who are looking for work). People are counted as in the labor force if they were working or looking for work during the reference week in which the Census Bureau fields the Current Population Survey.

labor force participation rate The percent of people in the labor force, which includes both the employed and unemployed. Labor force participation rates may be shown for sex-age groups or other special populations such as mothers of children of a given age.

legal form of organization In the business tables, there are five legal forms of organization: 1) C corporation, any legally incorporated business, except subchapter S, under state laws; 2) Subchapter S corporations, legally incorporated businesses under state laws. A subchapter S corporation is a special IRS designation for legally incorporated businesses with 75 or fewer shareholders who, because of tax advantages, elect to be taxed as individual shareholders rather than as a corporation; 3) individual proprietorships, unincorporated businesses owned by individuals. Also included in this category are self-employed persons. The business may be the only occupation of an individual or the secondary activity of an individual who works full-time for someone else; 4) partnerships, unincorporated businesses owned by two or more people; and 5) other, includes cooperatives, estates, receiverships, and businesses classified as unknown legal forms of organization.

married-couple family group Married couples who may or may not be householders. Those who are householders are "married couple households." Those who are not householders are married couples living in a household headed by someone else, such as a parent. Because married couple family groups include married couple households, the number of married couple family groups will always outnumber married couple households.

married couples with or without children under age 18 Refers to married couples with or without children under age 18 living in the same household. Couples without children under age 18 may be parents of grown children who live elsewhere, or they could be childless couples.

median The median is the amount that divides the population or households into two equal portions: one below and one above the median. Medians can be calculated for income, age, and many other characteristics.

median income The amount that divides the income distribution into two equal groups, half having incomes above the median, half having incomes below the median. The medians for households or families are based on all households or families. The median

for people is based on all people aged 15 or older with income.

Metropolitan Statistical Area (MSA) A geographic entity defined by the federal Office of Management and Budget for use by federal statistical agencies, based on the concept of a core area with a large population nucleus, plus adjacent communities having a high degree of economic and social integration with that core. Qualification as an MSA requires the presence of a city with 50,000 or more inhabitants, or the presence of an Urbanized Area (UA) and a total population of at least 100,000 (75,000 in New England). The county or counties containing the largest city and surrounding densely settled territory are central counties of the MSA. Additional outlying counties qualify to be included in the MSA by meeting certain other criteria of metropolitan character, such as a specified minimum population density or percentage of the population that is urban. MSAs in New England are defined in terms of minor civil divisions, following rules concerning commuting and population density.

millennial generation Americans born between 1977 and 1994. Millennials were aged 6 to 23 in 2000.

mobility status People are classified according to their mobility status on the basis of a comparison between their place of residence at the time of the March Current Population Survey and their place of residence in March of the previous year. Nonmovers are people living in the same house at the end of the period as at the beginning of the period. Movers are people living in a different house at the end of the period than at the beginning of the period. Movers from abroad are either citizens or aliens whose place of residence is outside the United States at the beginning of the period, that is, in an outlying area under the jurisdiction

of the United States or in a foreign country. The mobility status for children is fully allocated from the mother if she is in the household; otherwise it is allocated from the householder.

Native Hawaiian and other Pacific Islander The 2000 census, for the first time, identified this group as a separate racial category from Asians. The term "Native Hawaiian and other Pacific Islander" includes those who identified themselves as Native Hawaiian and other Pacific Islander and no other race (called "Native Hawaiian and other Pacific Islander alone") and those who identified themselves as Native Hawaiian and other Pacific Islander and some other race (called "Native Hawaiian and other Pacific Islander in combination"). The combination of the two groups is termed "Native Hawaiian and other Pacific Islander, alone or in combination."

nonfamily household A household maintained by a householder who lives alone or who lives with people to whom he or she is not related.

nonfamily householder A householder who lives alone or with nonrelatives.

non-Hispanic white The 2000 census classified people as non-Hispanic white if they identified their race as "white alone" and did not indicate their ethnicity as Hispanic. This definition is close to the one used in the Current Population Survey and other government data collection efforts.

nonmetropolitan area Counties that are not classified as metropolitan areas.

occupation Occupational classification is based on the kind of work a person did at his or her job during the previous calendar year. If a person changed jobs during the year, the data refer to the occupation of the job held the longest during the year.

occupied housing units A housing unit is classified as occupied if a person or group of people is living in it or if the occupants are only temporarily absent-on vacation, example. By definition, the count of occupied housing units is the same as the count of households.

other race The 2000 census included "other race" as a sixth racial category. The category was meant to capture the few Americans, such as Creoles, who may not consider themselves as belonging to the other five racial groups. In fact, more than 18 million Americans identified themselves as "other race," including 42 percent of the nation's Hispanics. Among the 18 million people who claim to be of "other" race, 90 percent also identified themselves as Hispanic. The government considers Hispanic to be an ethnic identification rather than a race since there are white, black, American Indian, and Asian Hispanics. But many Hispanics consider their ethnicity to be a separate race. In 2000 census tables, the term "Other race" includes those who identified themselves as "other alone" and those who identified themselves as "other in combination" with white, black, or another of the racial categories. The combination of the two groups is termed "other, alone or in combination."

outside central city The portion of a metropolitan county or counties that falls outside of the central city or cities; generally regarded as the suburbs.

own children A child under age 18 who is a son or daughter by birth, marriage (stepchild), or adoption. For 100-percent tabulations, own children are all sons/daughters of householders who are under age 18. In sample data, own children are sons/daughters of householders who are under age 18 and who have never been married. Therefore, numbers of own children will differ depending on how the data were collected.

owner occupied A housing unit is "owner occupied" if the owner lives in the unit, even if it is mortgaged or not fully paid for. A cooperative or condominium unit is "owner occupied" only if the owner lives in it. All other occupied units are classified as "renter occupied."

paid employees All employees, full-time and part-time, reported on a firm's payroll during specified pay periods in 1997. People on paid sick leave, paid holidays, and paid vacations are included as employees, as are salaried officers and executives of corporations. However, proprietors and partners of unincorporated businesses are not considered employees.

part-time employment Part-time employment is less than 35 hours of work per week in a majority of the weeks worked during the year.

payroll In the business tables, payroll is the combined amount of wages, tips, and other compensation including salaries, vacation allowances, bonuses, commissions, sick-leave pay, and the value of payments-in-kind paid to all employees during the calendar year before deductions for Social Security, income tax, insurance, union dues, etc.

pension plan Pension plan participation is collected by the March Current Population Survey. The CPS asks respondents whether pension plan coverage is available to them through an employer or union and if they are included in the plan. This information was collected for people aged 15 or older who worked during the previous calendar year.

percent change The change (either positive or negative) in a measure that is expressed as a proportion of the starting measure. When median income changes from $20,000 to $25,000, for example, this is a 25 percent increase.

percentage point change The change (either positive or negative) in a value which is already expressed as a percentage. When a labor force participation rate changes from 70 percent of 75 percent, for example, this is a 5 percentage point increase.

poverty level The official income threshold below which families and persons are classified as living in poverty. The threshold rises each year with inflation and varies depending on family size and age of householder.

Primary Metropolitan Statistical Area (PMSA) A geographic entity defined by the federal Office of Management and Budget for use by federal statistical agencies. PMSAs are the components of Consolidated Metropolitan Statistical Areas. If an area meets the requirements to qualify as a metropolitan statistical area and has a population of 1,000,000 or more, two or more PMSAs may be defined within it if statistical criteria are met and local opinion favors the designation.

proportion or share The value of a part expressed as a percentage of the whole. If there are 4 million people aged 25 and 3 million of them are white, then the white proportion is 75 percent.

purchase price The purchase price refers to the price of the house or apartment and lot at the time the property was purchased. Closing costs are excluded from the purchase price.

race Race is self-reported and is defined differently depending on the data source. On the 2000 census form, respondents were asked to identify themselves as belonging to one or more of six racial groups: American Indians and Alaska Natives, Asians, blacks, Native Hawaiians and other Pacific Islanders, whites, and other. In publishing the results, the Census Bureau created three new terms to distinguish one group from another. The "race alone" population is people who identified themselves as only one race. The "race in combination" population is people who identified themselves as more than one race, such as white and black. The "race, alone or in combination" population includes both those who identified themselves as one race and those who identified themselves as more than one race. Other government data collection efforts must offer the multiracial option by 2003, but they did not do so in 2000. Therefore, tables based on government surveys-such as the Current Population Survey-show different counts for racial groups than does the census. In general, census counts of the "race alone" population will be smaller than survey estimates. Census counts of the "race, alone or in combination" population will be larger than survey estimates.

renter occupied *See* Owner occupied.

rounding Percentages are rounded to the nearest tenth of a percent; therefore, the percentages in a distribu-

tion do not always add exactly to 100.0 percent. The totals, however, are always shown as 100.0. Moreover, individual figures are rounded to the nearest thousand without being adjusted to group totals, which are independently rounded; percentages are based on the unrounded numbers.

sales and receipts In the business tables, sales and receipts are defined as the receipts for goods produced or distribution or services provided. Excluded from sales are nonoperating receipts, returns on investments, and interest.

self-employment A person is categorized as self-employed if he or she was self-employed in the job held longest during the reference period. People who report self-employment from a second job are excluded, but those who report wage-and-salary income from a second job are included. Unpaid workers in family businesses are excluded. Self-employment statistics include only nonagricultural workers and exclude people who work for themselves in incorporated businesses.

sex ratio The number of men per 100 women.

suburbs The portion of a metropolitan area that is outside the central city.

Survey of Consumer Finances The Survey of Consumer Finances is a triennial survey taken by the Federal Reserve Board. It collects data on the assets, debts, and net worth of American households. For the 1998 survey, the Federal Reserve Board interviewed a random sample of 2,813 households and a supplemental sample of 1,496 wealthy households based on tax-return data.

Survey of Women-Owned Business Enterprises The survey is part of the economic censuses. The economic censuses are required by law and taken by the Census Bureau every five years in years ending in 2 and 7. The economic census defines women-owned businesses as privately-held firms in which women own 51 percent or more of the firm. The sample for the Survey of Women-Owned Business Enterprises is selected using lists of all firms in the U.S. as well as lists of individuals who filed 1040 Schedule Cs and other business tax forms.

unemployed Those who, during the survey period, had no employment but were available and looking for work. Those who were laid off from their jobs and were waiting to be recalled are also classified as unemployed.

value, of housing unit The respondent's estimate of how much his or her house and lot would sell for if it were for sale.

white The term "white" is defined differently depending on whether census or survey data are shown. In 2000 census data, the term "white" includes those who identified themselves as white and no other race (called "white alone") and those who identified themselves as white and some other race (called "white in combination"). The combination of the two groups is termed "white, alone or in combination." Because the multiracial option was not yet included in surveys and other data collection efforts in 2000, the white totals in survey data will be different from 2000 census counts.

work experience Work experience is based on work for pay or work without pay on a family-operated farm or business at any time during the previous year, on a part-time or full-time basis.

Bibliography

Bureau of the Census

—*Americans with Disabilities, 1997*, detailed tables for Current Population Report P70-73, 2001; http://www.census.gov/hhes/www/disable/sipp/disable97.html

—*America's Families and Living Arrangements: March 2000*, detailed tables for Current Population Report P20-537; http://www.census.gov/population/www/socdemo/hh-fam/p20-537_00.html

—Census 2000; http://www.census.gov/main/www/cen2000.html

—Current Population Survey, Annual Demographic Survey: March Supplement; http://www.bls.census.gov/cps/ads/2001/sdata.htm

—Current Population Survey, Historical Income Tables; http://www.census.gov/hhes/income/histinc/histinctb.html

—Current Population Survey, Historical Poverty Tables; http://www.census.gov/hhes/income/histinc/histpovtb.html

—*Educational Attainment in the United States: March 2000*, detailed tables for Current Population Report P20-536; http://www.census.gov/population/www/socdemo/education/p20-536.html

—*The Foreign-Born Population in the United States: March 2000*, detailed tables for Current Population Report P20-534, PPL-135; http://www.census.gov/population/www/socdemo/foreign/p20-534.html

—*Gender: 2000*, Census 2000 Brief, C2KBR/01-9, 2001

—*Geographic Mobility: March 1999 to March 2000*, detailed tables for Current Population Report P20-538; http://www.census.gov/population/www/socdemo/migrate/p20-538.html

—Housing Vacancy Survey; http://www.census.gov/hhes/www/housing/hvs/historic/histt15.html

—*Money Income in the United States: 2000*, Current Population Reports, P60-213, 2001

—*Number, Timing, and Duration of Marriages and Divorces: 1996*, Current Population Report P70-80, 2002

—*Poverty in the United States: 2000*, Current Population Reports, P60-214, 2001

—Preliminary Estimates on Caregiving from Wave 7 of the 1996 Survey of Income and Program Participation, by John M. McNeil, No. 231, The Survey of Income and Program Participation, 1999

—*School Enrollment—Social and Economic Characteristics of Students: October 2000*, PPL-148; http://www.census.gov/population/www/socdemo/school/ppl-148.html

—Survey of Women-Owned Business Enterprises, 1997 Economic Census; http://www.census.gov/csd/mwb/

—*Voting and Registration in the Election of November 2000*, detailed tables for Current Population Report P20-542, 2002; http://www.census.gov/population/www/socdemo/voting/p20-542.html

Bureau of Labor Statistics

—2000 Consumer Expenditure Survey; http://www.bls.gov/cex

—*Contingent and Alternative Employment Arrangements*, February 2001; http://www.bls.gov/news.release/conemp.toc.htm

—*Employee Tenure in 2000*; http://www.bls.gov/news.release/tenure.toc.htm

—*Employment and Earnings*, January 2001

—*Employment Characteristics of Families in 2000*; http://www.bls.gov/news.release/famee.toc.htm

—*Monthly Labor Review*, November 2001

Federal Reserve Board
    —*Recent Changes in U.S. Family Finances: Results from the 1998 Survey of Consumer Finances*, Federal Reserve Bulletin, January 2000

Higher Education Research Institute
    —*The American Freshman: National Norms for Fall 2000*, Linda J. Sax, Alexander W. Astin, William S. Korn, and Kathryn M. Mahoney, Higher Education Research Institute, UCLA, 2001

Immigration and Naturalization Service
    —*2000 Statistical Yearbook of the Immigration and Naturalization Service*, 2002; http://www.ins.usdoj.gov/graphics/aboutins/statistics/IMM00yrbk/IMM2000list.htm

National Center for Education Statistics
    —*Digest of Education Statistics 2001*
    —*Projections of Education Statistics to 2011*

National Center for Health Statistics
    —*1999 National Hospital Discharge Survey: Annual Summary with Detailed Diagnosis and Procedure Data*, Vital and Health Statistics, Series 13, No. 151, 2001
    —*Births: Final Data for 2000*, National Vital Statistics Report, Vol. 50, No. 5, 2002
    —*Current Estimates from the National Health Interview Survey*, 1996, Series 10, No. 200, 1999
    —*Deaths: Final Data for 1999*, National Vital Statistics Report, Vol. 49, No. 8, 2001
    —*Deaths: Preliminary Data for 2000*, National Vital Statistics Report, Vol. 49, No. 12, 2001
    —*Health, United States, 2001*
    —*National Ambulatory Medical Care Survey: 1999 Summary*, Advance Data, No. 322, 2001
    —*National Hospital Ambulatory Medical Care Survey: 1999 Outpatient Department Summary*, Advance Data, No. 321, 2001

National Opinion Research Center
    —2000 General Social Survey, unpublished data

National Telecommunications and Information Administration
    —*A Nation Online: How Americans Are Expanding Their Use of the Internet*, 2002

U.S. Department of Agriculture
    —1994-96 Diet and Health Knowledge Survey, Agricultural Research Service; http://www.barc.usda.gov/bhnrc/foodsurvey/home.htm
    —*Data Tables: Results from USDA's Continuing Survey of Food Intakes by Individuals*, Agricultural Research Service; http://www.barc.usda.gov/bhnrc/foodsurvey/home.htm
    —*Food and Nutrient Intakes by Individuals in the United States, by Sex and Age, 1994-96*, Nationwide Food Surveys Report No. 96-2, 1998; http://www.barc.usda.gov/bhnrc/foodsurvey/Products9496.html
    —*Foods Commonly Eaten in the United States: Quantities Consumed per Eating Occasion and in a Day, 1994-1996*, Nationwide Food Surveys Report No. 96-5, 2002; http://www.barc.usda.gov/bhnrc/foodsurvey/Products9496.html

Index

American Indians
  by age, 296
  degrees earned, 94–96
  share of population, 292–296
  with AIDS, 156–157
alcoholic beverages
  consumption of, 114, 124–125
  spending on, 319, 321, 324, 330, 335, 338, 344
alcoholism, treatment for, 148
apparel, spending on, 319, 321, 325, 331–332, 336, 339–340, 345
arthritis, 137–138
Asians
  by age, 297
  children's living arrangements, 258–259
  college enrollment of, 65, 83–84, 88–89
  degrees earned, 94–96
  educational attainment of, 65, 70–72
  households, 270–271
  income of, 166–167
  marital status, 247, 250–251
  share of population, 292–295, 297
  with AIDS, 156–157
assets
  by age, 352–356
  by income, 352–356
  financial, 349, 352–354
  homes, 349, 355–356, 359–360
  nonfinancial, 349, 355–356
  retirement accounts, 352–354
  stocks and mutual funds, 352–354
  vehicles, 355–356
asthma, 137, 139, 145, 148
attitude toward
  abilities, of college freshmen, 92–93
  abortion, 38–39
  affirmative action, 29–32
  death penalty, 38, 42
  diet, 110–111
  environmental protection, 43–45
  finances, 26–27
  God, belief in, 5, 33–34
  gun control, 38, 41
  happiness, 5–7
  health, 107–109
  helpfulness of others, 5, 9

important objectives, of college freshmen, 65, 90–91
  life, excitement of, 5–6, 8
  marriage, happiness of, 13–14
  physician-assisted suicide, 38, 40
  political party identification, 5, 46–47
  prayer, 5, 33, 35
  sex roles, 13, 15
  socializing, 5, 20–21
  standard of living, 5, 23–25
  voting, reason for not, 46, 49
  work, 5, 26, 28, 29–32
  working women, 5, 10, 12–13, 15

blacks
  by age, 298
  children's living arrangements, 258–259
  college enrollment, 65, 83–84, 88–89
  degrees earned, 94–96
  educational attainment, 70–72
  households, 270–271
  in poverty, 200, 202
  income of, 161, 166–167, 173–174
  labor force, 206, 210–211
  marital status, 247, 250, 252
  share of population, 292–295, 298
  with AIDS, 156–157
businesses
  as a financial asset, 355–356
  by state, 55, 62–63
  characteristics of, 55–64

cancer, 107, 148, 158–159
caregiving, 152–153
cataracts, 138
childless, 16–17
children
  and parents' work status, 214–216
  foreign-born, 313, 315
  harmed by working mothers, 10, 12
  hospital stays, 145–147
  households with, 247, 265–278
  living arrangements of, 258–259
  mobility of, 310–312
  number of, 16–17
  physician visits by, 142–143

school enrollment of, 76–77

  spending of households with, 319–334

  standard of living, 5, 23, 25

chronic conditions, 137–139

cigarette smoking, 122–123. *See also* Tobacco
  products.

cohabitation, 284–285

college. *See also* Education and School
  enrollment.

  attendance status, 85–89

  attitudes of freshmen, 65, 90–93

  degrees earned, 65, 94–104, 106

  earnings of graduates, 177–178

  enrollment, 65, 78, 80–89, 104–105

  enrollment rate, 78–79

computer use, 50, 53–54

contributions of cash, spending on, 319, 321, 327,
  333, 336, 341, 347

credit card debt, 357–358

death

  causes of, 107, 158–159

  penalty, attitude toward, 38, 42

debt, 349, 357–358

degrees earned. *See also* Education, College
  enrollment, and School enrollment.

  by field of study, 97–103

  by race and Hispanic origin, 94–96

  projections of, 104, 106

Democrats. *See* Political party identification.

depression,

  feelings of, 20, 22

  physician office visits for, 142, 144

diabetes, 137, 139, 148, 159

diet

  attitude toward, 110–111

  food consumed, 107, 112–115

digestive system problems, 138, 149

disabilities, 140–141

divorce, 248–257

drinking, 124–125

dual–income couples, 191, 193–195, 205,
  214–215, 217–218

earnings. *See also* Income.

  by education, 161, 177–178

  by occupation, 179–187

  of foreign-born, 313, 315

  of full-time workers, 161, 177–187

  of husbands and wives, 191, 194

  pension coverage by, 361, 363

  wives more than husbands, 191, 195

education. *See also* College, Degrees earned,
  and School enrollment.

  attainment, 65–75

  by age, 65, 68–69, 70, 72–75

  by race and Hispanic origin, 65, 70–72

  earnings by, 161, 177–178

  foreign-born by, 313, 315

  of householders with children, 277–278

  of husbands and wives, 247, 279, 283

  spending on, 321, 326, 333, 335, 341, 347

entertainment, spending on, 321, 326, 332–333,
  341, 346

environmental protection, attitude toward,
  43–45

exercise, frequency of, 130–131

eye conditions, 135, 137–138, 144

families. *See* Households.

fathers

  age of becoming, 16, 18

  by number of children, 16–17

  working, 214–216

feelings, frequency of, 20, 22

female-headed families. *See* Households.

financial satisfaction, 26–27

food consumption

  attitude toward, 110–111

  by place, 107, 118–119

  by type of food, 107, 112–115

food spending, 322–323, 329–330, 335, 337–338,
  343–344

foreign-born, 287, 313–315

gifts, spending on, 319, 321, 327–328, 333–334,
  336, 341–342, 347–348

God, belief in, 5, 33–34

gun control, attitude toward, 38, 41

wealth, 349–356

weight, 120–121

whites. *See also* Non-Hispanic white.
  by age, 301
  children's living arrangements, 259
  college enrollment, 83–84, 88–89
  educational attainment, 71–72
  households, 270–271
  in poverty, 202
  income of, 166–167, 173–174
  labor force, 205, 210–211
  marital status, 254
  share of population, 292–295, 301
  with AIDS, 156–157

widowers, 248–257

women working, attitude toward, 5, 10, 12–13,
  15

work. *See also* Labor Force.
  attitude toward, 5, 26, 28

working mothers,
  attitude toward, 5, 10, 12
  men with, 10–11

young adults, living with parents, 260–261,
  274–275